Whaea Blue

Whaea Blue

Talia Marshall

TE HERENGA WAKA
UNIVERSITY PRESS

Te Herenga Waka University Press
Victoria University of Wellington
PO Box 600, Wellington
New Zealand
teherengawakapress.co.nz

First published 2024

Ans Westra images courtesy of {Suite}. For details see p. 345.

ISBN 9781776920136

A catalogue record is available from the National Library of New Zealand

Published with the assistance of a grant from

creative nz

ARTS COUNCIL OF NEW ZEALAND TOI AOTEAROA

Printed in Singapore by Markono Pte Ltd

For Jim, Paul, and my darling Angus Tahere Hayes

Contents

He wāhine, he whenua,
ka ngaro te tangata.

For a woman and land,
men perish.

Echo Valley

Mum says they left me at the church by accident. I was not a real orphan left in a basket, but once they got back to the house, which reeked of the hogget roasting in the enamel pan, they realised the walking, talking baby was missing.

I wonder if they sat down to Sunday lunch before they realised I wasn't there. I was the only small child in the family then, so this seems unlikely. The problem was there were two cars: Mum and her boyfriend, Ian, had left the chapel in his, assuming I must be with my grandparents.

I wonder if Mum was white-knuckled on the drive back to the chapel—the fists are a habit of hers—or certain that I would be found safe; if she veered between both possibilities on the ride back to look for me.

At the Mormon chapel beside the cliff, they found me tottering around the breeze-block interior. I wasn't crying or disturbed by my solitude. I had probably been wrapping myself in the giant curtains that divided the main chapel from the parquet basketball court and the stage behind it. Later, visiting my grandparents in Dunedin, these curtains would be one of the only things I liked about going to church—that, and how icy the water was in the little paper cups during sacrament. I was intrigued by the baptismal suite, which I mistook for a spa. When I was eight I begged to be baptised so I could have a spa, but it didn't happen. I was a fatherless child.

I wonder how it is that nothing happened to me as I wandered the church alone.

Mum says that I wasn't alone, that I was holding a man's hand when they found me. But this doesn't sound quite like me, either—I hate holding hands. Unless it was my grandparents swinging me between them down the street in their careful cradle. *One, two, three, whee!* between their arms, over and over.

It's one of those stories about me that was told to me. Told to me so much it became a part of my memory. I know the freezing Chemico-pink toilets had a clean ashy smell that I hated. And that I used to feel frightened in there as a child, a fear that bordered on existential.

The first thing I remember is my mother. If I had let her edit this—a fatal mistake for any writer, especially with memoir—she would probably question my choice to single out the one time the family forgot about me, when the answer is that it makes a good story. And the truth is, it wasn't easy for Mum, having me. She had just turned nineteen when I was born and nothing about her Mormon life before that prepared her for being a solo mother to a brown baby. She was lucky, I suppose, that my nana was a sucker for babies, because there was no more talk of adopting me out once she clapped her large, baby-loving, icy-blue eyes on me.

I suppose one of my many problems is that I think I can remember everything when really there are all these holes. And I fill them in with the silly putty of my imagination.

When I was three, I broke my leg beside the lighthouse at Castlepoint. In my version, a man had been trying to throw me off. But Mum says I started running towards the cliff from the path, and he stopped me from going over the edge. Maybe I thought I could fly. After the averted catastrophe we went to the doctor's, and there I remember the tank full of tropical fish and smudging the glass with my grubby fingers.

That same year we went camping with Ian, the archaeologist, in the far north, near Tutukākā, and what I remember is the jelly. It was in the car on the floor of the backseat, and I plunged my red gumboots with the blue trim into its quiver by accident. I can't remember what colour the jelly was—red, or maybe purple—but I do remember the smell of the grass clippings on the soles of my boots. They ruined the treat Mum had made for me in a camp kitchen.

On the same trip I remember walking through a house when we shouldn't have—it was still tapu—and disturbing the whānau shrine to a kuia's old life. Below her whare we came to an opening, and I called across the valley and she called back to me through the cicada's song. This echo was the moment I fell in love with the sound of my own voice. But was it really mine?

Hiking out of the valley, we came across some men in the bush, singeing the hair off some dead wild pigs. There were little red slices, oozing like jam in their exposed baby-pink flesh.

I don't know why I always feel I am back there, in Ngāti Wai country near the Mermaid Pools, and in the valley, before and after the echoes—back in a place where I shouldn't be. I'm not sure if she is still with me, the kuia, but something holds me back from the edge.

Often Mum's version of the truth acts as a restraint. After the valley we went for a van ride on Ninety Mile Beach, and we were stranded by the tide coming in. Mum says I ran up the beach to bring back men with ropes. This does not sound like me either . . . None of these early memories can really be trusted, but maybe the story can? This urge to make details into a proper meal.

But there is proof of our trip up north into the thin spooky edge of the fish. In his field study of buried Māori gardens, Ian took a grainy black-and-white photo of us at the valley in Whale Bay, near Matapōuri: Mum is holding my jacket, while further down I cry and holler across the divide.

And I remember being on the ferry after the trip to Tutukākā, and coming into the Sounds, standing on the rail with chocolate dairy-food on my face, feeding my pottle to the sea, and a dolphin flipping and diving through the water and chasing the bow waves. It was thrilling to pretend to be an orphan. And now I can't bear to be close to any kind of drop, or balcony, in case I leap off—although I still love being on a boat. As long as I can trail my hand in the water I am not scared. Of myself.

Chicken feet

The day after I catch a plane from Dunedin to Wellington to meet Paul, we go for yum cha with my cousins. It is 1993 and I am fifteen. Observing him, I think: So this is what it is like to have money. I have lived in Wellington before with Mum, until I was ten, so I think of Wellington as my city, and it is strange to be driving around it with my father, Paul. I have even met my new cousin before. I was seven and tagged along to a friend's ballet class in Cuba Mall. Her mother—Paul's sister and my new aunt—was aristocratic and stiff in her seat when I was introduced as her niece in the mirrored studio, and my cousin rejected me, whispering to the other girls in the changing room while I stood there, sticking out like a hurt, pulsating thumb.

I wanted to be a ballet dancer too, but neither of us had the right body for that pretty and obsessive torture. It's a weird European phenomenon, to dance on your toes. Plus, the lesbians I was raised with in Wellington thought ballet was as evil as the Miss Universe pageant. I was lucky Mum bought me a tutu. I wore it for a year, aided and abetted by the gay teenager we lived with in a cottage on Arthur Street.

Now, eight years later, walking from the car to yum cha, my cousin is gentle and shy. Our birthdays are months apart and, all of a sudden, I adore her.

We walk past Toyworld in Manners Mall, a former sacred place of mine, where I used to covet the stuffed life-size

Dobermann in the window and where I would beg Mum to take me inside to the pink plastic paradise. I was not interested in Transformers or GI Joe. I wasn't interested in the gender neutrality of Lego. I was devoted to the colour pink.

Paul has tortoiseshell-and-gold wayfarer sunglasses perched on his curly head and a faded, soft denim shirt. Chambray is in. When I finally give something away about the Dobermann, he tells me he has a Rottweiler called Sophie. He is only thirty-three, which seems middle-aged to me.

The gap between who I was expecting and who Paul is in the flesh is a puzzle. I have ideas at fifteen about what it means to be Māori. I'm taking te reo for School Certificate, and my friends at school are often Māori, yet I have no idea about my whakapapa.

Because I am vain, I expected my father to be handsome. I will later realise that he was, or at least I will finally acknowledge his charisma. Really, I am a big child. Like my father. I have his curly hair and the same chin and a brow that can be heavy and sullen.

Later, at Paul's brother's house in Lower Hutt, I have to flee all the whānau so that I can cry. I don't know where the tears are coming from, but I heave and shudder as they pour out of me.

When I arrived to meet Paul, his father Mugwi was more excited to see the cricketer Martin Crowe and his glamorous wife come in through arrivals than me. He said, *Look, it's Martin Crowe*. Like my father, Martin was in his prime. I was the overdressed girl behind him, wearing black chiffon flares printed with tiny roses and an ugly velvet choker with a bent heart as a charm. There was more movement in my flares than my face.

But I found Mugwi's lack of guile endearing. I liked him on sight. Maybe love is the more accurate word for what I felt for Mugwi because it was so sudden and mysterious. Paul's mother, my new grandmother, held out her arms to me for a hug but I folded in on myself and ignored her disappointment. This woman was not my nana.

Mum says she almost went to Paul's parents' sandwich bar in Wellington when I was little. She stood at the bottom of the escalators and they kept on rising and rising without her. Mugwi, Māori as he is, reminds me of my Pākehā grandfather, and I'm conflicted by this instant fealty.

At yum cha the next day, I am entranced by the lunch—I have always loved Chinese food. Paul orders everything. He tells us we are going to love it. He lets me and his Mormon nieces drink Coke before lunch while he fusses over the jasmine tea, which is getting stronger in the pot. He insists it will help us digest the heavy food but we wrinkle our fresh, uncultured faces. We are too young to think about our insides. I absorb how Paul dotes on my cousins and feel abstracted rather than jealous. He keeps insisting the fragrant tea is just as important as the food.

First, we eat the BBQ pork triangles, flaky pastries stuffed full of crimson sugary meat sitting on a doily-covered saucer. I dip mine in the twin porcelain dish of soy and the slick red seeded chilli that Paul warns me about. He watches me eat so I have to hide the intense pleasure with my hand over my mouth.

We love the pillowy pork buns, too. We love all the pork things and are dubious about the coral prawns in their glutinous sacks and the shu mai topped with neon orange flecks. I have never seen a bamboo steamer or savoury food arranged in such a delicate, lovely manner and I stab at it all with my chopsticks using one like a spear.

Then the chicken feet arrive, and Paul dares us all to try them. We become girlier than our sex and shriek, but they are tasty when I give in and nibble at one. The custard tarts are an afterthought and Paul eats most of them as we find them too eggy.

I have had yum cha many times since this first meal with my father, in an attempt to recreate his largesse, and none of the chicken feet have ever been so *small.* The feet that came later were larger and far too reptilian to eat.

Later, when I'm alone in the car with Paul, he says he wanted to meet me so I would know who they were, meaning the Macdonalds, this massive Māori clan. I scoff at him, taking this to mean he has no real interest in finding out who *I* am. He was not that interested when he met me as a baby, yet here I am being lectured about the nature of family, having it *explained to me*.

We are staying in a three-storeyed villa Paul's friend has lent him in her absence. It is in Thorndon near the entrance of the Botanic Garden and up from the Chinese embassy with its pagoda. I wonder again at the marvels of being rich because my childhood in Wellington was so poor, moving from house to house and walking the punishing hills. I used to stub at Mum's Commando sneakers with my own as we scaled Bidwill Street to register my protest at not having a car.

Now I'm sleeping on the top floor of this house, in the indulged teenager's *wing* with white louvre shutters. A white girl who goes to a private school and whose diary reveals her to be a sociopath. The strangeness of it all comes in waves and I battle hurt and anger for Mum and the way these people, my new whānau, excluded her when she was sent back to Dunedin from Blenheim in pregnant unwed Mormon shame. One minute she was dancing with the cousins to 'April Sun in Cuba'; the next minute she was savagely out.

In the big house I watch my younger cousin nap with Mugwi, snug on the couch. The envy I feel drives me to smoke outside and I confess to Paul, who is horrified by my smoking, to also drinking gin because I'm a determined little adult.

Paul makes fresh pesto swimming in peaty olive oil to go with the crusty bread for a full Italian dinner. He lights all the candles in the grand, rickety house and I realise he is feminine. I think now that maybe the nineties were custom-designed for my father, his tastes grafted well to the age. He orders cappuccino because his Italian genes are the strongest. I fail to realise the flashes of generosity aren't real wealth but something Paul does for show.

Paul's mother gets drunk at the long rustic table because she has just lost her mother. My great-grandmother's death messed with the original plan, which was for me to meet Paul in Blenheim, on our tūrangawaewae. After dinner, on the drive to Lower Hutt, they realise my grandmother is missing her teeth, and they have to back up the car and pick through her vomit of Lindauer and pasta to find them. This becomes an instant family joke and I feel bad for revealing it. Even now I struggle with calling them my family, like I'm trying out a strange word in my mouth. Whānau seems an easier fit.

My father doesn't know what to do with me and my refusal to find him charming, so he takes me and the cousins to City Gallery, where all the canvases are white but *textured.* We are merciless in our teasing about this, so Paul drops all pretence and takes us to the video store. He confesses to not being a reader, but says he loves movies. Back in Thorndon, we watch Coppola's new campy *Dracula*. Gary Oldman as the vampire has hair like an albino fly and runs a knife along his tongue. Keanu Reeves is gorgeous, doomed and dim.

After Paul's grandmother's funeral, which I refuse to attend because being difficult comes naturally to me, we take the ferry back to Blenheim. The cousins are all playing cards—there are many of them now, from different branches of the clan—but I am reading a special sex issue of *Cosmopolitan*. My grandmother asks me what I'm reading and the awkwardness between us is intensified by the variety of sexual positions she quickly hands back to me. I have had to pull the sealed pages apart to see the sex.

When we get off the ferry in Picton, Paul's favourite cousin meets us at baggage claim and tells me to follow my dad. I reply, Paul is not my fucking father. The cousin hoots and tells me I must be a Macdonald because I'm fiery. Like *them*.

Before I was born, Paul's grandmother—a tiny woman from Bradford in the UK who sewed careful clothes for herself and my cousin, who also wasn't born yet—touched my mother on her belly, which was getting tighter by the day, and told her everything was going to be alright. But Mum took nothing home for her layette.

She was the only one, apart from Mugwi, who showed Mum this regard. And it wasn't alright—I was so big I almost split my nineteen-year-old mother like a peach. But Paul was the best person to dine with. I have never met his match.

Mum says he took her for a drive in his Volkswagen when she still thought they were getting married. But in the car at Lake Grassmere, looking at the salt flats, Paul told her he didn't love her and was not ready for any of this.

Later, she tells me very little about Paul except for the fact that he was a Steely Dan fan. The only song of his I like, or maybe even love, is 'Dirty Work'. I have had to construct my Māori father out of cultural clichés and he doesn't quite fit any of them. Except for the natural generosity.

*

Years later, during the plague, I am part of a poetry reading with a tarot card theme at Pegasus Books off Cuba Street. I sneak out before it's my turn and duck into the stairway of the same ballet studio where I met my cousin in the eighties. I pull down my leopard-print leggings and check for the potential embarrassment. But the blood is in my head.

We were meant to let Joy, who was organising the reading, draw a card for us to muse on. We were meant to use Joy's hands as a conduit for testing our fate, but she is a Pākehā so I sent her an email before the reading asking for the Tower. The worst card in the pack, worse than Death, which is really the white flower of rebirth and transformation, and worse than the Devil himself.

If you look closely at the Devil card, which signifies bondage, the chains around the necks of the man and woman he holds hostage are quite loose. They could just take them off, but they stand there fixed to the man who is half goat and whose eyebrows are heavier than mine.

I can't have something as cloying and clichéd as daddy issues. This can't be what this is.

Because it is Mum who always had the tarot cards out, spread in her favourite cross formation on a scarf for the lesbians of Wellington. I learned to read them at her knee or looking over a table, the only child under the table and the women who never stopped talking.

And it wasn't me with my ikura in my leopard-print tights, it was my new e hoa Becky, who had to tie her leather jacket around her waist before partying in another poet's borrowed jeans and singing karaoke into the night.

The Tower

Pegasus Books reading, Verb Readers and Writers Festival, November 2021

Katherine—who Mum had let move in even though she got naked at her flatmate interview, and who was often naked in the lounge or at the dining table, and never made any sense—made sense, just once. Katherine said the Tower tarot card is not a fall but a slow shattering like the crackle in a glaze.

That's fine, sister, but why am I falling and why is my crown of snakes on fire.

This is a secret, but there is a lotus inside Babel; it is as blue as the man under the bed—look, he spreads out his long, long fingers like a pelican. Oh no, he has such a big mouth! Don't let him in!

I stopped reading my own cards because I always pulled the Tower. I could do without the forewarning of colossal damage because that bell is already deafening in the belfry of my head.

I stopped reading my friends' cards because all they wanted to know about the future was if there was a man in it, or if their almost-man was going to stop being useless, and I had stopped believing in straight love so I found their quest for love boring and something I could no longer validate by encouraging it. Since female friendship involves blind validation, this was a tricky time. I announced that straight men are good for one thing: nailing to a cross. But the truth is, even queer love was boring to me.

It is my own fault all my friends ask me to read their cards: I have lied about being psychic for many years.

I told my Pākehā friend, who is no longer my friend, that I would read her cards if she paid me, and she said she would, and then luckily she never paid me because her love life was like *Thelma and Louise.* But with no Thelma and no Louise and just the sound of her whining into the canyon when a push would do. She would message me at 5am asking me to read her cards, which felt a little early in the day to be talking about men. The sun is a man: he comes and he goes, and even he wasn't up yet.

Men are only good for one thing and it's not opening jars—a can opener will help you do that; a can opener will stay where it's put in the cutlery drawer and the bonus is it will not subject you to psychological abuse. It just wants to help.

I tell one of my oldest friends to read her own tea leaves. I tell her to read the leaves because her conical fingers, which she calls square, have the gift and she sees the shapes, as sure as her shadow, just before they arrive; and even though I have stopped believing in love I tell her to ring me to say goodbye before she takes all the pills she's been stockpiling, because I do believe in braiding her back to the earth even as it starts to tremble and split—worse, I still believe in magic because magic is another word for sister; it's another word for hope, that tiny ridiculous blowtorch.

She tells me she can't do that because I will try and make her stay. I will try and make her pretend she doesn't hate every moment of being alive.

But I will be inside the Tower with her when it crumbles, guarding the lotus whose opal fingers are close to being singed by heaven for the sin of being that close.

It's been almost twenty years since we've seen each other in the flesh, twenty years since she watched me feed my baby from my own mouth in the toddler zoo of L'affare, nineteen years since we fought in the frozen aisle of New World about putting raspberries under the crème brûlée for the dinner party. I don't even know why we were having dinner parties—we were middle-aged at twenty-one—and I am still not as subtle as her; I was for the raspberries because my dreams are tart and pixelated while hers are fine as clay and just as prone to erosion.

But don't go e hoa, stay—I know you can't keep letting down your hair

Like a ladder into the darkness where there is no surrender and no sleep

And even though it hurts to look at your own hands because everything is ugly

I am trying to hold you here in the rubble of our pact, the man doesn't matter

the lotus does, the lotus is still blue and as unscathed as the air

Golden whare

I am reading a Robert Hass poem about his alcoholic mother and her nipples and I am remembering the crèche, Te Kāinganui, in Wellington where Mum worked and how I would fight Holly for the pink chair at morning tea. Huntley & Palmers crackers with margarine and strawberry jam should come with a trigger warning because they remind me of the war with Holly.

Even before I was an adult I wondered why they didn't paint the chair another colour, or paint another one pink. I think they added a purple chair later, and I watched, a detached, disgusted seven-year-old, as three little girls fought over the two chairs.

I should probably clarify: my mum is not the drinker—I am.

Mum used to lie in the bath a lot and was known as Late Kate. The bath was in a bathroom one door through the kitchen at Dorking Road, in a house owned by an ancient Russian woman who didn't seem to mind radical lesbians. Women would ring and ask for my mother and I would tell them she was in the bath. Very occasionally this was a lie. Gaggles of lesbians would sit at the table, getting stoned, drinking tea and coffee and talking the world down to a stub. They descended on my mother one by one so she could listen to their problems and flick ash into the bathwater and Mum would adjust the flannel over her breasts or her bottom half or not at all for some people.

Before Dorking Road there were other houses. And they were all filled with books. First there were the Little Golden Books read to me by my grandparents Gwen and Jim, and then Mum bought me a book a week and we went to the library. This is where the blame kicks in; this is where I learned the world. On knees being read to, being read to and read to and then I was reading—it was like stringing beads.

I would run my hand along the rainbow mural as we went down the stairs into the children's part of the Wellington library. JC Sturm was the most fearsome and unsmiling librarian there in 1982, but I don't remember her, so I fantasise that I received a rare smile from her because I was a half-caste girl.

I liked the pictures in the books as much as the sound of the text. *The Witch at the Wellington Library*, about the witch living in the basement, became a favourite. But the story that I demanded my mother read to me every night just before I started school was a little book with a pink doll's house on the cover: *Tilly's House*. The house is a doll's house that Tilly the maid flees from. She slides down the table leg using her umbrella and her escape is complete. Down at the end of the garden there is a glasshouse and she makes a refuge there. There is a jellybean packet for a bed and a doily for a tablecloth. There is a teddy bear who visits her who I later confuse with Corduroy, the bear who loses a button on his overalls. I have a Big Ted too, and a Little Ted. *Playschool* means a lot to me, and I already know that the Manu doll is my kin. Mum never kept my being Māori from me, and it was far more obvious then that I didn't come from just them.

We shared a bed at Arthur Street, and I would prise Mum's eyelids open before she was ready to be awake. I would keep on with this until she'd give in to me and the day. I was just as annoying with her hair. I would roll it around the brush until it was tangled and stuck, and she would let me even though I could feel her bristle when I tugged. It was still long and thick and dark, and I used to think she was Christina in the Andrew Wyeth print over the mantelpiece at my grandparents' in Dunedin. I would later learn Mum grew up thinking Christina was her Aunty Lorraine.

Mum still wore dresses then; I have a long red embroidered one I wear now that reminds me of her. I was horrified when she cut all her princess hair off into a spiky mullet. I was horrified when she started wearing dungarees, even though she dyed them pink and purple—her metamorphosis into a radical caterpillar instead of a butterfly. I felt betrayed by most of her sartorial choices.

Even though we moved from house to house, Mum was always drawing floor plans for her dream home, using a biro to denote the little swinging doors. We moved so many times that Wellington was like a Cubist painting to me; Mum had a Picasso Blue Period print in her midnight blue room. She had the painting of Katherine Mansfield and the girl in the poppies. She was quite femme for a radical lesbian. She was probably the most beautiful lesbian in Wellington but I didn't see it that way then.

But radical she was. The lesbians practised a version of 'Putting On the Ritz' in our lounge in Brougham Street for a cabaret to raise funds for the end of men.

The lesbian I loved the most was Jane Cool, a gruff, good-hearted dyke who had taken Mum under her wing when there was some fracas in a class Phillida Bunkle taught at Victoria University. Together they made a Reclaim the Night documentary. Except they forgot to take the lens cap off the camera they had borrowed and all you could hear was Jane panting as they followed the march, asking Mum what she had done with the Winfield Reds. They did not realise they had totally reclaimed the night until the premiere.

Mum used to smoke those Winfield Reds in the shower. There was nothing women couldn't do, then.

Except bring their children to softball. Mum's team, the Amazons, had a meeting about banning me from coming to their games. It was argued I was the product of a man. Luckily a consensus was not reached, but Jane still had to take Mum out the back for a Winfield before the meeting was over. And I was allowed to keep coming to watch the Amazons, when really, the highlight of my five-year-old week was walking Jane's miniature collie round and round the softball diamonds and paying no attention to the sport.

Mum had left the cult of Mormonism for another, more exclusive cult, where women could do anything and girls were not quite allowed.

Wake up darling, wake up

I guess that technically my copy of Ans Westra's *Maori* is stolen. I was thirty-eight and on the run from a life that wouldn't stop imploding and, while I shed people, places and things, the substitutes were whipped into my human tornado. Sucked into a chaos that took me months to register, and in the aftermath's grey, stinking wreckage, I was ungrateful to still be alive. But I loved my new book.

My possession of *Maori* was part of a larger argument between me and the gay man who had helped to raise me in Paul's absence. He was only seventeen when I met him at two as Mum's wary pāua, but he quickly won me over. They were at polytech studying early childhood education and we ended up living together in the old cottage in Arthur Street before it was pulled down. I can remember him putting food colouring in my bath to make it go red, blue and purple. When I turned five, he made me a gingerbread-house cake with chocolate fingers for the roof and immaculate green coconut grass.

He was devastated when Mum told him she was moving out and taking me to be with the real lesbians of Brougham Street. He threw stuff at her. He had even taken to wearing the lesbian little black dress, a shearer's singlet, in an attempt to assimilate into the lesbian army before he came out. He was the one who made sure I got a tutu, sneaking Mum away from the revolution to a dance school sale. I adored him.

Maybe it's ironic that we fell out as adults in Riwaka, a place I whakapapa to through Mugwi and where my gay uncle had offered refuge to me, his 'favourite niece'. Maybe it's ironic that, in the wall-to-wall kitsch of his cavernous whare, this Pākehā had so much Māori stuff—the kind you get from a second-hand shop or sieve through the 'funky' 'Kiwiana' listings on Trade Me for, to call treasure rather than taonga.

The book was in the backseat as I drove over touchy Tākaka Hill and away from Riwaka in a hurt rage. The new car—a silver Audi I'd named Ariel—was my other decent consolation prize in the tornado, but the kurī was already destroying the black leather upholstery with his anxious terrier antics.

Three years later, I found myself almost homeless and living with the kurī in the furry miasma of the car, but instead of Ariel I had a beat-up red Nissan that I had christened Bobby Jo. I drove her to my son's father Roman's place in Gisborne with the oil light on and my mental health companion-in-chief panting his ageing, rancid, Jack Russell breath over my shoulder as he perched on the seat like a parrot. I was running out of options and it was a sound offer from Roman, to come and stay with him.

On the way to the coast, Māori were everywhere I looked. Except for Tīrau, which had a Trelise Cooper outlet store in lieu of tangata whenua, and I thought, Why *is* Tīrau? The glib answer is horses, dairy farming and shit taste in clothes.

I saw Māori in Rotorua, Tokoroa, Whakatāne and Ōpōtiki, and then in smaller, more ethereal places like Nukuhou, with its roadside marae and the kēhua I felt at my nape driving through Tāneatua where a puppy trotted loose in the rain. I drank in the mythic promise of the road signs indicating the turn-off to Galatea and Murupara before I cut through the brooding valleys of the Waioeka Gorge. Roman had warned me about Waioeka, telling me I wouldn't want to break down there after midnight. I felt my eye snapping shut like a shutter behind a lens on the Māori I witnessed animating the cakey North Island whenua. And, in my madness, all these Māori everywhere were such a comfort to me. I did not need to open a book to find my own people, even though I still had *Maori* with me: my lucky, unlucky book.

In Gisborne, I kept trying to show Roman the images in *Maori* but he gave me Nāti side-eye and said, *No one cares about Ans Westra, Talia—write something positive.* It was as dismissive as the comment I found when I searched her name on Twitter, which remembered Ans as that hippie lady who turned up on the coast scrounging for a feed. My worry was how much that label also fit me.

And then, a few weeks later, because he likes to toy with me, Roman mentioned some aunties on a rohe Facebook group who were sorting out who was who in one of Westra's unnamed images. It had already occurred to me that this was one of the chief flaws of the book James Ritchie wrote the text for: this lack of names and identifying hapū and marae. It was the lacuna I wanted to write about. I felt that Ans Westra had gapped it on us and that her career was built on a simplistic, homogeneous view of Māori. A view that battled with my initial response to the photos, which was to feel seduced by their vibrating dream. I physically love some of Westra's images; I feel a pull towards them. This is a rare feeling for me when it comes to art.

And I was as anonymous as her photographs in Gisborne, lying on the couch in my freshly dead father's black puffer jacket, which was the bulk of my inheritance. One of the couch squabs sank lower than the others with the shape of my sorrow. I rarely moved. Sometimes I would heave myself outside to smoke on the porch and look at the panel beaters over the road through the straggly winter hibiscus.

Eventually I did leave the house. I bought cheap, cheerful, garish muumuus from a trash emporium called Art! Fun! Wear! on Gladstone Road, so my lying down had a more tropical, festive feel after that. I was exhausted and wounded but I was safe in this dingy haven. I hadn't felt safe for a long time. I bought a lot of leggings too, usually leopard-print ones because it had been almost a decade since I'd worn jeans. Gisborne is so far from another main centre the op shopping is excellent, with plenty of whenua-rich farmers and wealthy Pākehā in the greater area who have nowhere else to drop off their dead or unwanted loot. In the Salvation Army, this mixed with cheaper plastic plates ringed with kōwhaiwhai patterns and the sign on the women's clothes rack read *Wahine*. At the local auction house there was a golliwog in the rafters, and I squinted up at it wondering if anyone from Ngāti Karen, desperate to decolonise her thinking, had demanded that it be removed. I was not that bothered by the crass doll. It seemed like a toy for creepy old ladies rather than kids.

Yes, golliwogs are historically gross and racist, but easily remedied compared to the fact that there were almost no rentals available in Gisborne and homeless or precarious Māori were the least likely to be picked as tenants. On their own whenua.

I saw men walking or cycling the streets with everything they owned in a backpack, who slept under bridges or trees by the poisoned river. One day, a Pākehā man turned up at the front door with a raw steak in a plastic bag and asked if I would cook it for him, because he was living in his car.

But Roman had said he didn't want any homeless cunts turning up at his door, apart from me, and I was ashamed and relieved that his voice was in my head when I said no.

Besides, if anyone dared to jump the corrugated-iron fence out the back, Roman's pit bulls would have ripped them apart like lions. I kept a watchful eye on my kurī, only letting him piss and shit out the front. Roman lavished him with love. He'd given him as a puppy—with the name Tonka—to our son when he turned eight. Now, he called him Party Boy in a singsong voice while he fed him chicken necks and comically large bones on the rug.

Stanley, the guard pittie Roman had named after mass murderer Stanley Graham, would watch me through the kitchen window from on top of his kennel under the phoenix palm. If I met his empty gaze, it was like what Nietzsche said about staring into the abyss, except, after a while, the abyss got used to me and thumped his tail. Slightly. Turns out the abyss enjoys a steak.

Sometimes Roman would get us hāngī in covered foil trays from the shop around the corner. I would douse my steaming tray in mint sauce, a childhood habit I'd picked up from all those hogget roasts after church with my grandparents. The vinegar cut through the gassy cabbage, sheep fat, and starched smoky sweetness of the kūmara and pumpkin. And who doesn't love stuffing?

Our son was just relieved that his father had given his nearly crazy mother somewhere to live.

Near Art! Fun! Wear! was my favourite second-hand shop with its superlative Māori collection, a waka huia obscured by the travel cots displayed outside. Inside, there were whiskey bottles shaped like Te Rauparaha and other rangatira, a genuine find. There was a piccaninny ashtray and a weird print homage to Rachel Hunter, Dame Kiri Te Kanawa and KZ-7, beside jigsaw puzzles that, once assembled, revealed a stern Captain Cook being greeted by happy natives. I guess these finds were pretty offensive, but I coveted them all. I love Māori tat. And Te Rauparaha whiskey was less problematic to me than a golliwog, because his heke murdered so many of our iwi in the unfair game that war became for Māori with the introduction of the musket.

Meanwhile, in Gisborne, the local statue of Captain Cook on the port's waterfront had been branded with the words *Pakeha* and *Thief* in protest at Tuia 250. It was a dig at those in Tairāwhiti trying to celebrate (under the guise of commemoration) the 250th anniversary of Cook turning up in 1769 and murdering some locals with his crew, with the same poverty of imagination he used to rename their gorgeous bay. It is telling that most people in this country will have heard of Captain Cook and that there is a global scholarship industry obsessed with his voyages, when Te Maro of Ngāti Oneone, who was the first Māori to be killed by Pākehā on his own whenua, is barely known or talked about outside his own people. There were no macrons used over the two 'a' in the kupu 'Pakeha' defacing the statue, possibly because the graffiti artist was in a hurry.

Although I fully supported the righteous vandalism—the statue is rude af—my Kurahaupō iwi had a different story to tell about their encounter with Cook. Ngāti Kuia and Rangitāne o Wairau are far less visible within our own rohe than these mighty Ngāti Porou and Rongowhakaata iwi. Our Kurahaupō iwi chose to meet the Tuia 250 *Endeavour*-replica flotilla in waka near Picton, if only to remind people who the whenua and the wai truly belong to in Te Tau Ihu, and that, despite Te Rauparaha's tactical decimation of us between the arrival of Cook and the signing of Te Tiriti, we are still very much alive.

Cook was more understanding than a picky, plant-based eater when my ancestors, led by Kahura, ate ten of Furneaux's men over a grievance at Wharehunga Bay in 1773. He reminded the outraged crew they had probably insulted them. But that insight was only possible because we were equally curious about them and what was on board their big, buxom ships. We could have killed all those honky devils but chose not to. Since our arrival in Aotearoa from Hawaiki centuries before, fuck-all other people had turned up to visit and these clumsy manuhiri had nails, which we were desperate for.

I muttered to myself and to Roman from the couch that the real raruraru with Pākehā didn't start until we signed Te Tiriti and the settlers descended on us as a troubling mass. Cook was just the first to wedge open the gate using his silly naval flag. His impact on the whenua, apart from the immediate human tragedy, was negligible, but the legacy of his voyages to Aotearoa is immense and shattering. Roman replied to my horizontal muttering by reminding me that all my sentences began with the letter *I* and that no one likes a big head, pointedly watching YouTube videos about Emmett Till as he repeated the words *big head* at me, because he didn't want any of my trouble in Gisborne.

Still, I felt haunted by those men sleeping beside a poisonous-looking river, by the difference between the haves and have-nots I tallied at the two supermarkets. I studied a woman with a silver bob, the official senior helmet of the middle class, cramming a basket with all the bougie favourites. I saw a kōtiro, about seven, counting each grocery item too carefully as it moved along the conveyor belt at Pak'nSave. A man, who I assumed was her father, watched over her with the same stern regard. I caught myself staring and looked away. It's rude to stare anywhere, but it felt extra rude here on the coast.

*

One of the reasons *Maori* is so precious to me is that Ans Westra caught Māori men in the act of being good. And this is doubly poignant because the book was published in 1967. Over the next decade, the state accelerated its uplifts of our tamariki, almost collapsing the structures of Māori whānau by ripping tamariki from the heart of their harakeke and putting rangatahi in punitive institutions masked as homes. Now, gang members on television and half-broken people in print

media describe being 'interfered' or 'fiddled' with as historical wards of the state. These are subtle words when a tāne uses them like this in hindsight. But then Māori have this knack for subtext, maybe especially when it elides a horror.

When my mum was studying early childhood in 1980, Betty Armstrong, her Pākehā tutor, showed her class the Ans Westra image from *Maori* of a man pushing a wheelbarrow surrounded by kids, including one riding his shoulders and another laughing from the wheelbarrow. He is smoking, but everyone smoked then.

There is another image in *Maori* of an older man bending down to the same level of a little girl as they both corkscrew into the twist. And one—my own favourite, because it reminds me of Roman—where a younger man in a mesh singlet lets one toddler happily eat beside him, while the other has a tutū with his singlet.

It reminds me of those moments when Roman played much more easily than me with our son and freed up my fingers to do something useful. The roles are reversed in my other sentimental favourite from *Maori,* which shows a man under a tree fiddling with what might be a blade of grass as a woman walks past him in gumboots, slinging a toddler on her front.

They are such intimate, natural images, but how did Ans Westra get so close to us? The New Zealand she arrived in in 1957 was socially segregated by geographical and political factors. But this was on the cusp of change, as Māori were moving from papakāinga and smaller towns into the city. Ans became enamoured with a Māori family over the fence in Auckland, who were part of the new urban migration to the city. Her Eurocentric gaze noted how free, natural and spontaneous they seemed, compared to her own reconstituted family, and her camera started seeking us out. She moved to Wellington and found us at Ngāti Pōneke kapa haka meetings and became their official photographer. She would also catch the train out to Waiwhetū, the marae being built in Lower Hutt.

She saved enough money working at Rembrandt Photographic Studio on Cuba Street to buy a second-hand Volkswagen and began driving out of town on weekends to remote Māori areas. The car had just enough room to hunch her long Dutch frame into for a terrible night's sleep. Later, she would sometimes have her children in tow, tamariki with hair like wheat, heading off with their mother for the browner parts of the map.

Tall and stooped, with her camera at waist level, she would have seemed strange to Māori at first. This wasn't the usual behaviour for a Pākehā woman. And they would invite her in, because anything could happen to her out there. Children are often curious about a camera and would have been her first point of access, I suppose. It was canny of her really, to shoot from the hip.

The colour dust jacket of *Maori* shows tamariki looking down into her lens. They are from Ruatōria, a specificity she had previously disguised in *Washday at the Pa* three years before, giving them another surname, Wereta, and pretending they were from Taihape, to protect their identity, and, in doing so, adding her milk to their strong, dark tea.

The Māori Women's Welfare League met in Dunedin the year *Washday* was published then withheld because of their outcry against it. But it wasn't the anonymity of the whānau that disturbed them. They were concerned that the publication of these images by the Department of Education would make Pākehā look down on us. Even more. One image showed children lighting each other's cigarettes, but they were only copying the adults around them. The League's agenda was aspirational: they were going to show Pākehā how to be better ladies; they were going to beat them at their own domestic game. Most of the 38,000 copies of the booklet were guillotined in the furore. This is a pretty ghastly fate for images of happy children, to chop off their heads.

Ans Westra revisited *Washday* in a later series of images. One of the main subjects, called Mutu in the original text, told Ans she didn't need wallpaper or carpet in her whare because it reminded her of the safe, happy home she grew up in back on the coast. Her mother's consent for them all to be photographed by Westra also seems a bit lost in the historical fuss.

To me, as a contemporary observer, it is more anthropologically frustrating to change their names and location than to present children smoking or Mutu breaking tapu by warming her feet on a stove—tikanga tends to be a bit more flexible in private. But that image incensed the League. Yet, the mother in these images is so freely intimate with her children, and this Pākehā woman was allowed to record it. The story of Westra's perseverance with us hits me as a mother. Her pluckiness is admirable, I think; especially when she describes herself as a bit shy. I am shy too. And, like her, I am far more interested in what is happening in the neglected corners than on the main stage.

This is also why I am suspicious, because we have proven to be such a cheap date and Westra used her vulnerability—whether she was conscious of it or not—to engage with us, as much as any mandate for mahi from the Department of Education. And her gaze is not the same as ours, with its secret toughness underwriting the consent. Māori transcend her gaze. We are bigger than her, so it is a painful irony that Ans Westra's images are a collective taonga we rarely possess. We animate *Maori* unnamed by place, person, marae, hapū or iwi, the social circuits that form the motherboard of our being. Although, I have managed to recognise some of the marae in *Maori* by the women doing kopikopi in the Waikato or the mana wahine energy of the ancestral pou at Hiruhārama near Ruatōria. The nunnish habits at Rātana competing with the honking of the brass bands took less detective work because it was a large, well-known event. Our real stories should be this noisy; they should be spilling out the sides of her frame.

Ans Westra was poor and aspirational when she ventured off in her Volkswagen in search of our arcadia. When Māori became more radicalised in the 1970s, some were critical of her shy presence in our world. She argued she earned about the same then as a cleaner for her art. It is too humble a claim, when Ans Westra became a living legend.

The man in the mesh singlet appears again in *Maori*. He stands at the sink so you can only recognise him from the back. Two women and some kids sit at the stuffed table in the close kitchen. The children are working the meat away from the pork bones. They appear in other images of *Maori* and I recognise one by matching the cuffs of his pyjama sleeves. The child, these tamariki, are why Ans Westra got so close to us. But the man's turned back at the sink suggests something to me too. I wonder if they are a whānau from the coast from the angle of the sun hitting the door and the open face of the boy, but this answer is held mostly in the archives.

I couldn't reproduce Ans Westra's images here without asking for permission and I was reluctant to ask because of this history of her 'taking' our photos. It left me in something of a bind, but maybe I preferred an unsolved puzzle? Roman wouldn't let me near the closed Coastie Facebook groups, where they were clucking over who was who in some of her images. He was guarded because my nosiness was embarrassing to him. There was also the danger I would discover that he was making up this story of invested online aunties to distract me from my sorrow, which was stinking up his house.

What I remember most about being in labour with our son is this sudden involuntary turn into a wild animal, and having to surrender to my body's will. There is no getting out of it now, I thought, as Roman fussed at me to hang up my towel and I marvelled at the hospital's endless supply of gushing hot water to fill the bath. The water was my only relief from the pain because the gas made me throw up the Big Mac and McChicken I'd had for lunch before my induction, and there was no way I was staying still for a needle going into my spine.

When my son was a baby, I used to sing him 'Summertime', 'The Girl from Ipanema' and this song I learned at primary school in Foxton Beach, 'When the Red, Red Robin Comes Bob, Bob, Bobbin' Along'. The lyrics of the latter advise the sleepyhead to wake up. It was a contradictory song to sing as a lullaby, but he seemed to like it. Its forced cheeriness was reassuring to me as a young, new mother feeling the walls of the house close in on my isolation.

Funny, I guess, that two of my son's favourite songs have the phrase 'wake up' in them. Aaradhna's song 'Wake Up' reminds me of when we used to live in Aramoana. He thrashed it from the sleepout beside my annuals in the sweet courtyard garden. If I didn't water my flowers, they would sizzle off in the sandy soil like the mist that hung as a white woolly beard over the cliff in the mornings.

The other song is Mad Season's slower, droning 'Wake Up'. Roman played this grunge dirge when my son was fifteen and he brought it to my house with its view of the harbour and the monkey-puzzle trees. 'Wake Up' was the song on repeat in the weeks before the tornado and my new silver car, but I have fewer regrets now about not setting the house I left on fire. Still, I can't hear it without feeling for a warning that pulls much deeper than a siren.

But this sound is the thing I want to write into the images in *Maori*, as much as I want to solve the mystery of the man in the mesh singlet. Roman is not the right name for him; he would hate it. If I go further, and follow the music around the path down the side of the house there is a Māori girl on the back steps by the door. She is sitting there with a guitar, wearing jandals under the polite skirt tucked over her knees. She is playing the be-positive chord of D, and the kurī are gentler lions. They are ghosts the camera does not see.

The lake

Gwen could not let Jim die. Every time he got close—and there were at least five episodes where my grandfather seemed closer to death than usual—she would leave the rest home and her daily vigil beside him to walk up the road to their pastel unit inside the retirement village in Dunedin. They'd bought the unit and downsized their rose and hydrangea garden before he went into the home. In case he wandered.

Once home, Gwen would sit in her conservatory and not let him leave his body without her being there. This was their deal. They are both Geminis, so it was a twin thing, as much as the deal seemed freighted in her favour and unique powers. Because of the flat affect of Parkinson's, Jim's face was untroubled by lines. But he'd always had good skin—a Pākehā that browned as easily as the toast he barbecued on our caravan holidays.

As a child I loved my grandparents' morning bodies and good sleepy smells and the miniature Gainsborough padded silk portraits on either side of their king-size bed. Jim's portrait of the blue boy was on the left side and Gwen's was on the right, the woman in a white dress. Their lower-middle-class tastes suggest they were ordinary people, but they still feel like gods to me.

Now Jim was eighty-three and *lived* in a hospital bed. When his kidneys stopped working and his urine in the catheter bag turned an ominous pink from the blood clots, or when his chest started rattling with pneumonia and his face formed into the death cave, Gwen would pack up her devotion and her embroidery and vanish. Gwen—the former matron of day surgery, who took too much pleasure in showing the nurses and caregivers slumming it in aged care how to really look after someone. I ended up working there for over two years, first in the laundry and then as a caregiver, before I walked out in a huff.

The touch lamp in his room used to flicker and he would see his tiny dead mother and her hound-like jowls waiting for him at the end of the bed. Sometimes, when he wasn't dying, he would whisper to her, or think his children were trapped in a basement. The flickering lamp's name was Wee Nana. Everyone had loved her, even though she once mistook dog food for a cheap cut of meat and fed Mum and her brothers a stew of it. The dog, a Pomeranian, later had a terrible accident where its eye popped out. Jim took her to the vet and was so upset that he fainted on the floor.

There were no more pets for the children after that. Too traumatising. For Jim.

Big Nana was Gwen's mother. She lived in a mossy green La-Z-Boy that stank of piss all through my childhood holidays in Dunedin and the periods when I lived with my grandparents. She asked me who I was so many times while I tried to watch TV that I once made her a list of who I belonged to and my one real hobby: watching television. Uninterrupted. I wasn't sure why Big Nana wasn't in love with me like Gwen and Jim were. Big Nana was weird. She had a commode. She reminded me of the stepmother's real face in *Snow White*. We could not possibly be related. I would later learn the alien feeling between us was mutual. Even though she was demented she knew exactly who I was.

In the rest home, Jim would pretend to be asleep while Gwen sat there, because he could no longer drive up to the family history centre at the Mormon church to have some me-time with all the whakapapa. He helped a lot of people find out where they came from.

Gwen, who could be kinder than Jim, kinder than Jesus even, had the rest-home staff's failures to keep her busy, even though looking after Jim was a full-time job. She was locked in a war over pudding with Adrienne and Yvonne, the aged women we called girls and who ruled the kitchen. Except there was no cooking in this kitchen—it was a servery, so how things were done was the main thing at stake. They used fake passionfruit pulp the colour of bile to add some tang to the endless bowls of pudding and Gwen, who I call Nana, wanted them to sieve out the passionfruit seeds, otherwise Jim, who I called Grandad, might get lucky and choke.

Jim couldn't really swallow anymore; he couldn't move his neck, he couldn't stop Gwen applying Ungvita to his tailbone to prevent his sacrum splitting. I helped her turn him on his side and, while I fixed his pillows, I would bend down and look into his eyes and try to tell him, with my own silent pleading, that I was sorry that the people I imagined loved him most, me and her, were also responsible for robbing him of his dignity. But we all loved Jim. I was the only grandchild for ten years, and life since has never matched that first idyll with them.

Even Roman, who was suspicious of anyone except animals, some children and other Nātis, had a lot of time for my grandfather. Which maybe had something to do with how comfortable Jim was among Māori and may have been part of the reason he joined the Mormon church. Or maybe it was his father dying at the dinner table in front of him, here one minute and face planted into the cabbage and chops the next. Who knows what makes people turn to religion? Especially Mormonism, the most quango and semi-cultish religion of them all.

The church is where Nana met Jim. She says she joined because her new friend at Floriana, the florists where she worked, seemed so happy. She invited Nana to the beach and everyone there seemed equally wholesome and good natured. Jim, who was four years older, struck her as being too serious at first. Nana has a rebellious streak that is disguised by her intense approach to doing things properly. Instead of obeying her mother and remaining a dour Presbyterian, she shoved her hat in a hedge and went to the church where a hat was optional. Believing there were extra Israelites who left scrolls in a cave for deranged racist murderer Joseph Smith to discover in America, was not. Polygamy was officially banned by the church; Gwen was more than enough for Jim.

Even Adrienne and Yvonne had a cooing tender regard for Jim. This was the canal root of the problem. They imagined the tang in the passionfruit made life better for him—at least there was a consensus among the women that the food was worse than dogshit. So, we fussed at the edges as women who hated each other and found passive-aggressive ways to show each other what was best for him.

This present-day female carnage was destroying my memories of happy caravan holidays by the lake at Glendhu Bay. I went there every year with Nana and Grandad until I was twenty. Before Wānaka was overrun with rich Pākehā and their schist mansions, it was just a humble crib town in a grand place that was far prettier and less geographically intense than Queenstown. When I first heard this southern word for a holiday house—crib, or a North Island bach—I wondered why anyone would go on a holiday to sleep in a baby's bed. I was too literal as a child—when I found out a flying fox was not really a flying fox I felt robbed.

My grandparents didn't need a jet ski or a boat with a dawn-raiding outboard motor to enjoy being in the outdoors. All we needed was the lake. I very much wanted an orange lifejacket but I was too strong a swimmer; I feel more at home in the water or in a boat than on land. Instead of a lifejacket, Nana gave me an orange plastic cup to catch the cockabullies in the creek. I also wanted a net, but Nana was on the side of the fish: nothing lives in a bucket for long.

Grandad liked apricot jam and banana sliced on his toast with peanut butter; he liked chipolatas with piccalilli or chow chow (what is the difference?) and apple squares from the bakery in town and white sugar sprinkled on his custard like frost. He liked to read the *Otago Daily Times* during breakfast, back when nothing was happening in the world except the Honours lists. He enjoyed sitting up the back of the perennial spot during the dusk end of daylight. Jim on his low deck chair sighing at nature while he drew thin versions of the mountains with a whittled-down HB pencil. *Look at it Talia*, he'd say, meaning the all and awe of it. He was the same about the stars, the first person to show me a constellation on our way to the toilets before we split into ladies and men.

I understood the shape of the pot in the inky sky better than the twinkling Southern Cross.

There was the lake out the front of the caravan window and from the back window was the Valley of Kings—my name for it. Really, this is my name for it now; like a lot of psychos, my shadow is my gushing sentimentality. Thanks to Jim I love the smell of camp ablution blocks, which smell exactly the same all over New Zealand because of the ubiquitous concrete floors. And I like the sound of flies trapped at a window, because all these sensory buzzes remind me of being in the orange-and-white caravan at Glendhu Bay.

It seems a chore to describe the landscape, maybe because I spent so much time absorbing it and claiming it. I would bake for hours on my reflective lilo and float out past the buoy once I got older. When it got too hot I'd slip into the water and hold the rope of the buoy to test how far down it went, which seemed to be to a deep teal nowhere.

Lying on the lake I felt myself to be the centre of something magnificent. The hills were a limey green, rising up like Trashy from *Fraggle Rock,* and behind them the mountains seemed to hug me and the lake. In a poetry workshop at university years later, my friend Kay describes this feeling as lying in the lap of the mountains and I think,

Yes, that's exactly how it felt. But I was just as drawn to the tiny blue moths that clung to the muddy puddles outside the communal kitchen and the tree that brushed the roof of the caravan. Jim put its bristly cones into the red Thermette and fed them into the humble barbecue for another fried breakfast.

On my lilo I would quietly chase the blonde girl I was obsessed with, trying to make her like me back. But I was also thinking about boys. In the caravan, I'd look in the mirror on the fake wooden cabinet, pushing at parts of myself and sucking bits in trying to look thinner. When I later became thin, in my twenties, it gave all that thinking, which had felt so solid, a disjointed quality.

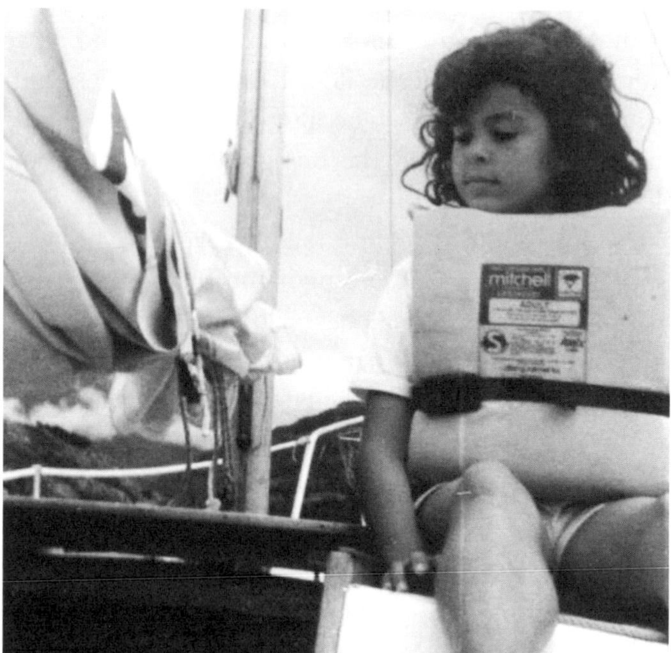

At university I would finally make a blonde friend. Except she dyed her hair all the colours and was tiny and thoughtful. She was smart and cool and strangely adult, and I had to have her in my life. She was one of the only people in Dunedin who ordered in Italian *Vogue* from overseas. Her name was Justine and she started looking almost pleased to see me when I pulled up a chair at the table in the glass fishbowl of the smokers' lounge and told her things about myself that would make her laugh and be my friend. We bonded over our grandparents, strangely. I didn't think cool people were capable of being sentimental, but Justine worried about climate change more than I did. I was worried about what would happen to my grandparents' caravan, to their blue-and-jade plastic plates and the tomato-coloured kettle. I was worried about what would happen to a whole way of life that already seemed to be disappearing, even though it was only 1997. Sunshine wasn't malevolent yet and no one did much recycling. Except Justine.

Working in rest homes, and especially the one Jim lay dying in, I became too aware of what happened to happy memories, to holding on to a way of life, and what happened to waste. Eventually all the memories are destroyed or lost, or turned to nothing and missing laundry.

It is Annie, who spits out one of her teeth even though the food we give her is soft. It is the way she fights you one minute and rests her head on you the next, and the way her head smells like a newborn's but overlaid with the trace of shit that is everywhere in rest homes, so much so that I become immune to it and forget to shower sometimes when I arrive at my new boyfriend Ben's, exhausted but saintly from proper hard work.

It is Rita rocking in her chair imagining she's still a gymnast.

It's Rosie, who is cute and mean and taught watercolours but has a son who never comes to see her.

It is Eva, who is my favourite because she is docile one minute pat-pat-patting at her side table and starts shouting and spitting the next.

It is Trevena, who begs me not to leave her emaciated stiff body lying there. And who is still beautiful even though her face is more lined than a notebook. It is being gentle with her knowing every part of her is sore.

It is June who, when she is finally let outside for a smoke, tries to light two at once. And who has to be accompanied because even using her good arm instead of the stroke-affected one she has been known to set herself on fire. She tells the nurse she hates that her perfume smells like arse.

It is another Annie, who is in her nineties, dying and crying for her mother. When I remind Annie of her age and that her mother is dead, she says, *So*. Annie sits with her comb stuck in her hair and her teeth black from tea; I like her, so I make the mistake of being honest about her mum, when she was out of it in her happy death delirium when I could have done the decent thing and promised she was on her way.

It is Liz, who fights you, then cries like she is being abused, once she is in the shower. She just gives up and I feel so bad then. The nurses gave Liz such a strong sedative that she fell and broke her arm the first week she was there. But Liz was still too wild to take into the fracture clinic, so her arm dangled as she abandoned the sling and walked the halls.

Working in a high-level dementia unit is to be where the *wild things* are, where toothless Annie's lost daughter wears the flat gaze of the dead in a photo on her wall. I catch Annie once by the sound of her singing as she uses a toilet brush to shove another man's possessions down the toilet. The stuff belongs to a man in his early forties, a Lou Reed fan with a rare frontal-lobe dementia. He is catatonic and can only remember his own penis and wanting to put every fucking thing in his mouth. I fall out with a nurse who expects me to lift him and his sweaty penis hands from his La-Z-Boy by myself. I hate asking her for help; I pride myself on being capable here, so I walk out when we are still fighting about it later and Jack, a demented old farmer who sings opera to his toy cat, pisses out blood in his catheter bag and the back of him smells like death and bowel cancer.

I adore Jack too; I walk out because it is wrong to openly fight in front of a resident, however demented he is. My feelings about what is best for people are getting in the way of caring for them.

It is Nola, who was a champion swimmer and, like Liz, hates showers so I am desperate to make her love them.

It is the women who told me the big one hurt them and how I did nothing except walk out when Adrienne and Yvonne thought they could get away with being nice to me while they tormented Gwen in front of Jim.

It is the way everyone ends up at the bottom of the lake. Disintegrating like Shelley Winters in *The Night of the Hunter*.

Even Ans Westra, my new Facebook friend, who, after my essay about *Maori* is published online, posts a long rambling message on my timeline telling me we should do a book about the child together. She writes that the man in the mesh singlet is a photo she took at Te Kaha. A place that is technically Whānau-ā-Apanui country. The Coast.

And then Ans dies, and I realise this book can no longer be about her.

Adrienne gave me a bag of Jerusalem artichokes once. It was generous of her; she had realised I was a good worker, as fanatical about care as my nana but far more erratic and less judgemental. I took Noeline, who never shut-the-fuck-up, with me in her La-Z-Boy while I dropped off the baskets of clothes room by room. I thought I was doing everyone a favour, but that's the thing about caregiving, no one really wants that, no one wants to be shown up. This is how Gwen got into so much trouble as Jim lay powerless beside her.

I pushed it too far with Gwen one day after work. I was yelling at her after one of Jim's failed attempts to get to Mormon heaven. I screamed, Why can't you just let him die?

Steve, her favourite, a cruisy evening-shift caregiver, Vietnam vet and former drinker, passed me a note from Nana near Christmastime, the punishing cooking festival that celebrates her other great love, the baby Jesus. Nana was writing to ask if I would be coming to Christmas. Steve was embarrassed by her note, and so was I, which was only half her intention.

I start working at Little Sisters of the Poor the day Jim dies. It is a Catholic rest home on the hill in Brockville. It was my dream to work there because I imagined care was something they took very seriously. Walking the corridor on my first day, I see a poor-quality, naive landscape of my favourite place on Earth, the lake at Glendhu Bay.

I visit my grandparents after this first shift, to let them know I have finally arrived as a caregiver. I work with the nuns now. I walk into Jim's room and he is close to death, so I don't get to brag to Nana about my day. Much. I'm not matakite, I don't have the 'second sight', but I've seen enough death working in the industry to know she won't be able to stop it now. Mum arrives. We escape to the conservatory up the road and she says, *Oh it won't happen this time*, and I say, *I think it will.*

I drive to my boyfriend Ben's, and sit under the rātā tree on the deck. I wait to hear that Jim is dead. Ben arrives home from being away on business and finds me in tears on the couch because a bird—I'm still not sure if it was a fantail or a sparrow—cheeped at me through the rātā. And sparrows mean Jim to me: Jim beside the rotary washing-line with a bread bag of crumbs as the birds crowded the lines before dropping for their feast. He explained that you can tell the male sparrows with the dark patch at their throat because they are surrounded by drabber flocks of women. His brown velour dressing gown was the same colour as the king sparrow's head.

Mum rings through while I'm still crying over the bird. Jim has died. Nana was with him and Steve was there too, the only caregiver she truly trusted. They were turning him on his side and—after six years in a home, of the bed-ridden misery that is unimaginable to me despite my being a partial and complicit witness—he exhaled and let her go.

The next day is Friday the 13th. In the morning I arrive at the rest home and run towards the big glass sliding door to shove it aside to face the fact of it. Down at the end of the corridor I used to walk swinging my care buckets full of used pads, some of my old workmates are laughing and shifting a piano in front of his room. Nana fought for Jim to have this room once his rotund frame was down to 38 kg and he no longer needed a ceiling hoist. The room has corner windows and sun, because they were both crazy for the light and the mood-enhancing benefits of vitamin D, the morning pour of it spilling over his newspaper and the smell of toast in the morning. The see-through colour of their former contentment.

My old workmates are just getting on with their day but stop laughing out of respect when they see me intent on his room. Inside it, I find the grey husk where Jim used to be. I start howling, a howling that starts around me and in me and isn't mine exactly; it's the same feeling I had when I met Paul and his family but much less alien this time. This belongs to Jim. Mum's youngest brother, the favourite, walks into the room and we hug, something we've never done. He is a quiet, reserved person and I am way too loud. He is probably trying to squash the howling with the natural goodness he inherited from them.

Someone, most likely the Australian nurse with great hair who Nana doesn't like much, has left the window open, to let Jim's essence out. These rituals are important when you work in aged care.

Later, after Grandad is taken to the funeral home, I go back to his room and slide my favourite Chopin CD of his into the relic of his Technics sound system. I am pretending to clean up his things, but I am useless again, the spoiled granddaughter and not the capable caregiver. There is a point in 'Tristesse', the étude I listen to, where the solo piano reaches a peak and moves into a piercing, gorgeous descent, and I wallow in it like a bath.

My grandparents are the first love story I have ever known, and on a whim I take a black comb from Jim's room because it was the last thing that touched the hair of his head. I take the Chopin CD too and some photos because I am a terrible thief.

Jim's funeral is held inside the Mormon chapel he built with Māori in the sixties, the same decade Westra's *Maori* came out. Three of his four children seem uncomfortable to be back in the modernist breeze-block temple with its needle as a steeple. But my Māori auntie, who is still a member of the church and also the favourite's wife, sings 'Pōkarekare Ana' to Jim with me. In the waiata, he is writing to his darling from across the water and we mouth the words.

Tuhituhi taku reta.

I am writing you this letter.

We take the liberty of changing Waiapu, my son's awa, the river he calls across to in the waiata, to the lake in Wānaka.

I'm not much of a singer. It helps that my auntie is Ngāti Kahungunu, an iwi known for their waiata and especially their plaintive counter harmonies. Jim used to conduct her in the choir. We practise the words together while she kneels beside her bed, putting on black pantyhose.

Now that Jim is gone, this auntie has become Gwen's favourite. The only church member left to keep her company on Sundays when her brood used to take up a couple of pews. Their relationship has not always been easy.

I start listening to an old Kiri Te Kanawa version of 'Pōkarekare Ana' obsessively on YouTube after the funeral because I have never known real loss. Aside from when I was seven, and the albino budgie called Measles from our lesbian menagerie at the top of Norway Street was brutalised by a cat. In the video Kiri wears a gaudy dress and the camera starts off close to her and moves further and further away until she resembles a pinpoint of light. Te Pō doesn't quite swallow her up.

It was Jim and Gwen's oldest son's idea to sing a Māori waiata inside the church. Māori had arrived from up north in the sixties to help with the church build and were billeted with these earnest Dunedin families who were also working for nothing for a rich American empire. In the small square photos Mum totters around a building site in a dress with her brothers. Nana learned to make boil-up and doughboys because Jim had asked the workers if they enjoyed her filled-roll lunches and they said they were very nice, but not what they were used to. It's funny, I suppose, that Mum grew up on a building site and should have been an architect but wasn't taught how to drive.

Nana, who has promised herself she won't speak at the funeral, gets up to remind us that Jim was almost too loveable. She wanted a fridge but he bought another hi-fi so there would be music in every room.

During their honeymoon period, spent taking home cassata cheese on the tram to share in their villa in Delta Street, Gwen turned some of Jim's beloved records into wavy sixties pot-plant holders, but she does not mention this at the Mormon tangi we have managed to pull off despite the fucking Mormons.

Nana is not one to brag about her craft. Sitting in the funeral home her pōtiki pulls off something too—he makes sure Nana doesn't hesitate too long about Mum's partner, Lisette, being listed in the death notice for the *Otago Daily Times*. He lists her name for the funeral director as Nana stutters. Lisette is the one who drove Jim's mobility scooter alongside bleak Hillside Road and into the shop in South Dunedin after it became obvious he wasn't able to use it to get away from Gwen and the constancy of their love. It was a great act of humility for a professor. Nana has been extremely fond of Lisette for thirty years.

Mum didn't lose it at Gwen like I did, flouncing around her territory and announcing she must let Jim die. She doesn't share those special privileges with me, but once she said with a great deal of anger, very quietly except for her loud bark on the last syllable: *My mother is a cunt.* We were sitting in Gwen's conservatory after Jim was first put in the home, against all our wishes. It was a hard time. After saying this about Nana, Mum pulled a thread of tobacco from her furious lip.

Another time I know Mum is crying before she rolls down the window of the car, because I am crying too. She says, *My poor parents, they are such good people, they have never hurt anyone in their life*. She has just come back from visiting their tortured demise in the sunny corner room.

These days Gwen's favourite, the pōtiki, plays a lot of golf.

Legs 11

We moved to Foxton Beach when I was ten because Mum and Lisette, this instant couple, a love story to rival my grandparents even, saw a house they liked one street back from the beach, and so they put in an offer. It was summer 1988 and the village seemed a proper beach town after Wellington's metropolis. It was just up the road from the high school in Levin where Lisette would be teaching PE. Mum, a refugee from a cult, had secured a proto-lesbian from Trentham. Lisette drove a Subaru. Lisette would sing and play 'Untouchable Girls' on her Swedish guitar. Lisette could yodel and do butterfly in the pool; Lisette could hang glide and play hockey and tennis. Mum made Lisette sit down and eat a packet of chocolate biscuits. Lisette gave up being an athlete for my mother; as usual, my mother gave everything and nothing away.

On the way into Foxton Beach, Mum and Lisette noted the macrocarpa hedges, which seemed to lean sideways the closer you got to the beach. They agreed the hedges were impressive and gorgeous because their new love gave everything a golden slant. Later we realised the hedges leaned because of the wind: for six weeks of the year Foxton Beach was so windy it drove us mental. There was sand in everything—sand in the sheets, sand under the sea-grass matting and sand between my teeth when I bite into the frittata because we are a family who has lesbian picnics now.

It was a great place to have a kurī; we moved there with my first dog, Zedra, a bearded collie cross who was still a pup. Grown, she would lie in the middle of the quiet hot road when she wasn't chasing traffic. I rode my pink ten-speed with no hands on the ram-horned handlebars down the gentle slope to the dairy. I watched *Neighbours* obsessively, but Kylie and Jason were minor characters to me. Mrs Mangel appalled and amazed me.

I make friends easily in Foxton Beach, and most of my new e hoa are Māori like me. They announce that I am their cousin. I have told them the father I don't know yet is a Macdonald. In response they say *We're all Macdonalds* but I don't quite believe them. Part of me is still convinced my father could be Paul MacDonald, the canoeist and famous blond Olympian. I am still fixated with blondes. Nana gets me a Malibu Barbie while I am staying with them in Dunedin just before we move to Foxton, but I give in and cut off all her hair and dye it with turmeric, so her mullet matches Mum's and her friends'.

Kara becomes my best friend. She has hair like Princess Tigerlily in *Peter Pan* and is the best dancer in the

Horowhenua area and sings along to Milli Vanilli in a raspy voice. She has leopards and cheetahs on her duvet because she gets regular ACC payments for the burns she got as a child, which missed her pretty, almost-adult face. Kara is my best friend, but she is also my nemesis. I make her and the other cousins watch *me* dance in *my* lounge.

Looking over our collection of Garbage Pail Kids bubblegum cards from the dairy, Kara asks me what Mum and Lisette *do* in bed? When I tell Mum about Kara's question, squeamish with discomfort, she says I shouldn't have to answer it but Kara is still allowed to stay over. I wake one night and see that Kara's hand is down her pants beside me on the bunk. But she is asleep; like me she puts her hand between her legs for comfort. I am too embarrassed to masturbate, even as an adult.

The rest of the community accepts Mum and Lisette and their mullets, and we even go to housie, where I get a kick out of the caller and their rhyming numbers.

I start hearing from the other girls that Kara is a better dancer than me but I still win the limbo at the disco held in a hall near the disused soundshell that hosted UB40 in the eighties. Kara tells me I am *up myself.* This is true.

We make up and break up, and her mum, Vida, has a joint with my mum and says *I know what you are, it's okay here in my whare*. Kara tells me Vida also got buzzed with UB40.

I start wagging school and hide all day in the dunes at the beach instead. This was never talked about. Mum had a job to commute to by then, and I'm not sure why I was so frightened of Kara's occasional annihilations, but I could make the beach last all day before I went home. One time the principal catches me hiding from Kara in a cul-de-sac close to the school. He makes me sit on the floor until I admit I am very good at writing and making up stories. I don't want a talent—I want friends.

There are nudists living on the corner of our street who decide to befriend Mum and Lisette. When Mum isn't at work she hides under the big round oak table from Dorking Road when she hears the woman knock at the door. Mum doesn't want to be around naked people if they are straight. That's sick.

At least the principal of Foxton Beach school wore clothes. He wore knee-high socks, short sleeves and shorts in all weather: the official uniform of the vanishing race of the sensible male New Zealand schoolteacher. Except he smoked. He would smoke in the corridors and stubbed them out before raiding another classroom to take over from the teacher. He told our class that around the age of eleven we learn to think abstract thoughts; we learn the moon is not really the size of a netball.

Kara had a cousin, who might have been my cousin too, who did not like the principal, or another teacher. Billy is fourteen but looks like a man, he is that big. He arrives at the school with a slug gun to shoot them both. Foxton Beach Primary has a flying fox, a pool, a trampoline and an observatory, but no war shelter, so they hide in the toilets in their knee-high socks, and Vida laughs about it later as her spotting knives heat up in front of us. Vida says they would have been better off hiding in the observatory because you wouldn't have seen their socks quivering below the stalls. And she's hacking through her laughter because she's cracked herself up again.

They were grown men scared of a Māori boy. I remember the fear dissipating under my desk when Kara whispered that it was just Billy.

This school had more than one village idiot. There was a girl with a big loose face and lank straw hair who could be as racist as her parents. One Sunday, bored and vicious, me, Kara and some other girls take the idiot down to the bottom field and make her kiss her little brother.

There is something wrong with us but also we are just girls who will forget, or know better than to remember, doing this. Kids can do some sick stuff when they are young. I'm sorry. One of us is dead now—she was the nicest one, the lightest one; she was so nice it was always a surprise when she was a bitch.

Years later, I spot a photo of Vida, Kara's mum, in an album on the Ngāti Kuia Facebook page. She and Mugwi were both at the marae in Canvastown, signing our Treaty settlement.

Kara was really my cousin—maybe this explains the rare bad blood between us.

The blue tūī

1991. It is 'Under Pressure' through Vanilla Ice and his sampled beat, it is the Fresh Prince, benefit cuts and MC Hammer pants, and it is also my first day at intermediate in Dunedin. All I can see is Kerry, flitting like a tūī around the other girls in their red jerseys and Macdonald kilts. Her curly, shoulder-length hair is so black it shines blue, and we are instant friends. I don't remember any awkwardness between us—just her teasing, the pranks and the mayhem. Kerry is a Gemini, too pretty and eccentric. Vika is half Tongan, and a Libra. She has a certain way she likes things to be put together. We all have curly, unmanageable hair.

At high school we graduate to wearing blue Anderson kilts and we absorb Delphi into our group. We turn the lounge at Mum's villa into a menthol-filled cathedral for music videos. We watch Boyz II Men, En Vogue and Betty Boo. We sing on the bus to Color Me Badd. We are loud, even when we whisper. And all we care about is boys—though Delphi, not so much. She does stuff to gross them out when she gets sick of them, like when she piggybacked me with our teeth blacked-out with chocolate self-saucing pudding and our boxer shorts around our ankles. Laughing and chasing our suitors away. Sometimes there is nothing better than being with your girls. Staying up all night with the sincere version of Delphi, listening to punishing R.E.M. Delphi was a Sagittarius, so was the most prone to hitching and unwise adventures, which meant having to run after her when she got into strange cars at 2am, so both of us could get murdered.

She still thinks this was wild, years later, when I'm in Gisborne at her place reminiscing with her and correcting her as I cackle that, *Actually, it was terrifying.*

Back then we shared everything except boyfriends. We swap Elle Macpherson boxer shorts, bodysuits and bras and give each other boils. We wear matching tartan tights in a primary colourway to the disco and Kerry writes Josh on her hands over and over and then on her desk. She asphyxiates herself to the point of blacking out using a scarf in Māori class and we are brown but not brown enough for some and too brown for others. We groom each other for nits and smoke more menthol cigarettes. Kerry has mandarin peels in her bed. In the bathroom in her house, where piles of our laundry are damp and stinking, the clay mask our skin is too good for oozes out of its tube. Charles & Eddie sing that they would never lie to us from the room down the hall.

Kerry's mum puts raw chicken feet in the beds to scare us one night for kicks, but none of us is ever told to go home. Instead, I microwave their pies and study the cat pawprint in the margarine and they take in Vika full-time. Dylan loves Brenda on *90210* and the LA night scatters stars onto the mink blanket and the dark we share behind the glow. 'Wicked Game'. 'Wicked Game' and the crushed-velvet heart-shaped bodice of youth.

We loll.

For Christmas, I give the girls a framed photo of us where I am the only one who looks good, because I am a Leo. Vika scrapes in but Kerry and Delphi look like ghouls.

We huff aerosol cans and Kerry kicks Vika in the face. *Hi-ya*, she cries, from down low, and her flat foot swings straight up into Vika's nose. Sort of by accident. All these ancient gags arriving pre-packaged into our girlhood. Singing Smokey Robinson and Sam Cooke, holding hands in the dark.

Girl, I'm sure I have known you from forever ago.

Kerry was just about to go to Little Waihi, to bury her Nanny Wiki, when I first saw her. Nanny Wiki had left Pōrangahau for an arranged marriage in Taupō and stayed in their mystic Catholic paradise.

Kerry and I lose each other from the everyday until I have my son, and then I need her again because she is already a mother.

Kerry and Vika look like sisters in the good photos; it looks like blood is keeping them together.

Saturn's return

I am twenty-eight and the cousins have been diving and bring back a sack of scallops and mussels to Hoani Bay. They shell them and eat some raw on the deck. Cousin Mark, another of Paul's favourites, looks so natural there, sitting with his legs wide apart and wielding the knife as he splits the scallops open. He is as relaxed cutting into their tight shells as a rainbow with hairy legs.

I have been feeling weird again. The bush talks to me; I hear whispers and hisses and I get in the hot bath on the deck fully clothed because I am thin now and feel naked all the time. Paul is proud of the huge egg-shaped bath on the deck. It is going to be part of his new venture.

Paul has fallen out with a Swedish billionaire and no longer sells collagen and soy-based fillers. He has bought a marquee business and used it to import a tent from India that looks like something from a Bertolucci film or *The English Patient*. He has raised it here on ancestral land in Endeavour Inlet. He fills the tent with safari-style fans and some Mies van der Rohe, Wilhelm and Wassily chairs; his cowhide Le Corbusier lounger; and a worn tan Chesterfield from a bistro in France. He is lucky he doesn't put his McCahon or his Hōtere in the marquee, having sold them to buy the land, because the next year it proves unworthy of the weather.

Worthy of an oasis but not worthy of the wind blowing in from Raukawakawa and the wet.

The floor of the tent is a large wooden platform and there is a claret-coloured Turkish rug tying the space together like a Calvin Klein ad. It has floor-length calico curtains that section off the central atrium from the generous rooms. He is still semi-rich and even Mum admits he has good taste. Out the back is a functional, subtle camp kitchen and an overwrought barbecue with a huge lid. I make a great show of cleaning it when I get there and then do nothing useful except comb knits out of my baby sister's six-year-old hair. Our children are the same age. As a brown solo mother it is pleasing to comb the nits out of the hair of her rich blonde mother's failure to do so herself. My sister has Māori hair like me, so I know what I'm up against.

Paul has a grand idea for Hoani Bay. He plans to build more platforms for smaller sleeping tents and offer a boutique glamping experience for trampers finishing the Queen Charlotte walk here in the Sounds. He has called it Hoani Bay after Mugwi's grandfather and ignores the old dwellings on the land, and the cousins who are angry with him for buying it. No one is really talking about glamping yet. It was Paul's downfall to be before his time.

We are under Mount Porororangi and across from Furneaux Lodge. Around the corner from where our ancestors ate ten of Furneaux's men when he accompanied Cook on his return voyage. I will later learn we kidnapped two patupaiarehe here and slaughtered the man and kept the woman to breed into our line for her beauty.

I spend New Year's at Furneaux Lodge partying with my cousins to ruthless cover versions. Cousin Mark says *Girl, you have had it hard*, because I have been describing being me to him. The family joke is to call Mark 'The Arab' because he got cavity searched at the airport after 9/11 for looking like he was from the Middle East.

After midnight, with the confusion of boats and water taxis in the dark and the small blinking lights of the jetty, I see how easy it would be to have multiple versions of a disappearance. Ben Smart and Olivia Hope went missing after midnight on New Year's Eve, 1999, on a night like this. Mark goes from yacht to yacht with his beer, knocking on windows with his free hand, looking for a party.

Mugwi arrives at the tent after the cousins leave and doesn't tell my kind of woeful, borrowed stories. On Paul's ex-surf-patrol boat he bought as a gag to scare the other boaties, we float around to the old homestead Mahana, where Mugwi was partly raised by his grandparents, Hoani and Polly. It is gracious with a veranda and a tennis court that was built for their son Jack. The first Māori to go to the Olympics. It is a habit of theirs to talk in firsts. I wonder if I was the first bastard to be ignored by a Māori whānau but will later learn there were more of us.

I wonder whether, if my mother was the one who was Māori, rather than Paul, I might have been kept by them. But to wonder such things is to enter a parallel dimension where I don't need to write. Or maybe I still would have felt like an outsider. I don't fit the narrative of the Māori child who is stolen by the state.

Mugwi just wants to talk about the cherry trees, and how many were in bloom here when he was a boy. Later, researching my failed novel, I will wonder when cherry trees first arrived in the Sounds. I will wonder which sailor had the stones in their pocket, or if it was a determined missionary with a small garden. Mugwi is unbearably pleased with my son. It is clear I am not happy and normal like all the other cousins so my presence is tricky here. But for the first time in my life I am thin. One of the cousins looks at me like he wants to eat me and I enjoy this.

The night after New Year's I help Paul with dinner. The cousins' scallops are bigger than the supermarket variety with glowing tropical tongues and Paul cooks them in wine and cream and lets me add some lemon zest at the end before he tips it into the pasta. Paul likes parsley and I like basil. He makes some lush bruschetta dripping with its oily aniseed for me and my baby sister. All his gestures are so abundant. We are hungover from our big night at the lodge but it is still one of the finest meals I have ever had.

Mostly I have been eating cherries and scorched almonds, because I like what not eating does to the membrane between me and the world, which is to feel both at once. I am being fancy about feeling skinless. That's what it was like, my eating disorder—it came with jumps. Flash cuts and those whispers.

I come back from the Sounds with a blue kēhua; maybe it's a patupaiarehe, maybe it is *not* a demon. Bad luck attaches itself to me like lint. It lives under my bed. This is the plainest way I can describe it—and no, I didn't invite it, and by the time I realise it's there it is too late.

People refuse to sleep at my house. I get thinner and thinner because I can't stop dancing.

Maureen, my neighbour, comes over before I leave that house and tells me about all the people who have died in it.

One in my room, one from the tree and one at the gate, at least.

Maureen drives a teal Mitsubishi and cleans white people's houses with cold water if they are too cheap to heat their holiday houses over winter. She is Ngāpuhi and said

Roman's people never made her feel welcome when she married into them.

This was when I lived in the deadly village by the sea. The kēhua made my son's Buzz Lightyear say strange things by itself, and his ball with an eye in it glowed as it rolled across the mantelpiece.

This is the way he walked into the darkest, pinkest part of the whale and cried don't tell the others

On the way to Nanny Shy's and Beau's unveilings, with our boy, who is seventeen, I fight with Roman. We fight driving through the black beech and green dappled light of Lewis Pass; we fight along the length of my river, the Wairau; and the next day after crossing on the ferry to the North Island we fight all the way to Gisborne. At one point I have to exit the car because the conflict is veering from malignant to dangerous. My son pulls me from the middle of the road in Nūhaka where I am begging to get hit by another car. It's dark, drizzling, and both his parents are insane with old shame and anger. He manages to coax me back into the car and holds my hand for the first time in ten years and says *I love you* in a way that makes me feel more whakamā. He defends my rage by explaining to Roman, his equally apoplectic father, that, lately, I'm sad all the time.

I suppose I should name the real reason for our fight, but I never will. Except to describe what kicked it off, which was Roman warning me before we crossed between the islands not to mention to his whānau that I wrote about what happened to them in Ruatōria in the eighties when I reviewed the *Ngāti Dread* trilogy and began my writing career, if you can call it that.

I am insulted that Roman imagines I would be that stupid and start ranting about the hole on the hill in Whareponga, which is meant to have no end. I tell him the only reason I wrote about them was because I *know* that hill.

I have never been to Ruatōria and Roman is right, it is no one's business but theirs. *Ko wai koe?* Who the fuck are you? But also, who the fuck am I?

Yet Roman had given me the books to read, when I lived in the deadly village by the sea. He had peered over my shoulder while I inhaled them in a weekend. Roman told me he knew who the prophet was. He also knew who the toddler was who left singed footprints on the marae ātea and who the nannies hid from the tohunga Pop Gage.

I should never have agreed to write about it; I was far too keen then. Not only did I know nothing about Ruatōria, I knew nothing about publishing online. But I have felt the obsidian slick of that bottomless hole once or twice, a horror expanding like an oil spill rather than contracting like dense matter in a galaxy.

In the car, in front of our son, I make another mistake when I accuse Roman of being as vulnerable as me. I say that we *all* have our vulnerabilities, and this enrages him even further. He replies, *I'll show you vulnerability*, and floors the accelerator while he eyeballs me instead of the road. It is rare for his pale eyes to blaze like this.

We are lucky to make it out of Dannevirke's outskirts intact, then we are lucky to make it out of Nūhaka and I can feel my son in the backseat hating and loving us for not being normal people like he imagines other parents to be.

We arrive in Gisborne late on Good Friday, and they leave me on the side of the road. Not in front of the mental hospital I beg to be taken to, or at the notorious gang street I then insist on being left at, having taken a wrong turn. Because I'm less scared of the Mongrel Mob in that moment than I am of myself and Roman. Instead, they leave me at Kaiti Beach and drive off in my car.

I have no money but I do have a gold tote bag and Tonka too—although the leash is long gone with the car. Rummaging through my bag I realise I also have wine, cigarettes, dog biscuits, a dead iPhone, a dead iPad and my spiralling sense of not giving a fuck to keep me company. I could die here tonight like this, I think happily. If no one attacks me I can walk into the sea.

My son feels bad for leaving me there and rings Delphi, my old friend from school. I hear her calling out my name from a house on the cliff, so instead of dying I spend the night with her, having a laugh and a cry about what's happened to our lives.

The next day Delphi drives me up the coast to meet Boy and Roman at the tavern in Tokomaru Bay. We are all contrite. They've just come from the place near Ruatōria where my son's great-grandmother Nanny Shy is buried for the unveiling of her headstone, and they are both aglow. My son is chatty with the wonder of the world he's just entered at the ceremony: the singing of an old love song for Shy, the light hitting the apex of Mount Hikurangi, and the uncomfortably hot girl cousins eyeing him up over the graves of their ancestors.

I finally get to see Ruatōria, a place Roman used to joke I would get chased out of, which sounded intriguing to me. Those fearsome women, capable of great spreads, running me out of town. At the superette I buy a pink toothbrush using a two-dollar coin and fall in love with everyone because I have a lazy person's tendency to romanticise service workers.

We drive on to Te Araroa where they are staying on the marae. I am shy and pretending not to be too much trouble when I meet his aunties for the first time. Before dinner I drive further into the village to get mobile coverage and at the store by the sea almost buy a T-shirt for my son that reads *Straight Outta Te Araroa.* I am late back and the last in the meal line for the sausage casserole, boiled potatoes, pūhā and sheep head, and when I sit down Roman whispers that the soft meat I'm about to cut into is the tongue, sticks his fork in it and puts it on his own plate. He says I am not to write about this unveiling but what he means is that I must not write about our fight. It is unfortunate for him that I have a lifelong hatred of being told what to do and that I still have my own tongue. But I appreciated his moment of marae chivalry, swallowing the sheep's tongue for me.

The next day we go to the urupā where Roman's grandfather Beau, Nanny Shy's husband, is buried. I stay in the car with my back turned, watching a horse in the paddock and making sure Tonka doesn't bark during the unveiling. I stay in the car because I'm frightened by the deep needling energy that is specific to this hapū and this iwi and the way everything in the air and underneath the ground is humming for me to know my place. I forget it is the anniversary of Jim's burial even though I keep catching the smell of his sweat when Roman sits anywhere near.

After the hākari—the hāngī, the coconut fish cooked in lime and lemon juice, the steamed pudding and custard—I go out to the carpark for a smoke. Singing begins to float out of the wharekai and across the marae ātea. It is so beautiful, particularly the voices of the women, I start to cry, possessed by the pentatonic harmonies Māori have uplifted from the tangi of the birds.

I forget it is Easter Sunday even with all this waiata rising like bread into the air.

*

I watched a documentary once where the white narrator said that Māori babies were given a meal of bellbirds, or korimako, to ensure their voices would be sweeter later in life. I remember hearing a talkback radio host say that everyone should go to the East Coast for a holiday because it is like going to another world.

Roman scoffed when I told him this and said *This is the world.* But our past is told to us by the settlers through the murky filter of their colonising sentiments, and worse, their anxieties. Except for in the parts of New Zealand that are still mostly Māori in cultural temperament, like the East Coast, places where time seems more slippery than an eel and older; deeper ways of being persist here.

At the marae after the unveiling in Te Araroa I heard this otherworldliness and the birds at its centre in the way the speaker began his whaikōrero to the manuhiri at the pōhiri:

Ka whakarongo ake au ki te tangi a te manu, a te mātui.
Tui tui tuituia. Tuia i runga, tuia i raro.
Tuia i roto, tuia i waho.
Ka rongo te pō, ka rongo te ao.
Tui tui tuituia.

Listen to the cry of the birds,
they are everywhere,
they are in us and above us,
they are stitching our humanness into the world.

But things change. Māori don't live as bird people anymore; we're not some lost, unchanging tribe suspended in a state of non-discovery.

Still. Listen to that sound. It's the humming that is and isn't the birds.

It is the tohunga hunched by the fire, unmoving except for the feathers of his cloak.

It is embarrassing, but the older I get, the more I notice the birds. When I was at university there was only one bird poem that I loved. It was in an American anthology I took out from the library and never took back:

There are no birds he remembers.
He does not remember owning a gun.
He remembers nothing of the past.

Writing this, I realised I had loved 'Linnets' by Larry Levis for over twenty years yet had no idea what a linnet actually looked like. I'd always imagined some kind of crow. But when I googled a linnet, the image search revealed that really, a linnet looks like a sparrow that has been dusted with red jelly crystals and has a cherry blush to its breast that resembles human lungs.

Levis creeps out over a salesman in two-tone shoes, snakes, and God getting balder, in the twelve-part epic about his brother shooting a linnet. The waist of a woman like a weasel slipping away.

He sold shoes, he sold soap. Nothing remained. He drove on the roads with a little hole in the air behind him.

But in the high court of linnets he does not get off so easily.

*

Before we left on the family road trip of doom, a pīwakawaka flew into my study and circled the room. It flew back to the balcony and repeated the circle and I saw this as a terrible augury. I told Roman about the fantail and he said it was just a visitor; the real omen of death would be if the pīwakawaka that had come inside was totally black.

I'm no one's father.
I whittle a linnet out of wood . . .

The next time I saw Roman he was standing in his backyard between Stanley and Copper, and the fruit tree behind him was full of fantails. I was uneasy looking at him and the circles the birds were cutting across him; magic like this needs water to make things ordinary again.

But over the bare table in the morning a glass of water goes blind from staring upward.

*

On the drive back down the country we pass through Tikitiki with its tiny church and all the carvings. Anglicanism took root here and it's hard to say who made the other more patrician: the missionaries or the local Māori. There is enough of a truce between me and Roman that I stare straight ahead and tell him not to hate me but that I suspect, or rather, have this feeling, that Nanny Shy watches over our son. He knows I mean the birds and my fear of the fantail and replies that birds are so much older than us; they watch over us, seeing everything we do, and when we die we pass through them.

Roman's words echo the chant of his relative back at the marae. He means that in the old, star-driven world of Māori we don't watch birds so much as they watch us. A song he likes, 'Midnight Rider' by the Allman Brothers Band, is coming through the car stereo and his bird religion has the same shape-shifting mysticism that Larry Levis channels in the Americana of 'Linnets'. The brief peace between us is like the mutual shedding of a skin.

Wolverines will destroy kitchens for pleasure.
Wolverines are so terrible you must give in.

The *O* trilogy by Maurice Gee, a fantasy series for younger readers, is one of my sacred texts. It means as much to me as *Ngati Dread* does to Roman. Gee conjures up a tribe of Birdfolk who were once so vainglorious and such merciless hunters that they were confined to a region of the world of O for their sins. They cannot fly beyond an invisible barrier, and bounce against it to their death when they try. It is one of the Stonefolk, a pudgy subterranean race, who leads them underground to their liberty. They are told they must learn to be as humble as the worm if they want to break the curse and fly over all of O again. On the journey, many of the Birdfolk die even as they come out of the earth for their first and last taste of freedom.

A pair of lovers live; they lie heaving on the shingle, their iridescence caked with mud that they are too exhausted to wash away in the river. Eventually, though, they take to the sky like it's a fresh sheet of paper.

Your shy father extinct in a single footprint,
your mother a stone growing a cuticle.

But Roman and I are not a couple anymore and I am not from the same hapū as my son and Roman—Uepohatu, the stone people who look like the finest Birdfolk of O.

I am not one of them and I didn't grow out of the mountain Hikurangi, which is the first place on Earth to be kissed each day by the sun.

But my place is defined by the space in their laughter that sounds so much like the birds watching our grim human antics from the canopy. The gap in Roman's mirth that he inherited from his relatives has always acted as a warning while I dangle.

Boy says he will never go on a trip with both of us ever again.

I will not have written these words,
I will be that silence slipping around the bend
in the river, where it curves out of sight among weeds,
the silence in which a car backfires and drives away.

When we get home, Boy, who is turning into a young man, keeps playing a song over and over on the guitar that he heard at the graveside of Nanny Shy. I realise the more I hear him play the song that I have heard it before. A night when, maybe, I got on the piss with one of the singers.

It's enough to make me cleave to the presumption Nanny Shy might be using us to walk the old love trail to that holy glitch in the river where Beau waits with folded wings.

It's the sound of Roman telling me that all I write about is horses and the water and that I should do something new . . . it's the space inside the silence of his hands making two circles from nothing in the air.

Who are you killing?

Before Roman, all my boyfriends were fairly nice and normal. In 1997, in my second year at university in Dunedin, I took about 120 dried liberty cap magic mushrooms with one of them. Like Ans, his parents were Dutch, so he was called Dieter. The mushrooms were in little see-through capsules and seemed harmless enough.

We had no specific plan and mooched around Woodhaugh Gardens waiting for the trip to come on. It got dark and I wasn't hallucinating but Dieter's Dalmatian started to weave through the traffic like a spotty ghost and we laughed instead of worrying the dumb, over-bred dog would get hit by a car.

We saw my flatmate near the shops and I was so pleased to run into her I realised what I really wanted to do was go home and trip with them and be around my music and my stuff and just be a girl instead of a girlfriend. I felt bad for wanting to walk away from Dieter, and realised I couldn't abandon him there because that's a stink thing to do to someone you're tripping with.

Walking back with him along the path that hugs the curve of the Gardens a solution came to me without warning: I realised I would be able to go and hang out with my friends if I killed him.

This thought was so sudden and unexpected something else happened in that moment that I've never been able to adequately describe, but I turned to Dieter, who was grinning at me more than a clown, and I asked him if he'd felt what had just happened to me. *Yes*, he said, looking into the eyes I wasn't sure I had anymore.

I did feel that whatever it was that had just used me as a conductor—whatever force, or dark energy—was stickier and more malevolent than tar. I looked down at my arms and it seemed the only release from the world and this horror of being me would be to split the skin of them open so I could flee myself and the force simultaneously.

We went back to his place and I locked myself in the bathroom to look in the mirror for signs of evil. I looked quite pretty actually, and thinner than usual, but my hair was starting to turn into snakes. I eventually came out and said I wanted to draw a picture. It was a very black, scribbly picture but it didn't encompass that darkness I'd absorbed on the street, maybe because I'm shit at art.

I rang Mum, who was in Christchurch working as a nanny for a family who had won Lotto. She was living with the gay man from Riwaka again, content. I wailed down the phone that I had taken too many mushrooms and that I was bad now. I'd hoped talking to Mum would take the panic and fear away and I calmed down after she said some good, typically sound stuff about what might be happening for me.

But after I hung up, I also felt a little cheated that I still didn't seem restored to my rightful self. I drew another picture of a blue translucent orb hovering over a dip in a plain. It seemed I was starting to come down because my shit art was becoming more peaceful and I eventually fell asleep listening to the Bach cello suites Dieter had put on, the cellist hacksawing away at the scales of my frayed nerves.

Dieter was a jazz drummer; we listened to *A Love Supreme* and Miles Davis, Art Blakey and Branford Marsalis and *A Night in Tunisia.* We listened to Satie and Górecki and his mother's copies of Joni Mitchell's *Blue* and we'd kiss to Roberta Flack. I had made him buy the Bach. I thought we were going to get married and I would take him to this hideous bougie homewares shop to pick out the Le Creuset pans we would have in our house. I started teaching myself to cook. I was turning into the father I hated. Dieter taught me yoga and did my astrological chart with his mother and my flatmate gave me some tarot cards.

I cheated on Dieter with one of the normal exes, a jock who always smelled cleaner than soap. Dieter went to Europe to get over it. His family had money. He came back pretty much over me, beatific and newly vegetarian and with an annoying new habit: meditation. I got rid of the boyfriend who was a lot more fun than him and made us get back together.

And now I'd taken some mushrooms and wanted to kill him. Oops.

For days after the trip I lay in my bed in the room that was more of a roost in the flat I shared with the girls. There seemed to be an invisible impenetrable barrier between me and the me I used to be just last week. Distant bits of self had fled over the skyline out my window and I was lying there not feeling right at all, hoping that no one would notice I seemed to be having the thoughts of a serial killer, that obsession so peculiar to the nineties.

When I did eventually present at psych services I was convinced I was a monster that was going to slash my family. They told me I'd had a drug-induced psychotic experience and prescribed me anti-depressants, sleeping pills and haloperidol, an anti-psychotic drug that made me feel even crazier, but diffuse.

I left university and lay down some more, eating Memphis Meltdowns, Fry's Turkish Delight and foul tahini-on-toast concoctions. I watched re-runs of *The Cosby Show* and played Tetris so much one of my flatmate's boyfriends hid the pocket game from me in an act of pious assholery. I eventually found it in the fridge.

Princess Diana died and I watched my flatmate Jaq emote. I had no emotions and no sense of smell but every night before I went to sleep I was plagued with visions I was some kind of wolf beast stalking through the forest killing everything. I put on 14 kg and barely washed and when I did have a bath I would flood the carpet and do nothing about it. I am still friendly with both Jaq and the other flatmate who tolerated my breakdown, which is a testament to their character rather than mine.

Jaq said my issue was minimal. She confessed she had a thing with wanting to stab people in the eye with a fork if they talked too much.

I trained myself to sleep well at nights and through most of the day. Sleep was the only escape from the plague of myself, a plummet into a velvety nothing.

Once I woke up and Mum was just sitting there, wondering, I guess, what the fuck had happened to her daughter. She moved back to Dunedin and I went to live with her. I had barely left home and now I was back.

By the time I had my son three years later at twenty-one, I was partially recovered from the notion I was a secret murderous presence in the world, but now, over twenty years later, I see my life, or rather myself, as hinged like a see-saw on that one bad trip. The before and after are like a photo and its negative. A jersey I've been wearing inside-out ever since and pretending my working circuits are still discrete instead of gaping.

Recovery theory insists there is a transformative aspect to mental illness, that the new stitches in old torn seams make us transcend the limits of our former shame or brokenness. I would very much like to believe this was true, but I miss myself at eighteen, so bolshy and certain in my own skin. I could have taken fewer mushrooms and not cracked my yolk.

I spent part of my nineteenth birthday at A&E, waiting to see psych services, convinced I was evil. I was there because I'd had to use a knife to slice a focaccia bread I'd made in an attempt to appear normal and entertain people. I'd never heard of a trigger warning but knives were my trigger.

But I also think when the professionals who dealt with my crisis told me I was having a psychotic experience and medicated me using the same language, it did not adequately house or dose the feelings and connections I had that night on the path beside the park. Using the psychodynamic diagnostic tools that also inform psychiatry, I was psychotic. But by their own definition my first response to those alien murderous thoughts was anxious and neurotic, the flipside of the antisocial paradigm they used to decide my treatment fate.

Later, on just anti-depressants, I would hide knives and hammers in an attempt to keep them from myself, ruled by this fear I would use them as a weapon to hurt someone I loved. I was a devout new disciple of the word 'psychosis'.

When you are psychotic, it is the external world that presents the problem. When you think you are the problem, the anxious self-surveillance kicks in with its inverse mimesis of insanity. It's the classical split between neurosis and psychosis that informs much of social psychology's approach to understanding internal strife and disorder. Freud goes in and out of fashion but his ideas run through us in the West like water.

But, for me, the most awful thing about my new affliction was that it was the people I cared for, mostly women, I imagined hurting the most. Men were a respite because I couldn't imagine overpowering them and of course being alone with children was the worst scenario and I avoided them, including the younger cousins I had happily volunteered to babysit in the past.

I had always been proud of my memory but it became a torment. I would hide the hammer and still know where it was. I should have told that pious asshole who hid my Tetris game to take the hammer instead but we'd already run into trouble over our divergent eating philosophies and it wasn't safe to tell him I was a monster.

I hated the flattened-out world of anti-depressants and took myself off them after six months. When I went back to psych services I described my withdrawal from Aropax as feeling like my teeth were fizzing and a seagull was beating its wings in my head. The elfin psychiatrist in a Hawaiian shirt told me he didn't think I was depressed. But I always think I know better than Pākehā men in corduroy pants, so I insisted I was and that I'd rather just be depressed without having to take the pills.

But in retrospect he was right: it wasn't depression; it was the force, the oily black pool opening up like a wound. The horror briefer than a second that had radiated out of me like a bomb and I was still stuck with the aftershocks, the wayward impulses and the fear of them, not realising the fear was the revulsion that prevented my acting on them. And so on. I couldn't differentiate between cognition, feelings, impulses and my imagination; I was swimming in alphabet soup.

Now I know thoughts belong to the head and feelings belong to the body and that feelings get in a tangle if they get stuck in your head with no way out of your body. But I still don't have much certainty that I *exist* as a continuous presence. My Facebook and Twitter timelines are an over-curated testament to this constant feeling of slipperiness. *Look at what I ate, look at what I think, look at my kid, look at me.*

According to recovery theory dogma we are meant to be able to change our lives because we make ourselves up as we go along, and if we are in charge of that storytelling, anything is possible. But equally, these constructivist, narrative ideologies fuck with the notion of having a soul, or pip, a special kernel that makes you *you*.

We read to know we are not alone—who said this? Did they mean that in our necessary solitude we experience the company of another world, a release valve from the unbearable parts of reality?

Certainly, all my reading has acted as some kind of map towards and away from the burden of a self, the search for and the escape of it, even when reading the back of shampoo bottles, phonebooks and cans. When I was unwell, I searched for books that would explain what had happened to me but none of them came close. Either too medical or too New Age.

For most of my late twenties I worshipped the great Canadian short-story writer Alice Munro and I still do. When I'm feeling morbid I google to see whether Alice—the same age as my nana, and from the same era as Elizabeth Taylor—has died. I take solace in knowing that Alice Munro's writing career didn't take off until she was in her late thirties. I survived seven years living on the main road of a small town I call 'the deadly village by the sea' by pretending she was writing me into the place. Each interaction, even a trip to the dairy for milk, had these layers. I learned to live off not much and I watched the traffic a lot because I was obsessed with someone I imagined to be normal. And I read Alice Munro like she was reading me.

And it was there in her last collection that I found my affliction, in a loose and frankly patchy set of stories called *Dear Life*. A semi-autobiographical tale about an adolescent girl who starts to fret she is going to kill her sibling after some bedridden illness. One night, or early in the witching hour, she flees to the kitchen to escape herself, but Alice discovers her father is already there, sitting at the table. She confesses her trouble to him. And he absolves her of the torment by telling her that, basically, everyone thinks stuff like this—it's not abnormal. He says less than this because he is a farmer like Munro's father.

We all think such things.

Your fear is not unique.

But after what happened at the park with Dieter—which could be described as *nothing* really—I started choosing men who were more frightening or damaged than me. Whether I was conscious of this or not. It's probably because my default settings are ambivalent. And I covet being a princess, so my romantic history is full of disaster.

*

After our son is born, Roman goes out to the phone in the corridor to tell his sisters the baby has arrived. When he returns, he says he has just seen Dieter. I didn't know he was having a baby too, a girl born eight weeks early, the same day as my boy.

The day before we take our baby home, Dieter materialises in the shared room where a woman has a baby darker than mine covered in fur like a gorilla that she sings to and whose song I can still remember and sometimes hum to comfort myself. Dieter brings me a white flower—I think it was a camellia—and tells me about his baby girl, who is upstairs in NICU but will be fine. Dieter used to meditate a *lot* and the white flower was what he used when he thought of me instead of the wolf I felt certain was lurking inside me. The flower was easier to deal with than the flesh.

I am not sure what I am thinking or feeling for my newborn—Roman is the instant parent, not me. I have never known anything like what I am feeling. I still imagine myself to be a detached person instead of ravaged by my own emotions.

But as my milk comes in, I look out the window of the maternity ward and the three red leaves left clinging to the tree are too piercing to be true. Autumn is a poignant season, but this was beyond melancholy; here was a tenderness.

At home, Mum helps me give my baby his first bath and something about her hands lowering him into the light steam, with my arms underneath him too, and his slight shock at the warm water helps me realise I *have* felt this before.

The fresh insane love I have for my son is her old feeling for me.

Lazy Susan

Mickey said he didn't start the fire. In Ōamaru, in their house by the sea. Mickey was four and home alone with his sister, who was only three and trying to seek refuge in a cupboard. Mickey pulls her out of her deadly hiding place and leads her from the house being choked by smoke out to the long grass behind the glasshouses. They watch as their parents arrive home from their shift at the fish-and-chip shop. Their mother spills like guts from the car screaming and screaming. She thinks they are lost inside.

Then Mickey and his baby sister emerge from the long grass. They run towards her, alive.

At their family Christmas I notice Mickey's mother never puts her elbows on the table. She doesn't believe in Jesus, much, but she bakes off massive trays of noodles in the oven to minimise the oil. She walked across China as an orphan eating grass and dirt after watching the Japanese murder her family. Now she looks to her left up the valley of Mickey's baby sister's house while her children and their children are noisy around her, and my piña colada trifle is a rum-soaked disaster but this family is polite.

Mickey is a builder and uses a wok to mix gib compound. He used to be a hairdresser too and finally gives my son a decent haircut.

Mickey is one of his mother's favourites—of all the

thirteen children she had with the shrewd businessman who rescued her as a refugee in Taiwan—but she still blames him for lighting the fire. Her children were all named by Pākehā and Māori nurses when they were born in Ōamaru, and they grew up knowing their mother's hakka name for them too. The nurse's naming was intended as a primer for Kiwi life.

Mickey was living with his mother when I met him. He'd left an older woman after thirteen years together because he wanted children of his own.

I wish his stories had been enough; they were all so true. He knew fresh pineapple with mint and sugar was a good cure for a hangover. But I lied to him. I lied to him. And his mother calls me 'Pretty One' in her Hakka dialect and feeds me a slice of frozen pizza done on both sides in the electric frying pan because she knows.

Mickey hopes that Kerry and I won't be pretty forever. It is a mean thing to be hopeful about, out loud, the inevitable loss of our looks. He has good skin and is twelve years older than me but he still tells me I have a wrinkle because I believe I have none. He pokes a finger at the wrinkle when he takes me out for an Indian meal near the Octagon, although he is almost as generous to dine with as Paul. Mickey orders things at yum cha I wouldn't think to but lets me hold the biro because he knows I love making the little ticks on the menu. Ben would order for us and I would feel anxious. Mickey is possessive in other ways.

I still go with Roman to the cemetery so we can be alone together with my back against a tree. But I finish before he's even started at me for himself.

The deadly village by the sea seems to think I am a retired hooker but I'm a feminist. It seems unfortunate no one can get past the leotards I wear; I have no women friends there at all. When Kerry arrives with her kids for the weekend their eyes narrow further.

There is no point trying to tell Mickey I'm a feminist because his best friend sees me from their white work truck and says, *Talia is wearing her fuck-me boots again.*

I still have the boots. They are vintage knee-high seventies reddish amber leather, round-toed with big wooden heels and were only eight dollars from the St Vincent de Paul in 2002. A hoko shop score! I am twenty-six when I'm with Mickey and I listen to 'Jealous Guy' and Dire Straits driving to Tīmaru to buy more stuff from the Warehouse. There are other, nicer shops, but I can barely drive yet, or park. State Highway 1 is easier than town. And I feel like the Warehouse is what I deserve for not enjoying Mickey's money. He is sadly wonderful to my son, who is four, and they have matching Red Band gumboots to leave beside each other at the door.

The whitebait and crayfish are also too good to be true. Mickey looks like Peter Pan when he comes back from the mouth of the river in his green wetsuit with all that white gold. I love him when he isn't near me. I love the wild salmon he catches—the farmed stuff is inferior. He bakes it in paper in the oven with capers, red onion, lemon and tomatoes. He couriers some whitebait to Paul and Paul decides he is a nice man.

And then I'm the rat chased out of the whare with a carving knife. Because he's come home from a long day and I've been getting stoned and thinking about someone who, despite the beanie, reminds me of Paul Newman. And I ask Mickey, *What's for dinner?*

She didn't know, she knew.

I can't live with what I have done and the nectarines in the fruit bowl start to feel like *magic* nectarines the more I stare at them. The rude question about dinner was a timed one.

Roman has a story about his father pulling an entire family from a burning house, but he didn't stop afterwards—he left them lying steaming in the grass and kept driving down the valley into Kaikōura.

It took a while to solve the mystery of who the hero was. No one caught his name. Singed footprints but no ātea, no ātea stretched by the grace of the unreal, at all.

The Queen of Swords

It took me three months to fall in love with him, but Ben wore me down. His manipulations were finer than the dust coming off the chisel chipping away at my resistance, and even more opaque. No one, particularly not a man, had ever listened to me like this before. Not even Dieter. Not even his fun replacement, Nicky Glynn, who listened to the Kinks and mouthed *cherry cola* at me through the smoke rings. Not even the blond jock who gave me hickeys while I clutched the handlebars as we doubled on his bike, hurtling down a hill.

No man had ever participated so willingly in the tomfoolery of my head or indulged my fondest memories and darkest secrets like they were a string of opal beads coming loose in his hands. Ben chuckled on his back in the blue of his room and claimed, in response to my stories, that he was just a nice, ordinary English guy. Like Ben was short for benign. I was surprised by how easy it was, just being there with him.

At a party two weeks later—by the kind of sheer coincidence endemic to Dunedin—I overheard a woman I already did not like much rave on in a distorted, freshly-broken-up-with voice about Ben to a friend, and I whispered in his other available ear: *Is Ben, nice . . . he said he was nice?* My friend nodded but might have been agreeing with her. And I blamed the fact that she wouldn't stop talking about Ben on her, not him, which reveals my feminism to be choosy and subject to karma.

She didn't know I'd slept with him a fortnight before, after a year-long drought of not fucking anyone. So the eavesdropping was the only habitual thing for me, not the casual sex. I am too high-maintenance to be treated casually—one of the few things I know about myself, and only by embarrassing misadventure.

But I liked Ben's room. It was a denim-blue den with good white sheets and a view from the bed of the harbour through the bare copper beech to the other, open side of the sea. And I was in love with someone who lived round the corner, someone who I had not slept with but stayed the night with a week after I'd been at Ben's, in another dazzling Dunedin coincidence.

In the taxi after the first night, Ben said, *Look at me*, and then after scanning my face added, *You're still cute*, meaning I'd survived what the morning does to strangers. Before the taxi arrived, he said he could not get enough of me, even just lying there. As a fool I read this kind of lush praise as my due.

I wasn't that interested in him. Apart from the fact that he had nice dope and made me come twice with his hand, he seemed very vanilla. In the daylight he reminded me of a bunyip, a woodland creature, chinless and balding, too shyly vain about his gym body as he went into the en suite and turned on the shower to hide the sounds of being human from me.

After a while I gave in to his persistent invitations to come back to his house and that convenient den. Ben's messages made the twin mistakes of addressing me as 'Miss' and using the word 'cuddle' in a sentence. So I put him off, which made me a challenge, I suppose. Before bed I confessed to being in love with the man round the corner and Ben was really good about it. Which I could have blamed just as easily on the Ecstasy we'd taken. We fell asleep grinning at each other in the shifting morning dark.

And he continued to be good about the other men—even Luke, my former obsession, the Paul Newman substitute, who came back from working the Australian mines for a holiday and also for sex. Ben was reasonable about this without the help of Ecstasy, so I turned Luke down and finally won the latter's respect. I mean, this had been the game: the heterosexual limbo that kept my ego lowering itself when I lived in that deadly village by the sea for seven years and used Luke and leotards to stop myself from losing my mind.

When I told Ben about the woman from the party raving about him and his kids, he said she suffered from anxiety. He said they went tramping together, and he got *cross.* He told her, *If you don't like it you can leave*. He told me the way I lay in his bed doing nothing all day was adorable compared to her grated beetroot and her anxiety. That he could smell me at work. He took a photo of how messy my ancient Nissan station wagon was before laughing at my holey tights under my expensive dress, and we went for drinks at a bar. He mistook my chronic levels of disorganisation for my being bohemian and sexy. Both words I despise. He confessed inside the bar in a low voice that he thought Margaret Thatcher was a wonderful woman and this was fresh information to me. *What?* I hooted, *You can't be serious?*

I think about those first early nights a lot, and sometimes struggle with the chronology—which night was I where? Who did I go home with first? I know I left my red gumboots and silver-and-sapphire sequinned butterfly top at the house round the corner as I snuck off early, left them there in his cosy, artful hut so there would be a reason to go back.

I stayed too long at Ben's that first night and in the afternoon, while I was getting ready to leave, he made me wear a jersey his mother had knitted for him back in England, because I'd lost my own grey cowl knee-length jersey dress dancing at the bar. Ben's jersey had the texture and look of muesli and was knitted with wool Mummy had spun from her own sheep. *You have to wear this*, he said, fully aware he was being a girl about it.

An adult should not blame the turn her life took on a jersey, but I still do.

I could also blame it on the moment I caved and went back to his house and I was disliking his business shirt and switching off as he yammered on before the Ecstasy hit, and he told me his mother had once stuck a carving knife in the table because he was sent to prison for shooting at pikeys—as he called them—when he was nineteen. Wait, what? Suddenly Ben wasn't such an ordinary guy. It is only later that I will realise he shot at, or near, caravans full of sleeping children.

It makes me wince to admit the concessions I made before I got used to Ben. When at some point my attachment to his presence became cellular. I liked the smell of his shirt coming off the hiss of the iron.

He seemed like a safer bet than the other men chasing me. He would drink cheap cooking sherry and burn Sunday roasts ready for when I finished my evening shift, and leave small greenstone studs, a gift not quite to my taste, beside the oven. It was sweet and non-threatening. It was cosy. I had no idea I was being seduced because being cherished through conversation felt so wholesome. One of my other men, Tama, scoffed and renamed Ben 'The Woman', which was both accurate and underestimated his power.

Ben agreed he was a lesbian when I told him he reminded me of Mum. His charm had a feminine, calculating quality, because deep down he fancied he was a silverback, the alpha and omega of the pack. He dripped sweat on me when we fucked, but his arms felt nice afterwards. He cooked full English breakfasts and insisted the black pudding on his plate was the best part. He ruined Rick Stein for me by making foul lip-smacking noises of possessive delight. Ben had been everywhere in the world I had not. I underestimated him too.

The man round the corner did not underestimate him. We went out for a drink and I tried to tell him I was sort of still in love with him, but then Ben turned up in the new Hyundai the company had humiliated him with instead of the Holden he wanted. The man sneered at me and said, *I don't want a lift with you, I'm not getting in that fucking car with him.*

Ben teased me about how the man was a *gyppo*, and must stink like patchouli because he knew that I was fussy about smells. I teased him back about being a freemason and the ridiculous aqua aprons they wear. The fact that he was right wing was still cute to me. Cute as his sermons about the high production values of ABBA as 'S.O.S.' tinkled on in the background with its jangly descending runs.

Ben let the dog sleep on the bed and really listened while I looked up another old childhood show on YouTube. He was not familiar with Manu, but his enthusiasms were equally infectious. He nattered on to a taxi driver about his childhood telly heroes Bagpuss and the Fingerbobs and, in the back beside me, Kerry, my true e hoa and sister, said: *Marry him.* Ben had given her Ecstasy too. All the drugs came from Ben; he was always sweetly shoving down my throat, in the name of fun, something I was reluctant to take, given my patchy history with psychedelics.

Ben was like Teflon on the comedown, nothing stuck—which did raise the uncomfortable question of whether he had a soul, an actual pip—whereas I'm like a strip of flypaper for a bad buzz, even on the up.

Ben finished me off by taking me to Glendhu Bay. I was restless about being alone with him in the hut he rented: it was not my grandparents sacred orange-and-white caravan. It felt a bit wrong to take drugs there. Jim was dying in his bed and here I was with a libertine. Gwen and Ben never warmed to each other.

I was squirmy while we took Ecstasy and played cards, something I used to do with kindly ageing Mormons. When he took me back to my river—a haunt even more special than the camp—I felt like I was splitting on myself, so I invited Kerry, who was having a genuine romantic crisis, to come and share our tiny hut. Ben was good about this and drove us slowly around the empty camp with Dire Straits blaring, which seemed hilarious. Kerry repeated that I should marry him.

I followed Ben back to Dunedin in the decrepit station wagon he claimed to find enchanting and thought, *Oh I love you, oh no, that's what this is.*

Nine months later I was at another party chatting with an old friend, and Ben came bounding up to join us, but the friend iced Ben, telling him he can never speak to him again after the way he treated the woman at the party. She was conspicuously absent from this party and her friends kept giving me the evils. This encounter was doubly startling because I had just dropped some acid with Ben and I knew the trip would hit differently now with this fresh information.

Once Ben skulked off I confessed to my old friend that the only thing that really worried me was Ben's attitude towards my son. I didn't confess that Ben had just made me have an abortion because he said we had been too wasted—that otherwise our baby would be perfect. He got a vasectomy a week later without discussing it with me, when I was youngish then at thirty-two and still wanted more children.

I didn't confess that getting ready for the party Ben had been fretting that we were spending too much time together, that I was on the benefit and working part-time, and it could get him in trouble. Even with his $150k salary package, he did not want to support my son while I cooked for his children. His father was worried I was a solo mother on the take, but Ben reassured him that I'd filled the cupboards and was a proper cook. In private Ben reminded me that really, he paid for everything.

As the acid Ben paid for came on in the bar toilets at the party I told myself I was a saint. I told my reflection that I was the good one. Perhaps the attraction of certain men is that they allow one to wear a halo.

At Ben's later, I found a begging, apologetic love letter from the woman at the party, where she thanked Ben for cooking her lovely meat and grovelled for not being grateful. She noted how nice his arms felt. And I wrote her off again.

I was stupidly in love with Ben. No sign or nothing anyone said really penetrated, even though I had already left him once, when my son met a famous rugby-playing cousin, Jamie Joseph, who gave us some tickets for a game. Ben seethed at me about it after watching us from the company car. He was jealous of a ten-year-old, which was both pitiful and insane. I went back to him because I was pregnant and he wanted to help me not have it. Babies, love: it's all dangerous and potentially disastrous. And instead of listening to my intuition I tuned out the inner voices; I ghosted myself. I split.

Disassociation is the only explanation I have for why I later let Ben call my son the dirty n****r—something he said more than once about my son, when once should have been enough. I would whip around and challenge him and he'd say *What are you talking about, I never said that, you're going mad, I can't have a mad girlfriend.* When I told Tama Ben used the n-word about my son, he could scarcely believe it—not that Ben would say it, but that I would permit it and stay.

If anyone praised my son in front of Ben, especially his own family, I would pay for it later. I would be reminded that my son was not special, brave or good-looking. Ben said he could not wait for him to fail. He wanted life to wind him out of his cockiness. None of these sentiments were acceptable to me and to repeat them doesn't really capture their stinging, dissembling poison. It was like I was stunned.

Five years later Ben's façade cracked in front of Mum and he banged his fist on her table about how he expected my son to behave. I can't remember his crime. I do remember being pretty drunk, the silent soaked kind of wasted, looking out the dark window at the port's giant blinking forklifts as they shifted containers. And saying nothing. Afterwards, Mum said *that wasn't like you* but who was I? I'd felt very certain of my worth going in.

I'm still unable to reconcile how Ben went from treating me as precious to filming me trying to cut my own throat as he snickered and promised to show the rich friends I had refused to meet. I was slow to realise how much Ben strove, above all, to manage perceptions.

The final text, where Ben called my son a 'boff head piece of meat' as he tried to kick him out of the house, is seared into my mind. As an IT guy, Ben rarely left a digital footprint, but I finally had proof. I can ignore what happens in real life quite easily—it is too shocking to be true—but I have never been able to ignore words on a page or a screen. Ben's text was the last fray of the string. I felt it snap.

Ben told me I could take his Audi up to Riwaka when I cried and told him that I couldn't do this anymore. I was meant to be driving up there for Easter to meet Mum. I wasn't usually allowed to drive the 'good' car. I was certain I was leaving him and was boiling with anger the next day on the drive up the island, but I was also anxious that my son was with me; I thought I would get in trouble with Ben for taking my son on a holiday. I could hear him in my head saying *That dirty n****r is sitting on my seats.*

Coming down the valley before the coast at Kaikōura my son was in charge of the playlist and put on our relative Raina doing a karanga to a whale. The whale called back to her. I laughed because it was Kaikōura but also because he knew I was waiting to see a dolphin. He changed the song to Real Life's 'Send Me an Angel' and then near a tiny island to our right a pod of dusky dolphins started flipping in the air and stalking fish in real time.

From Riwaka I rang Ben and told him I didn't love him anymore. When I talked to him again, stoned and less resolved, he sounded like he had been crying and announced that he was the one who'd had enough. He told me his son felt the same, which cut me more than his cowardice because I realised Ben was pinning this on him. I enjoyed being a stepmother. Our sons were the same age.

When I got back to Dunedin a few days later Ben was gone. I was already familiar with how much he needed it to look like he was leaving me—so that even he could believe it. I often announced that I was leaving him and Ben would say that I was mad to think anyone else would have me. Then he would counter that he was leaving me. He would remind me that when we got together everyone had warned him I was crazy.

It took two days after we split for Ben to ring his lawyer so he could argue we had never really been together at all.

He had taken his art, which were just prints, from the house, knowing I would deface them as revenge for not facing my anger. But he left his box of memories behind and, after throwing all his abandoned clothes out the window, I stuck his memories in the fire: the school reports, the love letters, the Father's Day cards in scrawly pen, his beloved postcards from Mummy where she described all the cheap cheese she was eating in France. Jaq watched, horrified, and tried to stop me by saying, *You might regret that later Talia*, and I replied, *No I will not.* It wasn't enough, I needed to scream in his face. I needed to erase him but like a magician he had already disappeared.

When Ben did answer his mobile he said in a small whimper, *I have been told I am an abused man.*

He hid down the bottom of the driveway and let the lawyer and her assistant pick up his mess. I had flour bombed all the clothes and ripped up his Steve Jobs biography with my hands and teeth; I threw eggs out the window that didn't crack, so I had to run down the path to crack them on the clothes. I spat all through the Audi trying to curse it. I screamed the n-word and *cunts* at the lawyers and questioned their feminism as they picked through his mess. Ben wasn't scared of me—he hid at the bottom of the driveway because he was scared his anger would show.

Jaq was wrong. I still wish I had blown up Ben's car as the grand finale to incinerating his palpable memories in the log burner. People hate Audi drivers in this country and maybe I would have had the sympathy of the nation. But this is where the age inserts a meme of me walking away gorgeous from a burning car. This is where the mask gets stiff because I was fat and crazy with crazier hair.

I told the lawyer I was made to get by Ben's lawyer that I just wanted people to know who he really was. It was a grandiose and pointless response to the separation agreement she read to me that stated I could have the thirsty Terrano and $5k if I promised never to speak to Ben again. In that calculating way of his Ben would have known I had plenty to say, and that I couldn't contest how long we had really been together because of my time on the benefit when he paid for everything.

I keep wearing down the old familiar grooves of the record, trying to understand how I could be so naive and this is where the literature gets in the way. Where we both become reduced to caricatures instead of flawed characters.

I was love-bombed—I could have just written that at the beginning. Love bombing is the technical term for the opal beads coming loose in his hands. It is probably better to be more precise and describe how Ben would smash cups in the garden if he found the mess of my forgotten weeds.

*

My friend and former neighbour Sam wanted three people dead so every day at lunchtime he set aside five minutes to pray for them. He prayed for their good fortune and for their families. Because otherwise the bitterness would consume him, and he was already recovering from a heart attack. There is something of the parable to this because it's true. But I enjoy my revenge fantasies too much to pray for Ben—and besides, it's a bit late now, for any of that.

I used to say, after his attempt to erase me, that it would have been easier if Ben had just died, or if I had—if there had just been some terrible accident instead. And then recently, I found out Ben is dead. And since you can't speak ill of the dead, I'll instead leave it up to Mum, who, between puffs on her rollie in the time of carnage and lawyers said, *He's gaslighting you. What's that?* I asked. *He's a narcissist*, she said. Maybe the word 'narcissist' has become so popular because it has such a satisfying, triple hiss.

Now I know everything there is to know about narcissists. I know enough to question whether I am one, when the answer is probably rhetorical: narcissists are not prone to self-reflection even as they seek their own image. As an empath it was my task to be Ben's body of water and mirror—but then, empath is a word that also vaguely disgusts me.

I have done the mahi though! I have done the deep dives into the pop psychology paddling pool! I have scaled down the ladder into the well of websites that promise recovery from narcissists. I have stalked through every Facebook group run by deranged lonely people sharing battle stories and I have watched YouTube tutorials where beautiful, formerly broken women break it down for me: why Ben was incapable of real love.

Did he really make me clean the brake dust off the wheels of my new car with a toothbrush while he stood over me with a running hose only to grab the brush from my hand and hiss that I wasn't doing it properly?

Was there a moment every Saturday after 11am when he would become septic with his hangover and tired of our *Come Dine With Me* TV marathon in bed and tell me to sit outside because I was fat, lazy and useless? Why else would I give in and clean the shower ready for when Bea, his older sister, arrived on her weekly break from work? And we would smoke and laugh in the garden or the den of our room with her and make fun of what a tyrant Ben was like none of it had ever happened.

Which parts am I concocting with too much reverb when I wang on like this? His sister never even used the shower. Ben was ecstatic the one time I cleaned behind the microwave and sorted the recipe books I didn't need to use.

I finally found the version of my 'us', the Ben that resonated the most, in an article on trauma bonding on the Business Insider website. I questioned the literature then—and myself. But then, none of the words we have for heartbreak adequately describe the wound and I would like to surface from the sea of other broken people with just a scar.

Instead, I am stuck with this malignant itch while I try to make the literature fit, try to knit my love story into the lexicon of the bad man with the disordered personality. And language like this tends to atrophy; the shorthand we use tends to define us more than the actual pain. Once people get their repetitive mitts on words like 'emotional labour', 'love language' and 'gaslighting', the mask dries and cracks form over our real face.

The End of the Affair by Graham Greene is one of my favourite novels but it makes love and thwarted desire seem better than life, more plush and realised. Greene uses the subtle shorthand of onions to evoke the secret language of the infatuated. So, it is a shame that reading my favourite literary fiction after my family ended was also of little use.

The last book I read when we were together was Richard Flanagan's *The Narrow Road to the Deep North* and I skipped the Burma death march bits while I absorbed the redhead wearing a glowing locket in her casket as easily as rain.

I couldn't watch or read anything romantic after I left Ben but I gorged on Holocaust and potato famine documentaries. I fell asleep on the solitary couch listening to the imperial crimes of the Congo on a podcast. I comforted myself with the thought that, throughout history, people had been a lot unluckier than me, had suffered much worse annihilation that was less privileged and personal.

I still struggle with any content or mention of romantic love. Instead, I cackled through *The War of the Roses*. What a wonderful movie! Especially the bit where Michael Douglas reaches for Kathleen Turner's hand as they lie dying and she rejects him. I was reduced to satire. Or Ashley Judd thrillers.

Elena Ferrante has described better than me how a betrayed woman becomes *coarse*. I swear a lot in real life—it's all fucking this and fucking that—but after it ended I would be like: that motherfucker needs to die. My language had become too specific; I was both the maggots and the corpse where Ben used to be. In my search for closure I ignored the black hole of the full stop. It had ended. The End.

Now I'm an opal in a shipwreck's lost chest, wishing I could ascend like the jellyfish hovering above, wishing I could shapeshift into their sweet empty rise to the top. Wishing I could shake off the literature as easily as a dog shakes off water.

Widows wear black so the rest of the village know to be careful of the void, of the loss she wears as a shroud. Victorians designed household manuals decorated with lilies and African violets to show people how to grieve—grief is one of the few things the Victorians were hedonistic about. In the current *Diagnostic and Statistical Manual of Mental Disorders*, the *DSM-5*, grief and loss are only registered if they become disordered, when really it is the world that is disordered; the medical model tends to pathologise the normal reaction to the harder parts of life.

Now the age is recycling different cosmic schlock, the zeitgeist says it's not me, but my Virgo placements. *Live! Laugh! Love!* shout the myna birds from the café art on the wall of our consciousness. But if I stand too long in my light and my power I might combust.

The older tropes are better and tell me to slash at myself with mussel shells until I'm running with red, that my task is to mimic and exaggerate the precise shape and feel of the wound. My ancestors cheer on my wailing and pleas to be tied to the funeral pyre, or maybe they shake me awake and tell me not to waste myself on Ben. It seems likelier that my ancestors want me to get a grip.

This is why Hinepoupou, my long ago tipuna, swam between islands. It wasn't a widow's drowning sorrow: she was chasing her tane down. Her swim was motivated by lust for vengeance.

Big Nana, my Pākehā great-grandmother, who refused to speak to Mum after I was born and instead asked the room who the pickaninny baby belonged to, spent the last ten years of her life in a La-Z-Boy trying to unpick a ball of wool, only to make even more of a tangle of it. I feel like this about Ben's death—that he should not be allowed to get away with it, but also, look at the tangle it makes.

But I struggle with resurrecting Ben, with breathing life back into him, when he died a nobody who wanted to be a somebody. It was his habit to divide the world using labels like this—not mine. And the very thing he found attractive about me was that I did not share his vulgar aspirations to be a somebody; I was smug that my worth was a secret. But if I really had more self-respect and was naturally taciturn instead of prone to self-exposure as a means of exacting utu I could let his name get wiped by the tide with my silence.

Ben also died not wanting to know me. I had obliged him in this sense by being terrifying, by digging at the dirt of his escape hole with my claws.

I have not been able to experience any pleasure from memories of being with him without it ringing with too much pain, but paradoxically, it was maybe the happiest I have ever been. The white tent of sheet over us in the blue den and the stories running between us like an orchard of stars. Writing this has been my first pleasure and cheap therapy.

But I cannot remember that brief happiness without feeling the same basic incomprehension I had near the end, when I was constantly frightened that something could happen to my son: an intrusive, obsessive thought that started to take me over the longer I was with Ben, because shame grafts better than skin and grows other, distracting protrusions. It is a malady I should have exhausted as my son is safe now and wishes I would stop talking about him.

Cheating death by casting futile spells—maybe this is my chief project here? Zapping the old stories back into life and lasering through the dust atrophied to my face as clay. Looking for a way to chip his real name off the cast to feel the light pricking my skin as a sweet, rather than piercing, thing.

But even to begin to entertain this dream I had to change his name.

*

Ben made me go to his twin Jasper's wedding. He told me he would break up with me if I didn't go. Not going to family weddings, like the dog being on the bed, had turned into a potentially excommunicable offence. This seemed cruel, because I wanted to marry Ben—not watch his twin getting married. Two years earlier Jasper had insulted me the day after Jim died, my first serious loss, by suggesting I should be over it already. I was not. Over it. Yet.

But I fantasised about the dog wearing a pointless tuxedo at my imaginary wedding. I wanted ten bridesmaids! After almost four years together I officially lived with Ben and was off the benefit! I had weathered watching Jasper leave his wife for another woman.

I agreed to do pudding for their reception, even though I found them and their love repulsive. I reasoned that I could do lovely food and not go—*I can send the food and my apologies*, I begged. *No*, he said. When I needled at him, Ben said if he was going to marry anyone again it would be me.

I could not understand why I had to go to this wedding when he didn't come with me to Mugwi's massive tangi: they were both over summer and weeks apart.

I made eighty-six sugar pastel roses to decorate Nana's recipe for ginger-and-lemon-jelly mini cheesecakes. I made two giant pavlovas: one topped with strawberries drowning in redcurrant jelly I had strained by hand; the other mango, slathered in golden kiwifruit and yellow passionfruit pulp. I dipped more strawberries in white and milk chocolate and made a tower of them with floating plastic cupids. I hate-made that food with love. I refused to appear in the wedding photos—I felt too fat—and emitted waves of hostility at the guests who kept asking Jasper what was wrong with the dark, angry woman.

I don't know how I became part of this heterosexual nightmare when maybe the fact that I was raised in a lesbian coven almost explains it. I couldn't recognise subtle danger signs out in the wilds of men. I had become a woman who cared about executing a pudding to perfection and managing perceptions, a pitiful rebellion against my sapphic elders. Pathetic as when I used to make Mum stop for an age while I browsed the bridal magazines at four. I would have been wearing my tutu; I refused to take it off, except for in the bath.

All the children and teenagers at the wedding—my sullen allies, who snickered with me up the back during the ceremony—said my pudding was delicious when I accosted them.

But I need the parallel recurring fantasy I nurse to be the real story . . . where I object to the marriage mid-vows, announce to the converted stables with its twee fucking bunting that the whole family is racist and fucked in the head, then walk out of their family compound at the former Seacliff Asylum, and drive off and away from their expat conceit, making sure, at least, that my impressive pavs were dressed in the wake of my devastation.

If I had driven off tooting fuck u in the mid-range BMW hatchback that was in Ben's name but that I paid for on his spreadsheet of love and had christened Eva Braun in the name of problematic relationships.

If I had made a scene, if I had just left in a blaze of incriminating glory. That would have been a satisfying ending.

But then I wouldn't have woken the next day and got on it with the wedding party, less rigid with indignant rage and even apologising to a woman who I had told to get fucked when she asked if I was pregnant in my big indigo smock. I wouldn't have endured Ben pissing out E on me in the toilets after finally catching me as I hooted and shrieked with laughter. I had run off with his drugs and given them away to the others to atone for being such a cunt at the actual wedding with my sour thunderous looks. Dancing all night while he said *Yes darling, yes*, in the old goofy way. Bea, who I loved, wouldn't have sidled up to me the first day of the wedding as she unwrapped the gladwrap from the couscous and the coronation chicken and said, *Don't worry, I'm hating this as much as you.*

Or if, even earlier, in the blue beginning—if only I had been brave enough to knock on the other man's door and ask for my gumboots back and my lovely butterfly top. I don't like taking Ecstasy at all; it is a hollow, carnival drug and the other man was my kind of orphan.

Or later, in the aftermath of the real ruin, if only I had not drawn the Queen of Swords doing my tarot cards and felt the shiver of recognition, thinking it was me. Months after finding a stray long red hair on Ben's coat in the blur where he used our children as a human shield and shuffled me into dead slippery space. I would not choose to ignore its livid presence between my fingers. Or that finally remembering the hair, and facing it, might make me the worst thing, wiser.

I remember a woman at the wedding who was so drunk she was swaying with flirty confrontation telling Ben he was the naughty twin, that she had *heard* about him.

After our first halcyon flush together, Ben stopped letting me play with his phone in bed, citing sensitive work reasons. He distracted me by reminding me I was the first woman he'd managed to be faithful to. He told me over and over that I was different from the others despite his habit of saying certain names and locations with a private frisson.

Ben's rhapsodies about my uniqueness were cut more and more by the undertow of my insufficiencies. I would sit in the car after being savaged not knowing how to leave because Ben paid for everything. Eventually I would go inside to the warm whare and let Ben redraw me as the princess I used to beg Mum for on paper. And I was often very low maintenance: I'd forget which city he was in when he rang, away on business. I enjoyed the oblivion of my solitude too much and the muted sounds of our teenagers getting on as brothers through the wall.

One of the few times Ben unlocked his phone with his thumb for me so I could put on a song for us I accidentally discovered that his top site was watching cam girls . . . when he hadn't touched me in months. We had just taken mushrooms, so I corrected this lack of physical contact by punching him in his malleable, drug-fucked face.

If I had just left earlier, then I wouldn't keep embarrassing myself into revelations like this.

I wouldn't have caught Ben after the vows at the wedding, quietly making sure Jasper mentioned in his reception speech my food and all those hideous sugar roses, having won my tenuous presence there by threatening to banish me.

Maybe then I wouldn't find it so shocking, how quickly he married a woman with red hair.

On our last holiday in the motorhome Ben had rented, we stopped at Cable Bay, a beautiful pale blue and stony place where my ancestor Tūtepourangi was murdered during the musket wars. Ben was indulging me because I kept threatening to leave him so I could write my novel about the wars, and I spent hours on that trip scanning the sea for dolphins. My search was futile: they only appear for me if my son is there.

I was imagining Tūtepourangi's daughter Hinekawa wrapped in a white sail and hoisted up the mast by a Scottish captain named Jock to hide her from Te Rauparaha's guerrillas, Ngāti Tama. I could see Jock reading 'Song of

Solomon' to Hinekawa from his giant Bible, and hear the sound of her laughter in reo as they tilted together, lying in the cabin of the ship. I was dreaming of being adorable to nobody and being a proper writer.

Ben wanted me to leave him. *I'll miss you*, he said, but when I remember it now, it feels sly rather than wistful, a sideways move away from me. Ben the crab, who didn't want me in his pincers anymore. And because all we did together was drink and smoke dope we took the dog down to the beach with our cans and spliffs and because we weren't watching, Tonka got onto a blue penguin lying in the rocks behind us and Ben had to wring the penguin's neck to end its misery.

Except penguins don't have necks. Like a heart, they are just a bolt of muscle, so it took ages to die and I couldn't bear to watch while Ben killed the innocent penguin and our buzz.

He said, *Darling, it's difficult to kill*, maybe because he was such a pussy.

The next day we are miles down the road at another bay near Rarangi. I can tell Ben is disappointed by the campsite, but it is my tūrangawaewae and I am happy to be this close to myself. We walk down the cliff path from the memorial bench named after the dead girl Olivia Hope to the tiny menacing beach at high tide. The cave there at the bottom smells like burning metal to me, the breath of an old taniwha foe in my whakapapa, but Ben cannot smell it. I am already teasing him about his inferior, colonising nostrils. In the cave, here at the edges of my whenua, there is another dead blue penguin, and the sea is licking at it.

A moment where I could have read the tohu and chosen not to keep taunting him back to life and his vanishing love for me. There was no penguin; there were opals coming loose in the valley between my ribs and, lying in the blue den, I am almost sure I am the only one who was ever, really there.

Cultural Supervision

'They said that Te Rauparaha was a god, not a man.'
—*A Record of the Life of the Great Te Rauparaha*

I should probably explain why I got so obsessed with the musket wars. Not the actual battles: a patu to the head, the head coming off, limbs twisting or impaled—none of it interests me, not even the carved handles of the muskets, which prove how adaptable and sophisticated Māori were. One exception is the mere pounamu, stunning greens and good for slicing, dicing and disembowelling the enemy. I hate all European weaponry. I hate tanks, most military dress, bayonets and B-52s, and I can't watch battle scenes or an impaling without covering my eyes. I avoided all of *Game of Thrones*, which Ben was obsessed with. I had to stop reading Graham Greene's *The Quiet American* after a baby falls apart in its mother's arms. Risk is a game I passionately hate. I also loathe chess, and anything resembling any kind of strategy. I have no fucking plan—and war is all about planning. But I can't resist a fight.

Te Rauparaha, the Ngāti Toa instigator of my people's demise, was a dreamer as well as a warrior, and the tohu were on his side, or he took their warnings seriously. On Kāpiti he dreamed of a black hawk that almost took out his eye; he reached up for its legs and snapped its neck. In real life, four hundred of Tūtepourangi's warriors were approaching the north end of Kāpiti in their waka as part of the first wave of a defensive attack. He was lucky Tūtepourangi chose to fight with the sunrise. To be in the light was my ancestor's first mistake. Te Rauparaha was ready for them.

But, like Tūtepourangi, I was unprepared for what was coming for me. I was oblivious to all tohu then.

After Mugwi's tangi, which was just before Christmas 2013, I am back in Dunedin, studying to work in social services. I have realised I could never be a counsellor, which requires having unconditional positive regard for people, a concept I struggle with. I have chosen the mental health stream instead because it is a struggle that is more familiar to me.

Regardless of our specialities, we all have to come together for a monthly compulsory Cultural Supervision session. Here is a chance for mana whenua to tell us how things are done down here in Ōtepoti—and for Pākehā to have a struggle session over us.

I recognise our supervisor at once: hers was the first house I got stoned in when I was fifteen. She was away for the weekend, but we found her Kleensak of dope. She doesn't know me, and I like this, at first. I feel like I am hiding something precious about her from her.

She seems nice enough, but she talks what Jim would have called absolute rot. I see a Pākehā with thinning hair in front of me, from the enemy counselling stream, nodding at all her lies. The Cultural Supervisor says normally Māori from up north just look out the window when she talks, like this is an endorsement. But I'm not quite like them, either—I'm from the in-between place. Literally.

Apart from her iwi, Kāi Tahu, there are eight other iwi in the South Island, all squashed into the prow of the waka.

Both the dark people of the north and the pale people of the south have one thing in common: pretending we don't really exist. Because during the musket wars our Kurahaupō iwi were almost erased, except for Rangitāne rangatira Ihaia Kaikoura, who signed Te Tiriti with the northern victors. They were almost as new to this rohe as the settlers in the 1840s, but many of them stayed. Ngāti Rārua, Ngāti Koata and even Ngāti Toa are often my cousins because there was so much intermarriage once the wars were over—and during them too, as alliances were brokered using women.

Back in class, I'm trying to look out the window at the city to appear authentic, but the cultural supervisor says something that makes me whip around to the front of the room. She announces that the Māori at the top of the South Island don't even bury their dead there. They take them home. *Back up north*, she says. This would be news to Mugwi if he were still alive. The urupā he is buried in is a mix of the conquerors and the invaded but they all seem to get along as the grapevines encroach on the tapu space from all sides.

Because of the whakapapa research I've been doing, which resembles a warren rather than a rabbit hole, I pipe up that Ngāti Kuia have been there for hundreds of years, before Kāi Tahu came down and absorbed the older iwi like Kāti Mamoe and Waitaha. Our presence here is almost as old as theirs. Ngāti Kuia share the *k* sound in their dialect instead of the *ng*.

I manage to say most of this before she interrupts me and says, *Oh no, that's not right.*

I can see the woman with thinning hair nodding her Pākehā head so I push the point and eventually the cultural supervisor concedes she *may* have heard something like this.

We leave it at that, and I wonder why she has started off our first session without a general round of introductions. But a mihi from the Māori students while the Pākehā sit there looking out the window would mess with her narrative, I suppose.

After enduring more of these monthly sessions I do something out of character, I hope: I complain about her to one of my Pākehā lecturers. She also sits there as I rave on about my whakapapa, her head nodding up and down like a car-dash ornament. I ask why our cultural supervisor is not teaching us to mihi, the thing that is meant to help you not insult people before you get to know them. Or to insult them with great purpose if you do.

The next session we do a round of where we come from. The cultural supervisor nods and smiles through mine, which is far too long because I'm punishing the thin-haired Pākehā, and I think, Ha! She won't be insulting my people again.

The cultural supervisor insults my people at the next session. She says we were grabby for their land during the Treaty settlement process, trying to claim as far down as Kaiapoi. That our Rangitāne / Ngāti Kuia boundary is north of the Clarence River after Kaikōura. No one is totally sure who lived where in that area because most of us were wiped out. But this is the problem with being dead. People make up lies about you: either sentimental fancies about your good nature or unkind caricatures. These become the facts and you have no right of reply. The consequence of an unfair battle is that sometimes the wrong people get the blame or are falsely glorified after the fact. And people you hardly know can pretend you were never even there.

The cultural supervisor says we all need to learn to paddle in the same waka. Which reminds me of something Tā Tipene

O'Reagan said to Mugwi at a hui in the early nineties when our iwi were trying to figure out which bit originally belonged to who. He told Mugwi to have a puff on the peace pipe. But Mugwi was a sportsman who hated smoking.

I stand up and shout at the cultural supervisor that I'm sick of having to sit here while she insults MY PEOPLE and I storm out of class with my laptop bag flapping open like a gaping mouth.

I insist to the Pākehā lecturer that I won't be going back for any more Cultural Supervision and, even though it's a course requirement, I still get 10/10 for reflecting on why I shouldn't have to go. The Pākehā's head probably needed a break from all the bobbing up and down.

The next year the cultural supervisor mistakes my much darker friend, Ruby of the North, for me.

When Ruby queries a point of tikanga, or tikaka as they call it down south, she says, *You! I just about didn't come back because of you.*

I enjoy that Ruby suffered in my place—it seems hilarious to me—but after I refuse to go back to Cultural Supervision my neck feels very twisted and my voice goes; my windpipe feels like there are fingers gripping it and I can't speak for a few days.

My hair starts falling out. And it hasn't really stopped falling out.

*

Paul also used to enjoy a tussle. In 2002 I'm staying with him at a hotel in Queenstown with my son, who is two and has a red cheek from an ear infection. We still bussed up here with antibiotics because I refused to miss out on a hotel. My solo-mum flat is freezing in the Dunedin winter and Roman is being useless.

Paul is over from Sydney for a plastic surgery conference, and in the hotel room next to us his nurse puts fillers in lips. Because smoking hasn't registered on my face yet, I think all the women thrilled with their plump new lips look like trout wearing lipstick.

Paul takes us into town and buys my son hundreds of dollars' worth of clothes and toys, and I'm delighted.

Back at the hotel, Paul goes downstairs and, over drinks and nibbles, he gets into a verbal tussle with a rep from a rival filler brand. He comes back up to the room afterwards, invigorated by the fight. Paul says, *I've got this mongrel in me, I just won't give in*, like this character flaw is a good thing. He is wearing a black jersey with yellow lettering that names him over and over as an 'aesthetic terrorist'. We all sleep in the king-size bed and it isn't too weird.

Delphi lives in Queenstown then, and comes to see me. Paul tells us we can order whatever we like from room service, and we do. Her vegetarian nachos arrive with too many sun-dried tomatoes.

Delphi is Kāi Tahu; Taiaroa Head is named after her tipuna. Although, its original name is Pukekura.

In her mihi the cultural supervisor mentioned Tūhawaiki, the Kāi Tahu chief and contemporary of Taiaroa. Tūhawaiki is her ancestor. He was also known as Bloody Jack of Ruapuke. He went to Sydney to arrange the sale of some land while my people were suffering on board one of his ships. Captain Jock and Hinekawa, Tūtepourangi's daughter, rescued them from Rakiura.

Tūhawaiki, who may or may not have taken the jaw bone of Te Pēhi Kupe, Te Rauparaha's uncle, to Tūtepourangi to make into a fish hook. This was before Kaiapoi pā was burned to the ground in retribution using the captured tohunga Hohua Rangireia's Kurahaupō dominion over the wind; before the pā was razed with all the women and children inside and when they were all still allies, odd foes and friends.

Pelorus Jim

In the eighties my grandparents take me for a long, terrible drive from Wānaka to Haast on the West Coast. I get carsick because I am determined to read in the car. The rātā are so red they are screaming, but I don't remember this. It is Nana who remembers the rātā.

I remember we are walking through a low canopy and I'm holding Nana's hand as Grandad walks in front of us exclaiming how beautiful it all is. The shaggy rimu and the taller podocarps. A kererū flies so low over his head, whooping and whirring, that it becomes a family joke but I'm still not sure why. Maybe because the kererū outdid his wonder, his authentic love of the bush. Grandad was also a happy swimmer, one of the only adults who actually played with me in the water. Pretending to be a shark and tipping me off my lilo into the lake while I shrieked with delight.

After the canopy we come out at a large swampy pond. There are dragonflies, hundreds of them, hovering above the water.

In the photo of this day I am holding Nana's hand and look much darker than her. I look like a little Māori girl wearing her light blue jersey, which dangles past my arms.

It looks like we are about to be swallowed by the bush.

*

Sunday afternoon was my favourite shift at the rest home. The boss didn't come in on the weekends and the afternoon 'girls' were a more relaxed breed than those who did mornings, when everything was all go-go-go. It seemed futile to shower and dress residents to go nowhere and receive no visitors, except maybe the reaper and his scythe, and I felt that all this activity was more for our benefit than theirs, to keep our own mortality at bay. But I learned to stay quiet about this because no one at work seemed to appreciate my existential reflections as we puffed away in the smokers' shed.

On my break, when I wasn't smoking, I would go down to Jim's room. The thickened Milo from Nana would be on his side table with an imploring underlined note for the staff and sometimes I would let it chug down the sink in my grandfather's tiny en suite instead of feeding it to him because surely he was sick of it.

Before she left for her unit, Nana would angle the pillows behind Jim's rigid neck then unclip the hospital bed wheels and turn it to face the television—her militant thoughtfulness extended even to when she wasn't there. Sundays meant nature documentaries, and one night I held the spoon as it trembled with Milo goo and watched the dolphins leaping out of the water and then shuttling underneath it like torpedoes. I don't know what Jim thought of the dolphins—not much probably—but we watched while I reminded him how much he liked *Das Boot*, the submarine movie, before I went to check another patient's pad hadn't leaked.

At Ben's later, after a spliff or two, I decide—or rather I gave in to the sudden intense intuition—that once my grandfather dies, he will become a dolphin. My therapist told me once that I still believed in magic and, instead of scoffing, I conceded he was right. It is easier to imagine Jim free in the ocean instead of in the rest home; magical thinking requires so little effort and is preferable to reality, the place where I am powerless against his decline.

Jim, the genealogist, became curious about my whakapapa when he began researching his own family history. It was before Ancestry.com and finding out where you came from meant scrolling through black-and-green microfiche rolls in the family history centre at the back of the church instead of the contemporary practice of sending your DNA to a dodgy data bank. The records would only allow him to trace his ancestry back to the 1700s and to illiterate Irish, English and Scottish peasants recorded in churches. The Irish were Catholics who were later dug up at the Symonds Street cemetery in Auckland to make way for the motorway. Jim knew my whakapapa here would go back further than his, and that somewhere there would be a record of it. And he was impressed by the oral traditions, where all the tīpuna rested inside a head to be passed on.

A peculiarity of Mormonism is their habit of 'sealing' the dead, so that people's ancestors could be reunited in the afterlife on their deeply uncool celestial plane. This is why they kept such meticulous family records. It was Jim's favourite part about going to church. And the hui ā-tau they used to have, where Maōri, who outnumbered the Pākehā, would converge and Gwen would ask everyone where Jim had gone: the answer was always off with the Maoris, in the big white tent, singing.

After Jim's sister Jean died, Nana went to seal her in the Mormon temple in Hamilton. Mum muttered that there was a fate worse than death because Jean was not a member of the church. Nana had to sleep in the dorms in a bunk bed and while she was eating by herself in the dining room a clutch of wāhine from the coast forced her to sit with them, because they remembered Jim so fondly. They poked her and told her she needed fattening up and her stay was less lonely after that.

After Jim dies, a kererū starts targeting the piopio tree outside Ben's bedroom. It chonks along the guttering and pokes its small curious head through the window. And I start figuring out exactly where I come from. I dive deeper than the stories Paul has mentioned as family lore and I find our taniwha to the beat of the kererū's heavy wings.

I find I can get as far back as the OG explorer Kupe, through his nephew Matua Hautere, our Ngāti Kuia tipuna. Another ancestor, Kereopa, abandoned Kupe at Boulder Bank near Nelson. Kupe was accompanied by a kererū on his first voyage here from Hawaiki, as he chased Te Wheke across Te Moana-nui-a-Kiwa. And Kaikaiawaro was the dolphin who helped him claim the great monster's eyes.

Later, Matua Hautere was led into the Sounds from up north by Kaikaiawaro, who nosed into Kenepuru and made the mouth of Te Hoiere, or Pelorus, River. Our Ngāti Kuia people, an iwi karakia, followed him to then settle all through the Sounds. Eventually their Rangitāne relatives joined them.

Kaikaiawaro had a lair near the entrance to the drowned bays facing into Raukawakawa. He could be raised from this place by the last tohunga, Kipa Hemi Whiro, with an incantation I won't write here in case a Pākehā steals it and it loses its power.

Jim used to play me the Limeliters' children's album in the Datsun on the way to Wānaka, and I loved the song

'Grace Darling', where the garrulous folk singers asked the children to yell during the chorus: *Help! Help!* A useful and less tapu karakia in an emergency than Kipa's chant. Sailors shouting to a woman for assistance in a crisis need to make it snappy.

Kipa Hemi Whiro, who is from the same Ngāti Kuia line I descend from, met James Cowan and Katherine Mansfield, and let both flutter off like cabbage moths with our taniwha story. Captain Cook brought the cabbages and radishes to the Sounds, but we were always fishing, not gardening, and the imports ran wild. The sea was our māra and the wāhine wove nets that were hundreds of metres long.

Kipa told James Cowan that the dolphin that had been helping sailors through the perilous body of water between Rangitoto and the mainland was not called Pelorus Jack, as the sailors had christened him, but Kaikaiawaro. Kipa accuses the French, who think they know everything about the dolphin, of being liars and calls them 'tāngata wīwī'—maybe to insult them further. He did not let Cowan know the taniwha could shapeshift between the dolphin and the kererū.

John Middleton Murry, Mansfield's feckless husband, wrote an account of her childhood holidays at Anakoha, near Kaikaiawaro's lair, and described the little girl meeting the tohunga with the club foot. Kipa was as generous to her as he was to Cowan but Murry was an unreliable narrator.

On the last motorhome holiday with Ben, we stopped at the Havelock Museum, which had a display devoted to Pelorus Jack. Beside it was a photo of Meihana Kereopa, a cousin of Kipa's who married his sister, Hana Whiro. Meihana built waka from tōtara to float down Te Hoiere River, and was often seen with Rupe, a kererū with two heads. Meihana: my great-great-great-great-grandfather, who died at 102, but not before he blocked the road at Pelorus River, his Hoiere, and said he was never made a slave by the musket war heke and that he would not be giving up his whenua to Pākehā, either.

The museum failed to make the connection between the taniwha and my tipuna. It was a quaint small-town hall with extremely well-polished floors, but my history had been divided into two separate exhibits, and so a vital connection had been severed—to Kaikaiawaro, who connects us to the

great navigator, Kupe, but also to the whenua and moana in ways Pākehā can only obscure or envy.

I am also an unreliable narrator, because you can't write about dolphins without seeking to inhabit them, and this is where my imagination comes unstuck. To describe a dolphin is to describe a lot of swimming. A special capable type of swimming. If you look at a dolphin it seems obvious it was designed for one thing: swimming. And even though I believed that Jim was a dolphin, I'm not fond of any art related to dolphins: the truth is, dolphins are tacky. I hate crystal ornaments with dolphins curving up and around them. I hate rainbows and unicorns collaborating with dolphins. No one has ever made great art from a dolphin, least of all those Renaissance painters who made them look quite unlike their real selves.

One great homage to the dolphins comes in *The Hitchhiker's Guide to the Galaxy*, where the dolphins are smarter than us. It explains all their swimming and, once the earth is fucked, they take off in the spaceship, saying thanks for all the fish. Who needs thumbs if you have been custom-built to have a good time? I have considered getting Kaikaiawaro to narrate my novel but he reminds me that he doesn't share my problems and my subject matter is way too dark—and what happened to all the free fish?

Maybe the only other great dolphin art is the retro TV show *Flipper*. And Flipper was part of the reason I had decided Jim was swimming around as my taniwha instead of enduring the white plastic paradise of Mormon Heaven. They had the same laugh. Grandad would grin whenever he made a terrible pun. But Flipper's famous laugh was dubbed by a kookaburra.

Despite my aesthetic reservations it became my project to see a dolphin. I was living in Aramoana when Jim died and I would walk the long defunct railway line, known as the 'mole', which divided the sea, quietly desperate to see a dolphin, a pod of dolphins—even killer whales would have been enough of a tohu that the afterlife was treating him better than his last years.

Instead, I saw a lot of seals pretending to be dolphins. I came to hate seals for their poor impersonation of my grandfather, and squinting into the horizon looking for a friendly fin accelerated the ageing process, triangles webbing from the corners of my eyes like the bird feet that used to hop over the awning of the caravan by the lake.

Pelorus Jack/Kaikaiawaro was last seen in April 1912, one hundred years before Jim dies in the same month, just before Easter. The century between them starts to mean a lot to me because of the coincidence. It means more to me than it does to the spokesperson for King Salmon, who justifies the expansion of aquaculture in the Sounds by saying that no one even believes in the taniwha Kaikaiawaro. He wants to clog his lair with salmon shit.

King Salmon is mostly owned by a Malaysian dynasty, who are also responsible for the destruction of the rainforest in Borneo to make palm oil. Responsible for the displacement of another indigenous people as they torch their homes. The Sounds are heating up, which is why King Salmon wants to expand into Cook Strait—their product is getting sick in their pens. I briefly consider writing about this environmental disaster for a magazine. But saving the world baffles me; even the idea of it is plain exhausting. I would rather scan the sea for supernatural sightings than crusade for a cause.

But when I research the changing ecology of the Sounds I learn the only thing thriving at the bottom of the moana are the mussels, which feed on the rich sediments caking the seabed. I discover that if a report were to be commissioned by the forestry industry it would blame this build-up—which is toxic to everything else, including the king shag Te Kawau-a-Toru, who came here with Kupe too—on the salmon farms. But the aquaculture industry blames the degradation on the fertiliser run-off from the forestry plantations going straight down the vertiginous hills and into the sea. It is like that meme of the two Spidermans pointing at each other in their identical Lycra suits: one of these things is exactly the other.

A rare white dolphin is seen in the Sounds after King Salmon begins pressuring the government to let it expand its operations, and I remember that Kipa said you have to offer the taniwha some fish to keep its favour. But I keep his chant inside my head.

*

One of Jim's first presents to me was a dictionary; he had some written some doggerel in the front about words being fun! And for everyone!

He was right, and I loved reading the dictionary as much as the phonebook or occasional Bible story. I liked the story in Genesis of the world being made in seven days and God using the Word to call the world into light. John the Baptist echoed him in the New Testament with *First there is the word*, as he baptised the rebel.

It is Jim wearing roman sandals and wading me up the Motutapu River in Wānaka. Jim is the reason I feel so at home in the water and believe in the power of words. He flips and laughs his kookaburra laugh and swims through the tangled kelp of my hair, before the grandfather I share with my cousins morphs into his other selves.

When I was seven, Jim helped me make a robot to enter a competition inspired by a new Margaret Mahy book. He got some chicken wire out of the shed and we shaped it into a little silver man. We covered the frame with tinfoil and, for the control panel on his chest, used Roses chocolate wrappers covered by forest-green gardening wire to make it official. The finished robot was about a foot high and kind of bent-looking. He looked more like a silver, needy alien, but came second in the competition. Margaret Mahy rang to tell me I'd won a digital watch, but I didn't believe my hero could use the telephone and I hung up on her. When the watch arrived it was too masculine for me, but I wore it until Mum sent me a Mickey Mouse one from Australia.

*

Kaikaiawaro would only let you fuck with him once before he left you to your fate. This is what happened in 1904 when a sailor on board the SS *Penguin* tried to shoot at him. The taniwha refused to help the *Penguin* after that. It seems tasteless to mention that, in 1909, the *Penguin* wrecked itself on the rocks near Wellington, because a lot of people died—seventy-five of them in fact. The women and children mostly, because their lifeboats capsized on the rocks that stick out like deadly crystals on the coast at Pencarrow.

Others say that Kaikaiawaro never actually swam through the French Pass, that he would veer off from the boats he was guiding to let them squeeze through the swirling plughole between the mainland and Rangitoto. It is thought that

Kaikaiawaro enjoyed carving up the bow waves, that he was just having fun.

I think of my son when he was one, running through the grass at Mugwi's brother's tangi, and me running ragged after him, trying to look like a devoted mother in front of the other cousins. Even Paul's mother noticed—she told him, *That girl is running herself stupid. I can't help her, I'm in the kitchen.* She was making sticky, fluffy trays of cherry clafoutis for the hundreds of mourners.

Paul took us to the department store in Blenheim to buy my son some real shoes with decent soles. Running through the wet grass of the paddocks down at the pā had ruined his soft aqua leather baby shoes.

On the ferry over to the tangi we had added a stray girl to my attempts to play inside the children's area of the *Interislander*. Her large whānau watched us from the safety of their seats, but kept playing cards. At the tangi they took me aside and told me they could tell I was one of them because I looked so much like Paul's sister.

*

Three years after Jim dies, I drive Nana to Riverton for their wedding anniversary. This is where they went for their honeymoon in 1956, and where Jim was born. She tells me my favourite uncle was conceived in Aunty Lou's bed. Aunty Lou, who ran the sweet shop and who Jim had an attachment to, even though he left Riverton before he started school.

Because Nana is telling me about her ancient sex life, I decide to do my own terrible sharing, spurred on by the fact that there is a pair of kererū on the power lines and she remembers the one who got the better of Jim.

I tell her that I think Grandad is a dolphin now, and I'm surprised when she accepts this, but maybe she's just happy to be talking about the husband she fell in love with instead of the man who spent six years dying in a bed. We recolour that day with all her red and the way she says rātā, without the macrons.

When I tell her that my relationship is falling apart and that Ben seems to hate my son, she is certain that our job is to love all the children.

The War of the Rātā

Someone interrupted my monologue midstream one summer to ask, *Why would you want to write about that?* Meaning the musket wars, and my failed attempt to write a historical novel. Maybe she meant I might hurt my feet on the rocks while wading into such murky water, because her question seemed to contain a vague rhetorical warning—Māori in flavour—to be careful of bad juju.

'Bad juju' was Paul's name for *that* trouble about our bones down near the mouth of the Wairau River. He did not mean our ancient kōiwi over the other side of the bank at Te-Pokohiwi-a-Kupe, but the bad blood that ran under the whenua behind his childhood home, mucky and silent as tar.

It was the very thing I could not—or rather, would not—shut up about.

Paul's other Wairau stories were more hardcase, endearing and comical when he talked about growing up there, over the relics of Kowhai pā. Mugwi had played there as a boy, too, living close by with his grandparents Hoani and Polly, who were old lovebirds and distant cousins. Hoani's grandfather was Meihana Kereopa; Polly descended from Meihana's cousin, the Kurahaupō ariki, Tūtepourangi.

Once, Mugwi and his older brother Cappy found some taonga and adzes in the loose sand out the back near the beach. They ran into the house to show Polly their find. Someone told me that Polly went blind until they put those things back.

When I was in Te Tau Ihu after leaving Ben, Paul picked my son and me up from Cable Bay and drove us back to the old whare at the Wairau bar. We looked through the windows while my son sulked in the car, and Paul was upset at what the rats had done to his mother Polly's formerly spotless kitchen. Their fluffy mess on the bench fuelled his desire to go back there and start again. Her succulents were still thriving beside the desolate water tank because the land is so hot and dry. When our tīpuna arrived from East Polynesia it had been a swamp teeming with bird life and eels. Polly used to cook swan eggs for her moko that took up the whole pan.

Beside the whare was a reserve for landless natives that was occupied by people Paul called 'squatters'. They lived in house buses and tents with no running water and Portaloos. A tenuous existence between our cousin's grapes and the river. Paul cursed their presence with his familial hot-bloodedness—the same way he cursed the sewage running into the mouth of the Wairau where the whitebait had once run into the bar, fresh with the brisk, iodine flavours of the moana.

Paul was working on the cousin's vineyard and what was left of his art was in storage. I liked him a lot better for his losses and resisted the pity that was becoming a complicated part of my love.

One night, a woman came back to the landless strip, maybe drunk, and her car caught fire and set the bleached tall grass ablaze; it snaked to the white whare, setting it alight. The chimney stands like a lost pou now, and the kitchen where Polly saw the end of her people in the dark glitter of her head has been released into the same void as her vision.

I like to think of Polly sitting at the table jiggling her leg and cocking an eye until the scared boys had learned their lesson and she could perform the miracle of regaining her sight. I find that the other option is more frightening, which is that some of our history is so dark it has the power to blind us.

Paul told me our iwi, Rangitāne o Wairau, were called ditch diggers by their captors, Ngāti Toa, during the musket wars, that period before the Treaty was signed that no one ever really talks about except online Pākehā trolls. The Hobson's Pledge Facebook page shares the article I wrote about Paul as proof we were savages and I wince because that was not my intention.

The ditches Rangitāne dug as new slaves were war trenches really; Te Rauparaha knew Kāi Tahu were coming up from the south to stop him taking the rest of Te Waipounamu after his tauā had carved through Te Ūpoko-o-te-ika-a-Māui and taken Kāpiti as a war base, capturing its vantage point between the two islands.

From Kāpiti, his attacks on Te Waipounamu came in waves and were assisted by Ngāti Koata, Ngāti Mutunga, Ngāti Tama, Te Ātiawa and Ngāti Rārua. Mugwi was Ngāti Rārua through his mother's taha, and our tipuna Pukekohatu was an ally and whanaunga of Te Rauparaha through their connections at Kawhia.

After the trenches had served their purpose, my people were split through the head by one of our beautiful brutalist weapons and eaten or buried standing up in the used holes of their whenua to desecrate the mauri and wairua of their departed being. Te Rauparaha was punishing us for the arrogant double-insult of our rangatira Te Ruaoneone, who had threatened him with a root pounder, a vulgar patu. He was still punishing anyone he could for the death of his children at Lake Papaitonga and his uncle, all butchered like piglets in front of him. Eyes plucked from the heads of children and displayed in front of their fathers could drive anyone towards a cold psychopathic insanity.

Before Pākehā arrived, our societal weave had been hierarchical, as much as it was described as communal by liberal, admiring Pākehā when they rewrote our histories to suit their tastes. Yes, Māori lived communally, but it would be a stretch to call us Marxists—and if Judith Butler, the high nonbinary priest/ess of theory, were transported back in time in a DeLorean to Kāpiti and Te Rauparaha's hospitality, she wouldn't be able to comprehend why there was so much pork piled up on her plate at a hāngī or even be sure it really was pork.

The pork and potatoes Te Rauparaha cultivated on a massive scale using my people, formerly high, as slaves were as useful as my ancestors' heads to trade with Pākehā for muskets. Rangatira were already richly tattooed. It would probably surprise Te Rauparaha that his descendants are now seen by the visitors he used to trade freely with as dysfunctional peasants in need of saving by bureaucrats. When we were once the most glorious, isolated people in the history of the world and live between this myth and the very margins of the sea.

Before Pākehā arrived in overwhelming waves, Māori society had already been fatally altered by the introduction of their destructive technologies. Te Rauparaha could be described as a rampaging, psychotic war leader at best—and at worst, a capitalist and vengeful opportunist. Te Rauparaha had his reasons, but very rarely did he counter for Pākehā morality in his schema. That way of thinking just didn't exist here.

In contrast, our Rangitāne ancestors had arrived peacefully in their Kurahaupō waka from Hawaiki to settle at the tip of Te Waipounamu. Once established, we treated human burials as sacred. Resting in peace is not just a Christian notion, but those bones are over the other side of the awa. At Kowhai pā, six hundred years later, we were treated as grave diggers and slaves. The Wairau, the river Paul loved, divides the dream from the nightmare.

Manny—Polly's son and my great-grandfather—married into Ngāti Rārua through one of the Piripi girls, Horina, Mugwi's mother. She had three other children with Manny, and then died, far too early, from cancer. Manny quickly married her baby sister, Tauru, and they had seventeen more children.

I wonder how Polly judged her son. He often acted as her chauffeur on her trips to see all her moko. But all the ties between former foes were blurry there at the Wairau: war had turned into sport, amazing spreads and games of cards that shook the few riverside houses down to the sea with their teasing and their mirth. Sport was taken just as seriously as God. Probably more so.

Talking about this with a suddenly touchy cousin I make the mistake of calling Tauru, Manny's second wife, 'Darky'—my grandmother's name for her. My cousin, who is from her line, bristles and says, *You mean Tauru?* I then make another crucial error, which is using my father's term for Horina's children: the first family. *What do you mean, cuz?* I mean Manny's twenty-one children. I mean the spares. And it was briefly tense on her porch with its tino rangatiratanga flag, which obscured the sight of her bucky bongs but not the smell.

When he died in the late seventies, Manny was still sending tonnes of potatoes as a tariff up to Ngāti Toa in Porirua, and cousins would work on large-scale plantations, crossing between north and south over Raukawakawa for the harvests of crops and kaimoana. On Facebook whānau pages cousins reminisce with other cousins about sacred and scary aunties and the mahi: on the farm, in the kitchen, in the washhouse; outside scalping through spiky kina on a trestle table at sports days; and the thrills of diving for crays, scallops and pāua.

Manny was a godfather, with palms like dinner plates and fingers bigger than sausages. He would sit beside the lemon tree stabbing for something he needed, while the children would run and run and run.

One of our biggest cultural myths is that Māori are lazy and in need of saving, especially when first observers of us couldn't get over how busy we were. In their ethnographic hierarchies Māori rose to the top like cream, which reveals more about the bias of the outsider than any truth about our

collective character. We were busy on our own terms, but our past is filtered through a Pākehā gaze that begins with Captain Cook and is then painted with words by artists like Augustus Earle, who wrote fanciful accounts of our sudden savagery for keen readers back in Britain.

Yet even Augustus Earle noted our hospitality. In 1827, he and some companions got stranded on a mud flat and came across a clutch of wāhine cooking shellfish. The women invited them for a kai because there is maybe nothing ruder in Māori society than eating in front of someone without sharing. Augustus and his men slept the night on the flat and in the morning the wāhine, laughing, carried them to their boats. Like James Cowan, Augustus is a deeply unreliable narrator and yet it feels accurate. Those wāhine feel real.

Māori only became 'Māori' in the presence of others; before this we were normal and there was no need to qualify it. Now being Māori is an umbrella term for historically disparate iwi and hapū. And while it is correct that Māori were accomplished gardeners, like many sophisticated peoples we also tumbled like wolves. The Romans were administrators of a massive military complex; and so was Te Rauparaha when he set up his trading post on Kāpiti to feed his avarice. 'Ka Mate' is a greedy, life-affirming haka as much as it celebrates his cunning and ability to get out of tight situations. Māori have only been characterised as a lost, Stone Age race since people have imagined they 'discovered' us.

The technological progression of Western society was driven by war; the invention of the bra is adjacent to the Holocaust and the Manhattan Project. Māori were skilled fighters; the British adopted our winning methods before they sent us off to fight their wars. Erwin Rommel praised the Māori Battalion soldiers after fighting against them in North Africa. But the balance tipped more than a waka with the introduction of the musket. Our tikanga had not caught up with the musket's capacity to cause mass destruction. Einstein and Oppenheimer encountered the same issue—albeit at some distance from Hiroshima.

Te Rauparaha's son, Tāmihana, would later turn to the cup of Christ because we were all sick of the taste of our own flesh. We were first colonised by the musket, but then we still had our agency. The Treaty of Waitangi would not have been possible without the musket. The British used trade to colonise Māori before they resorted to force and legislation.

Unfortunately, Māori proved to be better traders than them.

I missed out on the industrious gene, and Paul hated the hard work of the dairy farm and the crops around Manny's homestead. Mugwi would be up at 4am milking the cows while his younger brothers rose later and sat on tractors harvesting the corn and peas. The children got to play together, but they had never been on a holiday. The other option was church. Or sport. Manny became a Mormon after his little girl Kuia died at three. But he still lived like a godfather, driving his white Ford Fairlane first onto the *Aramoana* ferry on its maiden run with Mugwi's younger sisters, Chicky and Kahu, on the sofa of the front seat. Nosing on like when Kaikaiawaro swam into Te Hoiere and Kupe left Rupe, the kererū, behind to feast on berries.

I'm proposing that before we signed Te Tiriti, te ao Māori was magic. I mean this in the truest sense of the word, and not the stale hamminess of a magician. Our world was still supernatural. Christianity latched onto this tradition of prophecy and karakia and used it to subject us to their larger fairy story. But we were not fools. Te Rauparaha's dream of the black hawk the night before the 1824 battle of Waiorua had meaning.

Tūtepourangi, Polly's great-great-grandfather, helped lead three thousand warriors to their death against Te Rauparaha's force of three hundred at the battle of Waiorua at Kāpiti. The numbers simply don't make sense because there weren't many muskets then. Although Te Rauparaha had a mere pounamu, Te Tuhiwai, that could chop water and read the wai for a way. Tūtepourangi was found at a waterfall on Kāpiti hiding his jaw-twisting mere, Kauae Hurihia, only to be revealed to his captors by the emerald halo shining above it in the waterfall's mist.

Tūtepourangi negotiated his release by using a tuku whenua and handing over the mere. He gave them millions of acres. Millions. He was allowed back on the island

Rangitoto, the head at the frilly edge of the Sounds, and the tip of his former empire. A tuku whenua is also a peace deal so that warring parties can live together in peace once the fighting is over; like most things Māori, it is reciprocal.

*

Speaking of lost islands, I played a king and an earth goddess in a production of *The Tempest* in my last year of university. I was pregnant and didn't know it. As the ship went down at the beginning of the play we sang Psalm 23. The Lord was our shepherd even on the water. It was the only directorial touch I agreed with, and Jim loved it in the audience; at home he got out his *Collected Shakespeare* from the shelf. I had missed out on playing Ariel, the role I wanted, and made a listless king, dressed in white cheesecloth, which is not flattering.

But later I learned that *Ariel* was one of Captain Jock McGregor's ships. In the Whanganui Museum they hold his two huge Bibles and one of his warning bells.

I imagine Tūtepourangi as a Prospero-type figure on Rangitoto island, effeminate like Paul, which is telling, I suppose, because Paul was a mongrel on the rugby pitch. Tūtepourangi, living out his days on Rangitoto and through to Cable Bay with Ngāti Koata. Tūtepourangi as a reduced, maybe comical figure. A big barrel of a chest that Wahapiro from Ngāti Tama shoots through the heart on their way down the west side of the waka, on a heke to slaughter Kāi Tahu that Te Rauparaha didn't fully approve of. The route—not the intention to take Te Waipounamu. He coveted that waka for himself.

Hinekawa, Tūtepourangi's daughter, seems like Miranda, Prospero's girl, in *The Tempest*, and I find it much easier to inhabit her. It is foolish to reduce Tūtepourangi, our common ancestor, into a comical failure and Hinekawa was also better served to survive. She was saved by the sea captain Jock McGregor, who rolled her into a sail to hide her after her father was murdered. She died in Wellington, the year the Treaty was signed, at twenty-five, just after the birth of their son, Teone. Teone settled in Foxton Beach and had been raised by Ngāti Raukawa. They kidnapped baby Teone from the ferryman at the Manawatū River after Jock left him there, promising to return. Years later, Jock would arrive on his horse from Whanganui with presents to take across the river for Teone's children. Teone was an orphan who was wanted. Teone was Polly's grandfather.

*

Apart from Hilary Mantel's *Wolf Hall* trilogy I don't have much of an appetite for historical novels, especially if they are about war, or political intrigue—but I could have stayed in her incarnation of Cromwell's calm cool head forever. I wonder how I can enter the consciousness of a rangatira, when I do not think like a chief. This is my first real concern as a writer, more than any irate cousins.

My other failure to write the novel is, quite fatally, an issue of language: my characters would have to think in Māori. Despite their strategies being as sophisticated as a Tudor court, there is no appetite for historical novels written in te reo, when not enough of us speak it. I am conscious that I am dubbing this story with English and not its native tongue.

I did imagine a battle scene at Kāpiti with the Bach cello suites on the movie soundtrack, and herein lies the problem: my brain is too white to conceive of a world untouched by Pākehā for six hundred years. Even as I can sense and smell the sea at Kāpiti swimming with the metal and milk smell of my cousins.

I read about a sailor from a crew of six on the *Samuel*, who may have survived being eaten in 1824 and may have ended up on Rangitoto. I name him Thom and imagine him as a tutor for Hinekawa and Meihana—her cousin and Hoani's grandfather. They are staying at Whanganui Inlet, below Farewell Spit, and Thom shows them how to play cards and whittles chess pieces. Most sailors weren't educated so I have to imagine he is on the run from something, and in disguise. An amorphous Shakespearean hero.

When I try to get past Polly through to Hinekawa I have to ask the internet: *When did fruit first arrive in New Zealand? What was the first fruit?* The answer is peaches and watermelons, and they arrived in the technologically sophisticated north; cherry trees prove harder to trace. *Did sailors play cards? When did they start playing cards?*

The images of cards are a sweet distraction from the war but I order the people into suits: Hinekawa is the queen of hearts; the queen of spades is Hinepoupou, the tipuna I admire who swam from Kāpiti to Rangitoto hunting her men down.

I split the pack of cards into my whakapapa to try to make the war spark into feuds and bloodlines, black and red and white and back into life.

It is easier to imagine Polly sitting at the table, shuffling the cards and preparing her insults. Polly grunts then chuckles when another player, Aunty Lady, reminds her it is her turn and because the game is hearts she plays the queen of spades; she had been hanging onto her just to take out Aunty Pushy, who licks the cream and coconut from her fingers, always bragging that her lamingtons are the best.

*

In Kaikōura, Polly kept dry goods and worked the pumps at their general store. She raised her son Manny's children alongside her own younger ones and would whāngai others. She sends her daughter Hannah to Murupura, where she is raised with Hirini Moko Mead. There is a photo of Polly holding Hannah before she gives her away to Hoani's auntie. Her eyes are big and round with her impending loss.

Manny would drop Polly in Murupura to collect duck eggs with her moko; she taught them how to play cooncan and other simpler card games. Sometimes she would bring a child home with her to be looked after, atoning for her son's mistakes or a cousin's trouble.

During the Depression, Polly bought herself a Chevy Roadster taxi, which was driven along the most extraordinary coast in the world. Polly didn't have much time for Pākehā, even when they were ferried in her car or when she acted as

a part-time bootlegger for them. There was no impetus to pretend to be blind; she needed all her wits about her.

Like the night in 1948 that Polly spent at the salt flats of Lake Grassmere. She was already a kuia then, and waiting for Hoani to return with the swan eggs they both loved to eat. She would have been wearing the fur coat her daughter Kuia would later wear in a photo digging for toheroa at Hōkio Beach—with her knife up its sleeve. But in the morning their grandson Cappy finds Hoani dead, missing one shoe. Hoani was lying a bay over from Polly's frozen midnight vigil.

I read about this sad end in a newspaper clipping at my grandmother's house after our visit to the old whare. It seemed apt that it fell into my hands, and the sad romance of it equalled Gwen and Jim. But I must have been brave enough not to beg Ben to take me back after he had eviscerated me using my son.

Five years later, to the day that I read the clipping, Ben dies.

It was the same day in 1898, when Polly was twelve, that her father was gored by the bull, and the day I came home in 2016 from Riwaka and stuffed all Ben's memories in the fire. Or maybe this was the day after.

To the new writer friend, Alice Tawhai, who asked me why I would want to write about all the killing—it's because Tutu, a kupu that can also mean a person who doesn't know how to leave stuff alone, wasn't even born yet.

Who are you killing? is a better question to ask someone who looks like they are staring into nothing at all.

I keep asking the other cousins on Facebook if Polly could drive, but no one remembers. And I think of the night Hoani lay without his one shoe in the dark. Why is it that she couldn't move? What is it that she was so frightened of that she could not see.

PLUME
PLUME

Widow song

Autumn 1898, and Nicola Sciascia, the assistant lighthouse keeper on Waikawa Island, spends his last day on Earth with the animals. I like to imagine my tipuna was fond of them. Another assistant will later describe coming off his shift and seeing Nicola's bull tossing something 'like a sack' into the air. But when he gets closer, he realises it is Nicola being gored.

Paul told me it was Riria, Nicola's wife, who saw him being tossed through the air, wondering at first if it was just her washing from the line loose in the island's constant wind. Then the horror of what was happening really registered, and she ran to him, too late, and cradled his head in her apron as his blood soaked through it to the tartan. Riria was pregnant with their eleventh child. Polly's teina Tutu was born Pirihira Waikawa Sciascia back in Riria's rohe at Koputāroa, her middle name bearing her mother's grief from the island.

The puzzle and problem with attempting to write historical novels is that you have to describe what people were wearing, and decide whether the bull was destroyed when the record isn't forthcoming. *What happened* wrestles with *what if . . . ?* I have come across another, better account of Nicola's death than my imagination's because it involves gallant animals. The bull wore a heavy chain around its horns, which the head lighthouse keeper had added a log to. The account drily notes that this arrangement with the log may have further enraged the bull. It adds that Ruby, a cow, and Judy, a mare, tried to charge at the bull to stop it from goring Nicola. But maybe this would have to be seen to be believed—the animals turning circles around Riria, who is hunched over the heap where her husband used to be.

Judy was the companion of a toothless old horse called Punch, and she would bite and kick at the bull if it tried to worry her mate. She had been brought over to the island to replace Punch, but proved to have a mind of her own, and was prone to taking carted loads right to the edge of the cliff on a whim. If I could pick my fighter in this story, I would choose Judy. The bull is unnamed, so I have taken the liberty of calling him 'Toro', which is Italian for bull and has the double delight of a rolling *r*, like te reo.

Nicola was stationed on Waikawa for the crime of falling asleep at the light at Pencarrow Head, near Wellington. When he was punished by the marine board he had the mitigating excuse of influenza. He was already far too old by keeper standards, but his wisdom was respected so he didn't lose his job; Nicola's large well-behaved family was sent to the even-more-remote island instead. Life there sounds lively when his fourteen-year-old daughter, Margaret—Polly's older sister—writes a letter to an Otago newspaper describing the shipwreck of the *Pirate*, the canary that survived, and the captain's dog then appearing three days later. The hungry, shivering dog would have seemed part mirage, part miracle.

On Waikawa there was porridge or crayfish for breakfast, vegetable and flower gardens to tend, animals to feed, and the mail boat's riches to wait for. There were picnics and Bible and astronomy lessons. Nicola's children were well educated despite their isolation from the mainland. There was a decent school and their father kept poems and recipes jammed together with his thoughts about learning the English language and the stars. But his notebook has since been lost.

Nicola was the only one unafraid of the bull, believing its moods and calculated hormonal charges could be fought off with a stick. Otherwise, the Italian is described as thoughtful, gentle and intelligent. Nicola had left his Catholicism behind in Trani when he married Riria McGregor. She had been christened an Anglican in the Rangiātea church at Ōtaki by Octavius Hadfield after her Ngāti Raukawa people swapped the musket for Bibles. The church had been established by Tāmihana, the son of Te Rauparaha.

Nicola was the pilot based at the mouth of the Manawatū River near Foxton Beach. He lived in quarters over my former school and, in his journal, described how the sand got into everything. He befriended Teone, the 'half breed' son of Hinekawa and Jock McGregor. Teone lived by the river with the children of his first and second marriages to two Ngāti Raukawa women. Riria was Teone's much darker daughter from the first wife, Pirihira Poutu; eventually Riria was old enough to marry Nicola. At a tangi, a cousin describes them to me as a love match.

I probably need to describe Riria's face, which was cut with sharp fine angles and the heavy brow of her Ngāti Kuia whakapapa. It is a face we all carry versions of; there are thousands of descendants from this one marriage. Nicola is just as recognisable in relatives I meet—his quizzical forehead softens the intensity of Teone's brow.

In 1997, a whānau group, including my Macdonald relatives—Manny's brother Enoka and Piri Sciascia, matua of *Te Maori* exhibition—went to Trani in southern Italy and met their distant relatives. They were told Sciascia was not pronounced *see-ah see-ah*, but *shah-shah*. I still have to say it both ways to figure out if I've met another cousin. But then, Māori have a knack for tipping the pōtae of a name askew, for nicknames and the endless joke of them.

Nicola's lighthouse on Waikawa was later shifted to Wairoa, where it sits beside the river, deep into Ngāti Kahungunu rohe. It has a copper dome and diamond-framed kauri windows. From inside it, Nicola would have stared at the long changing nights of the sea. It is probably best not to romanticise the howl of the wind at Waikawa when it likely drove him mad as Mum in Foxton Beach.

After Nicola was buried on Waikawa, Riria semi-settled in Pōrangahau, east from Waipukurau on a narrow road cut by blind corners towards the Hawke's Bay coast and further down the motu from the lighthouse at Wairoa. One of those places where to go across the bridge over the river is to cut off one world and simultaneously enter another.

But at the time Riria arrived with her brother Hokowhitu, Pōrangahau was a busy hub for Ngāti Kere. Hokowhitu had been called to Pōrangahau to carve the marae complex Rongomaraeroa after a kuia saw his work on the whare whakairo in Koputāroa. Hokowhitu's pou have the googly, unblinking eyes of owls and the strong graphic style of the Tainui carvers from his Raukawa taha.

Riria would criss-cross like tukutuku from coast to coast between her brother's pou and their own people back in Koputāroa, Hōkio Beach and Foxton, where her children married distant and not-so-distant cousins. In Pōrangahau her children married into prominent Ngāti Kere whānau, like the Tutaki and Rōpiha.

Riria never married again, and as a kuia she smoked a pipe. I can see her sitting with her daughters on the porch, the dusk deepening into a smudgy peacock blue, wearing her green and red McGregor tartan like a sari. She cackles and raises an eyebrow between puffs, sweeping a stray moko in for a smoky kiss after tricking them with a lethal strip of toffee.

Riria and her daughters were fine weavers, and I want to have them weaving in the dusk, but what idiot weaves by bad light? A lot of what passes for tapu and tikanga is just plain common sense. My tīpuna were busy women, busy people, and I am not busy. I just like to watch or ask annoying questions, hoarding details and pressing them into the silly putty of my imagination. And I get it wrong sometimes. I am still not certain that Polly could actually drive but it suits my story if she has her hands firmly on the wheel. Polly is the tipuna I feel most akin to, despite our differences, and she was a proper matriarch like her sisters and mother. Riria and Nicola had sons too, which is why Sciascia has become a Māori surname here—except the tika pronunciation died with Nicola's tongue. Their son Charles died in Belgium's rotten fields but not before he posed in front of the Sphinx in Egypt, riding a donkey while his superior rides a horse.

When Riria died in Pōrangahau she was taken on a flatbed truck with a guard of honour, taken over the bridge across the river and back to her own world of Koputāroa, where both of her taha had spilled blood into the whenua.

Polly was at Foxton when she met Hoani, her distant cousin, through Meihana, who tied her back to Tūtepourangi, the ariki for Ngāti Kuia, Ngāti Apa ki te Rā Tō and Rangitāne. Hoani was hacking at the flax. He just kept hacking and hacking.

This is why, when I move to Foxton Beach with Mum and Lisette when I am ten, everyone tells me I am their cousin.

You are a Macdonald, they say. *This place is full of them.* This is what Paul was talking about when I met him.

Dolphin Princess

After the unveiling for Beau and Shy, we are on the ferry crossing back to Te Waipounamu. I have picked a fight with a couple because it is very early in the morning and people around them (me) are trying to sleep but they are very loud about their love. I have already had to endure a marae sleep—I shouldn't also have to encounter a couple in love.

They call me an overstayer, and she tells me it's clear that I'm not getting any. So I almost start a movement, even as my son and Roman move to another part of the open lounge so they don't have to defend my honour. Fuck those two, I think—and fuck these two, because the others in the lounge are on my side: heads start breaching the surface of blankets to tell the couple to shut the fuck up too.

My leadership of the movement is brief, because I get a bit excited and mortify my new followers by hissing a war cry, telling them all I'm tangata whenua, when no one has asked. Over the other side of the lounge Roman is shaking his head at me, but it's too late for him to pretend not to know me.

It is not even 7am and I've ruined the rest of the day in the car for my son with my self-destruction.

But the woman was wrong about both things. I was *getting* plenty. Roman remarks once we are in the safety of the vehicle that they must have thought I was an overstayer because of my hair and clothes. He decides the pyjamas I'm wearing are too tropical, that I look like a Pacific Islander. This is almost a compliment from him because he loves anything to do with Tonga, insisting that Nātis came from there, when they weren't growing out of the mountain.

There is a video he is fond of watching when I stay with him in Gisborne two years later. It is a big event for the Tongan royal family, but most of the video is just the preparation of the feast. When I ask Roman why he enjoys it so much, he counters that it's the tinkling of the cutlery because he retains the ability to surprise me. He changes the video to a blind boy taking part in a kava ceremony who can sing and sing and sing.

Blue. Mother. Orange. Go.

Isaac, always drifting, takes a wrong turn and gets stuck wandering around the shopping village at Kaiapoi. An older couple see him, this furtive waif, and offer to give him a ride as far as Culverden.

The woman has a greying braid under her white headscarf, and she turns to talk to Isaac often. The waggly skin tag near her ear distracts him with wanting to pull it off. She tells Isaac her name is Eleanor, and the man is Matthew, and goes into some spare detail about their small farm. Matthew is silent except for a nod and drives staring ahead at the road, which begins to bend into the jutting stony outcrops.

God loves you, Isaac, Eleanor says, as they drop him off on the side of the road to hitch to his new job thinning pines further north. Sometimes Isaac doesn't even need to stick out his thumb before a man slows to give him a ride. Eleanor has been slightly harder work. Isaac had to look lost rather than found.

A week later, Isaac is staying at a holiday park in Blenheim with the rest of the forestry gang when a package arrives for him. It is from Matthew and Eleanor, and contains good work socks, a khaki jacket, a Bible and some DVDs they tell Isaac to watch. Eleanor writes that they love Isaac like God loves him, and if things stay rough for him, if it gets too hard, he can come and stay. Isaac would be able to work on the farm; all their children have left home. He would be helping them.

They name Isaac on their account at the local Farmlands store in Blenheim and he buys a pair of expensive hiking boots that make him almost three inches taller as he walks out and away from the staff's suspicious looks.

But Isaac has a habit of throwing things away—even stuff he loves—so he chucks their Bible and DVDs in the communal kitchen bin without a thought in his head apart from scoring. He is only superstitious about Māori things, as much as he transgresses this system too because he is hapless. The boys laugh at the letter he reads out as they pass the glass pipe. *We love you Isaac*, they parrot.

When Isaac tells me about the couple I wonder if they are refugees from a cult, and a man writing me the odd letter and many, many emails tells me about the Camp David kingdom near Waipara, another strange and uncool sect that contributed to cults becoming synonymous with sexual abuse. I wonder how long Isaac would last in any cult, given his history of being passed through the hands of ghastly adults. Isaac calls the couple 'the Gloriavale people' when he rings me, but they seem even weirder than that.

The forestry gang moves on to the West Coast and Isaac gets caught stealing some pounamu in Hokitika, from a factory shop where you can make your own pendant, and he gaps it, leaving the motel room in Ross in a state. The woman who runs the place tut-tuts at the cigarette butts she finds under the bed. She was initially soft on him, even with the meth smile breaking the perfection of his pale Māori face. When she interrogates the rest of the boys, they say they have no idea where Isaac has gone or who will pay his bill at the motel or over the road at the pub.

Isaac is already in Culverden with the couple, ringing me in a desperate state. He tells me he hates the food they make him eat, that he might kill them for it. He hates their chopped olives, their apricots and their nuts and seeds. I try to reassure him there is nothing sinister about almonds. The DVDs turn out to be material telling him Jews are evil and run all the banks, but Isaac doesn't give a fuck about any of that; he is just desperate for a cigarette and a piece of meat.

Isaac is coming off meth and has no weed left, and the couple won't buy him more tobacco or let him work on the farm. As usual Isaac insists to me that everything would be alright if he could just work some mythical farm. Matthew and Eleanor have told him it is more important that he watches their DVDs, but he tells me he is going to kick their shed in and then Matthew's head, too, if he finds him. Isaac says he does not like the way the man talks to Eleanor, which grates a bit given the way Isaac talks to me.

I yell down the phone at him, pleading with him not to do anything stupid. I tell him to just walk out of there. I remind him he can always find another lift. I consider ringing the police. Even though Eleanor has told Isaac I seem like a witch they don't deserve to be attacked like this.

But what if I do nothing and Matthew finds him busting up the shed and when Isaac comes at him waving their machete Matthew shoots him? What if, when he wakes hours later, Isaac becomes aware he is not alone, and there are young women in headscarves set up to milking machines like cattle, and Isaac can't tell if they are giving him eyes or pleading for help? A breeder for the brave new sect. But where are the babies?

Or, what if finally my pleading worked, and there was no shooting or underground milkmaids? And Isaac just walked out of there, tired of his own tantrum. And in the aftermath, Matthew and Eleanor stood together and absorbed what had happened to their shed and forgave him with little fuss. They are just good country people, after all, who, despite their anti-Semitic fanaticism, keep putting money in Isaac's bank account so he can continue to drift loose around the motu and back to my door like a dandelion's loose, wispy pin.

Everything that happened to Isaac could always go either way and it didn't matter because nothing stuck. He was touched and prone to disasters that could also be read as miracles. I met him less than a month after leaving Ben. The man in Riwaka offered him up to me and then instantly regretted it because he had wanted to keep Isaac for himself. Before I got to Riwaka, he'd told me Isaac reminded him of Roman, but—although they are both Sagittarius, and vaguely horsey-looking Māori—Isaac seemed much softer to me. Roman is insulated by his chronic levels of suspicion.

Isaac lolled on the day bed in the Riwaka man's lounge, watching kapa haka and wearing the dark red cavern of it like a second skin. All he owned was a bucket of shearing tools and some new day-of-the-week underpants from the Warehouse. I could not decide if he was a boy or a man, even though he was the doomed age of twenty-seven.

It makes me flinch to write anything about sex—I am less squirmy writing about cannibalism. But it is also impossible to write about Isaac without writing honestly about fucking. I could not register how desperate Isaac was for love because I was having such a good time using him to forget myself. Even though he would ask over and over if I loved him, I could feel only my own needs. I was also desperate to be alone with my grief after the savagery of the break-up with Ben. I complicated this by taking Isaac back to our holiday haunts.

But Isaac could make time turn into hot fuzz with just his eyes and a soft invitation from the couch. Isaac believed in auras, ghosts and his father's steamed puddings. He could find pāua and drugs anywhere. The beautiful, natural way he let a bottle of beer dangle from his hand like he was holding the curve of a hip.

Isaac said, *My father is the Jesus of Dannevirke.* It was a great sentence.

I made the mistake of describing Isaac as being my school project and he never forgot it. He was the most damaged person I have ever met, and I took far too much delight in his damage. As if I were keeping him as the prize specimen in my trauma petting zoo.

I also need to confess that I am blaming him for my cigarette butts under the bed in the motel room in Ross. But he had made me go to the West Coast. He paid for everything just so I would stay with him for a few days. He was even worse with money than me. Paler and more generous. He bought my son a motorbike.

*

I liked the way Isaac looked at me. My capacity for worship, which Ben had slowly eroded, was back. It was Easter and I was writing a story for *Mana* magazine about the crowdfunding campaign to buy the beach at Awaroa. Isaac had a disqualified learner's licence but I eventually let him drive the Audi I had bought with Ben's hush money. Isaac drove us down into Abel Tasman National Park, his hand as gentle cupping the gear stick as it was with my knee. He moved the car through the twisty roads and past the giant shuttlecocks of the nīkau with ease.

Before I let him drive, he had kept pressing into my thigh

and staring at me and I accepted this as normal, even though the woman at the petrol station refused to serve him smokes and assumed I was his mum when I went in and insisted that they were for me.

I did not enjoy the way Isaac could demolish an ounce of weed in days. I could not see anything resembling a future with him but there was no *future* for me; this was how I liked it. Isaac could burn through time using sex, but afterwards I would hide so I could cry alone. Any escape from the present tense was brief and any reminder of the past was torture. Driving through there with Ben in summer there had been the bluest hydrangeas.

Isaac's language was as limited as his circumstances, but it was also effective and subtle. He often made me laugh with just three words. When I asked him why he imagined he was in love with me he replied, *You **read** to me*. A revelation that collided in a fatal way with my vanity.

I had been reading Ron Crosby's book about the musket wars to Isaac in the red cavern at Riwaka. It was a violent passage where my people's heads were tied as trophies to waka in the Sounds so the cousins dwelling deeper there would know they were in for it next when the waka taua nosed into the bays. I asked Isaac if he thought of us as a savage people. He said yes and didn't seem insulted.

Isaac had told his story of abuse over and over, at home and within institutional settings, and no one believed him—especially not his mother. He pitched a tent in a neighbour's yard at nine to escape her and the lure of motorbikes from his abuser. In the chaotic underbelly he moved through as an adult, the abuse became his prime mode of seduction. Using his tragic, subtle, poor-me stories on a damaged or bored woman when he was trying to escape another man. His sexuality seemed more fluid than a woman's.

He only really turned on me after a sensitive claim to ACC was rejected; he'd cried with relief when he thought he might finally receive some compensation. He'd wanted a house truck and some dogs and to work as a mobile shepherd. But he was signed out of the claims system without a cent by a psychologist who met with him for an hour. He'd spent hours with a counsellor to get this far. Like me, she had told him his pain was special and would be seen. It was frightening when he started ringing me telling me he was going to cut my bits out, but I felt partly responsible. I had tricked him into believing the world could be fair.

Isaac had been using drugs as a trapdoor for his trauma since he was a child. Addiction is a genuine means of survival for some, and he was happiest shearing sheep with just the buzzing sound of the comb filling that deadly space between his ears. Shearing also funded his habit and the hearty shed life. He loved the piss-ups after knock-off on remote high-country stations. Nights fuelled by laughs, waiata and Steinlager. Shearing meant cosy sex with the rousies or a blowjob from a stoic closet case. Isaac was not fussy.

Isaac was also content with dogs. One of his first stories to me was of a jealous farmer who had shot all five of Isaac's dogs when he worked as a shepherd. And the missus then shot herself. I renamed Isaac's bitch, his favourite and the head of the pack, Lark, when I first wrote about him; she roamed through a dream I was skirting the edges of, as I used her to sniff out my ghost.

But I was pulled to the graceful point of his chin, the tawny freckles on his shoulders and the perfect V of his back, where I ignored the tattoo of a jester with skulls for a face and skulls for bells. Later, when he was back on the pipe, I would also ignore the bleach smell of meth filling up Ariel, the declining Audi, and the way his grinding teeth made his jaw ripple. From the side, his ears were small and almost undercooked-looking. Now, I don't care if a man is beautiful—that is just another fatal, empty trap.

If Isaac disapproved of something, he had one word for it: Yuck.

Being abused as a child did not stop Isaac nudging at my tailbone all night on crack, harassing me for the sex I was sick of.

Isaac turns up at my ranchslider holding a cricket bat a few months after he leaves Culverden. The bat is swinging like the machete did in my unhinged, paranoid vision of the farm. It's his eyes I look to after the bat, and they are mad.

I have just woken from a nap on the couch when I hear the rustle of his footsteps, but I am not surprised to see him there. I've spent the last few days trying to escape him, having one mishap after another involving Ariel, which is now dicky from lack of maintenance.

My colleague had to rip the phone out of the wall when Isaac got patched through to my office because I collapsed into tears. The cop at the police station believed I was the crazy one when I turned up telling them Isaac had breached his non-contact order. Maybe I am crazy. I believe I can make the car start with a bump of my fist like the Fonz in *Happy Days*.

But I was right—they weren't just empty threats, because here he is.

I put my hands in the air when I see him, like he is holding a gun, not a bat. Internally, I make an inventory of all the things out in the open that could make Isaac use the bat on me: there is a letter from a man on the table; a large, serrated knife with a spiky pronged end on the butcher's block trolley; my cell phone is in full view if I reach for it to dial 111; and my computer is open with multiple incriminating tabs. Tabs that show I still feel entitled to interact with the outside world.

I pass him cigarettes out the window beside the locked door and beg him not to hurt me. I have been locking my door for six months when it's not my habit. Eventually, I open the ranchslider, go out on the deck and convince him to sit beside me. I cannot even look over at my neighbour Sam's place. Isaac has already threatened to kill him, my dog and any man that talks to me on social media, telling the recent one he'd slit his throat. I am surprised when he doesn't just smash the glass.

If I blocked Isaac on Facebook for messaging me countless times in a day he'd pop up in the open sea of Twitter. Yet he barely touched me with his anger; that's why it was so crippling, and it's not the cricket bat I'm scared of, it's what the meth has done to his eyes. His fresh, insane paranoia that, now I am a lecturer, I must be fucking one of my students.

I tell Isaac, despite his menace, that it's okay—he can put the bat down.

I live half an hour out of town and the next two hours, talking him down, are among the most frightening of my life—scarier than giving birth or driving with a flat tyre on the motorway, although all these experiences induced the same uncharacteristic calm coupled with the inward, boiling desire to live. It is news to me that I want to live, because most of the time I'm ambivalent. Roman used to tease me about this, offering to kill me on any of our rare bush walks.

I manage to convince Isaac to have a shower. We are both filthy from days spent chasing and being chased, and, once I hear the water running, I text Kerry from the phone I have slipped in my pocket. I ask her to ring 111. I live so far out of town it seems likely that I will have to pretend to enjoy being raped to live.

I take a Valium that Isaac is carrying and so does he, and he starts to fall asleep on the couch after his shower. He has been awake for days and I feel some old pity for him when I adjust the blanket. His eyelids keep fluttering awake like a child's to make sure I am still there. He has been threatening to kill the dog, but the dog still wants to curl up behind his legs and I have to coax him away from the couch.

When I see the patrol car from the deck I run to it with the dog tucked under my arm.

Isaac bays like a shot animal when the police wake him, oblivious, on my couch, and then he screams *I love you* from the back of the car as they drive him away. I am reassured by the cop taking my statement that he will be held in the cells for what he has done. That he won't be popping up like that at my door again. I do not make too much of the fact I have been warning them for days that Isaac was coming back for me as the Valium is working and I am probably in shock.

Isaac is released from court two days after being arrested and returns to my house within the hour. He runs towards me from a car I have never seen and I make it to Sam's, running with the dog under my arm like I'd run to the police two days before.

I hear the car screeching down the thin street, gunshots and then yelling down at the bottom of the inlet, and later the police lose him in the bush. Their dogs find his T-shirt.

During the night, after Sam has driven me out of there, Isaac hides in my house, steals my phone and reads through my computer.

The next day, Isaac walks along the mānuka-hedged railway line, and then through the old tunnels on the cliff by the sea out towards the open road, where someone always gives him a ride. The grotesque jester tattoo on his back bare to the weak, early winter sun. He can get anywhere in the country on foot within a day.

Even though I felt cursed as Isaac was on the run and I escaped Dunedin, and even though I was medicated for the nightmares of him where he appeared from nowhere and anywhere like a slippery goblin, I found it hard to hate him. Even when I was forced to resign from the lecturing job I'd had for six weeks and thought I was going mad from fear and lack of sleep, I didn't hate Isaac. Isaac saved me from having a career and being faithful to the deadly language of the social servant. He saved me from explaining Te Tiriti to Pākehā and mopping up their tears with its fraying parchment.

Even though I was terrified of Isaac, I still *felt* for him, and was a little awed by his intuition that I was interested in someone else. I was. His ghosts were real and blended with mine.

Sometimes Isaac smelled like blackcurrants and nothingness and sometimes he smelled like the metallic cave at Rārangi and had the breath of its taniwha.

On the ferry I drank a cider chunky with ice and on the lounge's flat screen I watched the mumsy fashion of the milling guests at Harry and Meghan's royal wedding. On the deck outside in the dark I tried to smoke, scared that Isaac would emerge from behind the lifeboats but scared also that I could just jump into the water to make all the splitting stop. On the drive up the island I'd stopped recognising my hands gripping the steering wheel.

I was jumping out of my skin like a banana at any sudden noise or peripheral movement. I bobbed to the beat of PTSD. But, after a while, I also really wanted to fuck him. Isaac is still the only person I can imagine being in bed with, apart from Roman, without pain.

I met the man who has been writing me love letters, but he was like a noodle in person, a boneless vampire. Chemistry is impossible to fake. He tried to impress me about the art world and his reading of Kierkegaard. I named him the Aesthete in my head. I thought briefly that Isaac was right to send him a message threatening to cut his throat.

After my bad trip, I was only really attracted to dynamic, mercurial bullies. I was not interested in Ben until he told me he'd been to prison.

*

I miss Isaac's light but firm touch and economical way of sleeping, like he was under a bridge or a camellia by a church. I miss his tongue flicking at me like a lizard. I miss the way he would say *I love you* at the dinner table while I fed him the cockles we'd collected from the inlet, cooked with wine and cream and mopped up with rēwena bread from the supermarket. He seemed so innocent when I first met him in Riwaka and I watched the slope of his chin pretend to read the newspaper over mushrooms and eggs at breakfast.

Really these rituals were the barest simulacra of my old life. Ben didn't read the paper; he read his phone beside me after bringing us coffee to have in bed.

And I never quite trusted that Isaac's voice, which had a deep echo, was really his own, as he was always transforming before my eyes. And despite his longing for a home, rather than just somewhere to *stay*, he could never stay put.

The first time Isaac touched me was uncanny; the way he felt for the right place on my back, the only place I can relax into being touched, and he rested his hand there, and then he waited and waited for me to turn to him. I thought I was ageing and disgusting but I saw none of that when I used him like a mirror. I'm not sure I'm attempting to metabolise my fear back into desire so much as trying to suggest they are the same thing.

I am not just an unreliable narrator: I am a complicit one. Being broken is not a reasonable excuse for someone like me to use someone as desperate as Isaac. I mean, I was genuinely *loved* as a child. I had people who took the daily project of raising a child very seriously. His own terrifying wanting could not be solved by me, for the sound of it was bottomless.

I still have periods where I jump at nothing and am consumed with intrusive lurching memories of Isaac and his deft first self. I hoard some of his sentences, like when he said he wanted to taste me when he was fucking me. It is appalling that I still find the memories of such talk exciting. Maybe I just admired Isaac's economy.

So far, I haven't complicated matters by leaning on any talk of the curse, but I did believe I was cursed for a while, when Isaac was at his worst. My friend Ruby sniffed at me like I might be cursed when she let me hide from him at her place before I left town. Yet I feel like I still haven't conveyed his Māoriness, or how Māori the whole thing between us felt.

I'm not talking about the 'domestic' violence—I'm talking about the curse. Like naming Ben, it is perilous for me to name the tohunga at the centre of my personal vortex as it risks calling him back into being.

Why would a tohunga even bother with me? Unless it is another thing I shouldn't be writing about. I am often anxious and half-convinced the ancestors want me to keep my mouth shut, especially if they are Māori and not directly related. But forbidden topics are like catnip to me.

Nana was hit by a car the day I finished writing an essay about Isaac, but I didn't make the connection until later. She was expected to die but her tiny pelvis knitted itself back together and she surprised everyone by not just living but walking again. She says the night before it happened was the first time she had dreamed about Jim in the four years since his death.

It also seems necessary to confess the gunshots I heard when Isaac was on the run from my house were just a farmer having at crack at the rabbits. Trauma, when recalled after the fact, is usually overripe with fantasy. Because belief has to be courted in this arena of competing wounds. This is why I reach for the past. There is so much horror there and it is easier to describe than real sorrow.

All the old trouble, bubbling and boiling away.

Isaac's Ngāti Tūhourangi people were from Tarawera and sheltered from the volcano's 1886 eruption in Hinemihi, a whare whakairo that was later transported to a country estate in England. When a fire took out the main house a few years ago, Hinemihi remained unscathed. Hinemihi is a plucky little survivor who has become a touchstone for Māori overseas. A whare that became so rich during the tourist age of the Pink and White Terraces that her multiple pāua eyes were replaced with gold sovereigns. Lately there has been a lot of talk of bringing her home.

I have to concede that Isaac did have gold flecks in his eyes. And the ghost waka Guide Sophia saw prior to the Tarawera eruption had people on board with the heads of dogs. The tohunga who despised the tourism and foresaw Ngāti Tūhourangi's demise survived the eruption away from the others, dying only once they cut his ancient hundred-year-old hair in the sanitorium he was taken to. The tohunga had been reluctant to leave the fresh happy pit of his whare, a place where he had survived with no food or water for four days. It was Pākehā who dug him out; his relatives just wanted him banished for his malicious predictions. He was rescued on the condition he be taken away.

The whare Hinemihi is the body of a woman who kept a powerful lizard as a mōkai. And I was seduced and therefore blinded by all this scorching mana that was not mine to touch. Isaac was as out of control as lava, always on the move and consuming anyone who got too close. And there I was, oblivious to the seething flow, reading to him about his ancestors from another book I'd been asked to review. Isaac insisted to me that the picture of Hinemihi on English green in the book about whare whakairo was a place he knew, but Isaac had never left the country.

After Tarawera buried the wonder of the coconut-ice-coloured terraces, Ngāti Tūhourangi were exiled south to Whakarewarewa in Rotorua and became known as penny divers. Jumping into the steaming pools to search for the eyes of their former whare. They were already versed in the performing village version of us; they were used to working as living souvenirs and immune to the smell.

*

On the run from Isaac I try to rid myself of the curse at St Faith's, the church at Ōhinemutu near Whakarewarewa. I am deranged and living on McDonald's coffee and Burger King. Mayonnaise oozes out of the haggard wreck of me like stigmata.

The tohunga Tūhoto Ariki lifted the tapu of an old burial ground so St Faith's church could be built. Inside, its Anglican surfaces are embellished by Hinemihi's carvers, but it's the later addition of a sixties frosted window of a Māori Jesus I have come here for. I pray to the optical illusion of him walking from the lake to the shore because it is my kind of kitsch. It vibrates with the too-easy, deadly meanings of the plastic.

My prayer in St Faith's has a begging apologetic energy. I apologise for writing about Tūhoto Ariki and using the image of the Māori Jesus when I first wrote about leaving Ben; I apologise for describing the tohunga as pissy at being discovered in his pit. Really, I am asking the lizard to release me from its mouth. But I am useless at prayers and get distracted on my pew by the tourists and the fatally loud reo version of 'What a Friend We Have in Jesus' piping in through the speakers.

Outside the church, I walk the kurī so he can piss somewhere that won't reactivate the curse and an impressive-looking Māori man with dreads, who looks about my age, waves to me from one of the dinky little whare of Ōhinemutu. He calls out, *Kia ora, Whaea, are you Sam's mum?*

Ōhinemutu was the end of my being a girl but I am still a sucker for any kind of superstition. My whole face lights up like a bulb at any talk of a curse and its giggling whispers of preternatural doom. To shiver is to feel alive.

*

A cousin once told me that whakairo, or the process of carving, refers to what the worm does to wood submerged under the water. He is used to hauling native logs out of the inlet we whakapapa to in Pelorus Sound. My cousin takes them back to his workshop to reveal the āhua of our tīpuna in their flesh. He told me we were inspired to carve by the little round pockets the worms make in the logs, which also resemble the mottling of tā moko in our skin. Whakairo refers to the digging, to making those little pockets of air.

Isaac had holes where the worms had eaten away too much of the wood. Including the hole in his gums he could whistle through to call to the invisible dogs. He was not my lost treasure to dredge up from the pit—especially when I was still mining it for the opals I'd left there with Ben. Sometimes his eyes echoed the pit and sometimes they were changeable liquid aqua like Hinemihi's discarded pāua. So perhaps, despite all the drama, my cosmic punishment, distributed through Isaac as her walking pou, has been slim.

When Isaac was on meth his ghosts got closer; they started breathing down his graceful nape and I should have known better than to tutū with them.

I did try to refuse once. It was dark and I was living south of Dunedin in a one-door crib right on a coast rich with southern kēhua. Isaac kept disappearing in my Audi, ostensibly because he had a job hosing down the slaughter in a local abattoir. But his moods had become quicksilver. The sight of his white gumboots through the side window of the crib had become a relief and a problem. He had already stabbed my tyre, and another time he'd put the handbrake on when I was driving, but I'm used to motoring disasters and scary men and switched from being lippy to calm.

This night Isaac was home. He'd been out walking, and said we had to help a woman who was buried near the beach. He said something was wrong with her neck. I countered that it was too dark to leave the house and go looking for a ghost. It was asking for psychic trouble. But he was like a kid with a dogged whine and insisted that I come and look.

Maybe this was the same night he tried to put lipstick on the dog and the dog snapped at him. For once. I mean, theirs was a genuine love affair but even the kurī knew he was back on crack before I did. Smell is the sense that is tethered the most to intuition.

We walked through the low dunes with the kurī towards the beach and I paused on the track to indulge Isaac, but also, I felt a coolness there, a depression in the atmosphere above the clumps of tussock.

I said, 'Here?'

'Yeah,' he said. 'Here.'

Later, I will learn the buried woman had lost her head to the waka as she jumped from the cliff to the river to meet her lover.

She was already too far gone to be helped.

The Greenstone Room

Ben uses company money to take me to Auckland while he does business. It is 2011 and the height of the John Key years, and by accident it is also Paul's birthday, so while Ben is at work we take my baby sister to the Langham, an almost-posh hotel. Paul is wearing a black Comme des Garçons suit with red silk lining, but he has no front teeth under his new moustache, and we are here for the buffet. He is huge now—bigger than his grandfather Manny, the godfather of Blenheim. Paul has started to resemble Manny even though they could never stand each other. Paul was the only one who would refuse to get Manny a lemon from the tree. Paul is turning fifty-three, but his hair is still lush and curly with only a few threads of white.

The Langham buffet is special, the kind of treat my baby sister has grown used to. A friend, Luna, tries to join us and it's the first time I experience my father being hostile at a table. She leaves. When my teina, Mamie, goes back for more high tea and to charm the staff, Paul leans over and says he did not like Luna's hat or the way she was looking at my sister. He says she is not a disability or a specimen. Usually, he accepts people being captivated by her.

Mamie is tiny and eats a bit of everything. The desserts are cute and extraordinary, and the Indian is proper Indian served by chefs in tall papal hats. There are a lot of Asians in neighbouring booths and tables, which is what Paul always notes when he shares dining spaces with them, whispering too loudly that they know the best places to eat, a habit of his that didn't die with the nineties.

I am trying not to feel sorry for Paul. It is impossible to pretend he still has money. This is a fine-dining buffet, but it is still a buffet.

The next day Paul takes me down a back street in Ponsonby for Italian toasted sandwiches and pizza. It is one of the comfy hermit holes where he hides from the high-living set he used to run with in Auckland

After lunch, driving me back to the hotel, Paul hooks a quick left into a carpark. The police have been tailing him, bored in heavy traffic, and have flashed their sirens. It has been a long time since Paul paid a parking ticket and he knew he was being followed. He is arrested while I sit mute in his ancient Land Rover, which I then have to drive through Auckland's CBD to the police station. It is a manual, not an automatic, and I am a bit stoned. This distracts me from feeling my father's shame. The difficult task of driving behind the cops in a city where driving requires all your senses. I watch him being taken inside and realise that my sister will need picking up.

I walk from the station to Freeman's Bay and wait for my sister at the gate of her school. She is much smaller than the other pre-teens and says hello to everyone as they ignore her. It is too obvious to state that this hurts my heart because I am battling my default urge to be blunt and tell her our dad has just been arrested. She is so happy and proud to see me I pretend that coming to pick her up is my surprise. She tells everyone that is ignoring her that I am her sister.

She has never caught a bus before; public transport is a novelty. All the adults on the bus match her effusive friendliness, which compensates slightly for being shunned by her peers. I tell her that Williams syndrome, her disability, is what Pākehā describe as being a fairy. I insist to Mamie that she is a patupaiarehe because we are Māori. She tells me she loves being a Māori. *Same sis, same.*

I take Mamie to the hotel room and she goes straight to the fridge. She is used to hotels and loves flying and has a yearly trip to the Royal Hawaiian with her blonde doll of a mother, who is the same age as Paul but never ages. The Royal Hawaiian is Joan Didion's favourite pink palace of a hotel. I became transfixed once by Mamie's mother's breasts over yum cha at Grand Harbour near the viaduct, because they seemed as round and hard as cricket balls and the lazy susan kept sending small bowls past them. She refused to eat the fatty duck, but Mamie wants everything in the fridge at the hotel and I indulge her.

Later, Ben tries to tell me Mamie has Prader-Willi syndrome and that's why she eats everything in sight. Ben's dyslexia overlaid with his arrogance means he has it all wrong. We are already tipsy and bickering is still a novelty between us, but his habit of knowing better than me is starting to show. His benign mask is slipping. Our first real argument will be about the IRA, which I am obviously for, and Ben is against. I will tease him about the negligible difference between war and terrorism. I will say it's just a matter of names as the vein in his temple throbs and snakes into his bald head.

In our last year together, Ben says he is going to an important board meeting with the Māori, who don't know how to be grateful, and that he will have to do his mimi, which of course means piss, not speech. He is on a board to protect the penguins and the giant albatross, because being a director looks good on his LinkedIn page, but really, he is zealot for tanks and military history. The gun emplacements built into Taiaroa Head meant a lot to him.

I don't correct Ben by telling him that he means to give a mihi. I am tired of the fact that he never seems to shut up. If he wants to embarrass himself in front of the Māori he imagines he is saving, that is on him. I imagine Ben doing his mimi and I chuckle on the inside. We don't laugh together like we used to.

Eighteen months after our sad buffet and Paul's arrest, Paul's younger brother gets up before dawn to dig a hole for Mugwi in the sand at the urupā at Māori Island. The island that is no longer an island. The brother is wearing Paul's suit with the flamboyant red lining as he digs.

Ben refuses to come to Mugwi's tangi. He can't risk being impressed by us. He has been telling me for months that the famous All Black and Highlanders coach Jamie Joseph isn't really my cousin. But Jamie will be one of thousands at Mugwi's tangi, the biggest tangi in years, even though it is the day before Christmas.

Polly and Hoani, who raised Mugwi when Manny married his son's auntie, are ready for him as he is lowered into the ground at their feet. Mugwi chose to be buried with his grandparents, not Manny, who is already getting crowded by the other branch of the family. We throw golf balls into the grave after him so he can beat his brothers in Hawaiki. As his granddaughter I am given a lily to throw in the hole by the same favourite cousin who claimed my Macdonald fieriness was familiar. Mugwi is buried deep so my grandmother can join him.

The new family joke is that during Mugwi's tangi my grandmother doesn't know what to do with her knickers at night—we are sleeping in the old school hall of the wharenui at the pā—so she stuffs them in Mugwi's coffin. She has to retrieve them from under the cloak before they close the lid.

Normally my grandmother would be the one doing all the catering in the kitchen but even I am marched out of there when I try to put away some milk. This is proof I am too close to Mugwi at last, because it is tapu for immediate whānau to be near the preparation of food. There isn't a lot of reo on the pā but the old tikanga persists.

My grandmother becomes fixated on a cat hanging around the wharekai. Calling to it and fretting for it instead of letting her grief show in front of the whānau who Mugwi used to lend all their stuff to. A smaller family joke was when she used to ask Mugwi in her softened Yorkshire burr what had happened to the spade or the chainsaw, even though she knew by then that Māori share everything with each other.

Me and Boy leave early on Christmas Day so the immediate family can get on with grieving. Before we leave, Paul goes out to the chiller trailer full of leftover kai and chooses me the biggest crayfish—it is massive—and packs it in ice to take back to Dunedin. I am desperate to be alone. I want to be with my real family, Nana and Mum and the pōtiki's mute children, to absorb my grandad's absence, which is still too fresh. Being in the car with my son is as good as being alone. We see dolphins at Kaikōura and I'm so excited to see my grandfathers I jump up and down by the aluminium railing and almost get clipped by a truck.

Instead of making it back to Dunedin, I stop at the Asylum after a ten-hour drive and serve the crayfish with mayonnaise from a jar and some limes I stopped to buy on the way. Ben's family make a great show of eating it and Bea calls it 'ambrosia of the gods'. Which grates slightly, but I am also grateful for some recognition.

*

I will never forget how right and sad it felt when Mugwi was lowered into the sand. Because when Paul dies five years later, and is testing the straps and the sand's collapsing sides, it feels the complete opposite. Paul was only fifty-nine and he wasn't finished yet.

The cousins sing a dismal version of 'Whakaaria Mai' for my father, which is embarrassing to Māori everywhere, and I almost don't include this detail here, but I can't help myself.

I'm not asked to speak at his service, and I can feel my son seething beside me and my little sister crying as I put my arm around her. I am already deciding how I will write about this, because that reptile inside me never sleeps.

I will eventually describe myself in the story I write for *North & South* as the missing piece of a jigsaw puzzle with the same semi-toothless grin. I won't describe his last room in Auckland, the one he died in, when he'd lived in so many great places in the city he loved. Or the peculiar agony of walking through it ten days after his tangi and seeing how he had been living when he still had such big plans to go home to the Wairau River to reclaim the section with the chimney and the desolate water tank. Instead, I go heavy on the metaphor, I let the water laugh through the door of his room and then Paul is back there, sinking into the little stones.

I take a pounamu cross from his room and another darker piece that feels and looks like an anchor. It has weight but the cross is light—the cross might be jade from overseas and the anchor obsidian. I sit clutching these taonga at the top of Symonds Street, feeling too devastated to cry. I make it to a random gastro pub and destroy happy hour for some tottering women by crying into my bowl of mussels. They turn around like penguins and leave me to my misery. The

Aesthete comes to pick me up, and when we get back to his own tiny flat he cries at my tears on his way out the door to meet up with his ex and go to an art opening. I don't ask him to stay with me, even though, for the first time, I really don't want to be alone.

Paul met me beside the river when I arrived late for Mugwi's tangi. I got out of the car and rushed to him, and it was one of our only spontaneous hugs. I am not a hugger. If I know a hug is coming, I will think, sometimes for days in advance, about how the hug can be avoided.

After Mugwi's burial, Paul said, *That was a hard day for me Talia, burying my father.*

It was Mugwi who came into the room one summer, when I was nineteen, after I'd shouted at him, my grandmother and Paul that they were the biggest fucking hypocrites in Blenheim. He came into the room where I was crying with my nineteen-year-old rage that was mine and my mother's and told me that, even though I needed to learn how to behave, I was one of them. He said, *Girl, you're my blood.* He hugged me and it felt like we were a ship going down and I still can't decide who was holding on to who.

When I start to feel haunted in Gisborne I realise that it was wrong to take something from the room my father died in without having it blessed. The pendants sit on the mantelpiece at Roman's under the picture of his relatives. I put them in Paul's puffer jacket when it feels like the whole house is starting to rattle and shake.

*

When I first arrived in Gisborne in Bobby Jo, Roman drove us up to Ruatōria for Easter, and we even stopped at the Ngarimu homestead after visiting the urupā and the cool wind circling Nanny Shy's white wagon-wheel grave. We looked at a house to buy. There was a mock orange invading the front bay window, like the mock orange I got to strike from a cutting of Truby King's from Bea at the Asylum. Mock orange reminds me of running the path when I was three at my grandparents' house: there were blue and pink hydrangeas, then the mock orange, and the honeysuckle tangled in a flowering pink Albertine rose over the trellis gate. Mock orange, with its hint of gardenia but something softer than satin and more subtle than jasmine. I would run that path like it was a haunted gauntlet, despite the beautiful smell that could breathe you into one world from the next.

A fantail was swished by a horse's tail when I turned back to leave the house we didn't buy, with its pepper tree, and the coral and wasabi-green vintage lino, and an aspect to the river like *Washday at the Pa.*

Five moko said *look at me, look at me* as they dangled and hugged the pepper tree like leopards. On the drive back I studied Roman's tattoos. I suppose I would be happy if I could spend my life studying men's arms. But only if they chose the right song.

*

Paul's brother drives up the motu to bring my father's body home to the Wairau from Auckland. His large coffin is put in the back of the brother's courier van, where his Rottweiler lies on it like a sphinx.

At the poroporoaki, I am relieved when the same brother apologises for how few photos of me they have, but more so when his Rottweiler smooches over for a pat, and my father puts his gentle sorry head in my lap.

Orphan girl

I am carless now, with Roman in Gisborne, because I have abandoned Bobby Jo, the red Nissan. Roman has our son's van, which he saved his student allowance to buy after winning a scholarship. A couple of months ago I was trying to get to a fancy press lunch in Hamilton, when smoke started puffing out of the front of Bobby Jo. I was parked in Matawai before the gorge, eating a pāua pie, decided the smoke wisping into the air was just exhaust fumes from the car idling in front and drove on. When I stopped at roadworks the lollipop girl eyed Bobby Jo, and then me, like we were the same problem. I realised I was not going to make it to any bougie lunch and turned around, but the car got worse. I managed to pull over somewhere safe as it went *tick-tick-tick* and the engine cut out. Except it's not safe to be a woman alone in the gorge so Roman had to come and pick me up before it got dark.

One of his hi-vis colleagues sees the car every day on his way to work. Roman relays his updates to me with a told-you-so snicker. First, someone kicks in the side door, then the windscreen gets smashed. Finally, someone takes the tyres. It is proof of my failure and my innocence about what life is like here. I am wiser when I'm surprised it isn't torched. When I finally get back to it, my makeup bag with my stash has been stolen. The stash was worth more than the car.

So now I don't have a car, and it is the day before my birthday, and I am on the bus from Gisborne to Hamilton.

After the twisting Waioeka Gorge the driver stops for a rest at the tearooms in Ōpōtiki. An older Māori woman gets off the bus here as her neph taunts her from a skittish horse right beside us. The rest of the passengers on the bus are mostly Māori, and laugh at his antics, and the growling she gives him isn't serious. Up high on the double-decker Intercity, I'm still wondering how I can take it all in, and the moment is over before I can get a decent photo.

Later, in Hamilton, I am sitting at my mother's outdoor table and we are talking over good coffee in small cups about transphobia and how to make sense of what happens on Twitter. As a vintage lesbian she is still getting used to some of the new words. We are laughing and animated, not apprehensive because no one can hear what we are saying.

I hear a fantail's familiar cheeping and without looking I dread that it is black. When I twist my neck to look for it, it has flown back towards the Mongolian silk tree and then out of the garden. I cannot see what colour the pīwakawaka is, as the sun coming through the tall trees behind us is low and blinding.

I turn forty-one the next day but I am stuck in this teenager's situation of needing to be picked up and dropped off. I am going to Auckland to stay with my cousin, who is out protesting at Ihumātao. She has promised me a cake in the middle of a political resistance. I don't really care about cake—getting wasted is my sugar—but I appreciate the fact that someone wants me around them.

While I am waiting at the bus station in Hamilton to get to Manukau I see the stranger walk towards me. She totters along in an outfit that is outrageous considering it is the middle of winter. She wears silky purple boxers high around her waist with a butterfly belt, a worn white T-shirt, dirty sneakers with thick rugby socks and a short pale pink mohair scarf that she has tied over her baseball cap and then under her chin in a bulky knot. A cross between a rapper and a kuia, and Pākehā to boot.

I feel a terrible knowing that she is going to sit beside me. I curse myself for dressing like a hippy, for looking approachable and open to the universe in my waistless loud rags from Art! Fun! Wear! I don't care about the universe at all, and I suspect the feeling is mutual. I care about the dead Māori kuia in charge of everything.

The apparition wears lipstick in a cheap chemist shade of hot pink and it is pasted on like the Joker well above, and below, her lip line. When she grins and asks me for a cigarette, I notice her gums are bleeding around the metal of her braces. Not dripping, but there is a bright red seep that shocks me.

I know what it's like to need a smoke, though, and always give someone a cigarette if they ask me for one—in fact, I usually give them two, or even three, because it's my lucky number. A ciggie for the one she's missed and been craving, one for the now, then one for the future. This is how time works, and smoking. She feels like a girl, this strange interloper, and about the same age as my son, but she also feels reanimated.

She says, *You're nice,* and I realise I'm being misread. She follows me to the back of the bus, where the two Māori women in the seats facing us keep subtly raising their eyebrows at the young woman's monologue, at the tricky stream of consciousness I have been made sudden subject to. Some of her sentences are so startling I make an internal list of them, even when I am pretending to be asleep:

After Saudi I'm going to Africa to hydrate everyone

I plan to only drink sparkling grape juice and eat grapes the whole time I'm there

We need to move whole populace

Waikato is a great place for training

I'm an orphan

I did my own makeup

They complain about me at the backpackers' because I won't talk to them (I cock an eye)

I can block anyone on Twitter and get them banned—I have a special button (I gulp)

It was nice to meet you, read my page, I know everything about politics and history but wait until the morning so you can really concentrate

I bet you talk about me

Near Mercer, and just before the long, congested drive into Auckland, she announces she has a rash and starts scratching theatrically at her arms. I offer her the chalky nappy cream made out of calendula that I use for the rash I have developed from wearing the same green sandals every day. I used it for my son when he was a baby and fed him organic baby food because I was determined to be a perfect mother. She applies the cream to her arms and claims the itch has disappeared. She accuses me of being nice again. She says that she went to the same school in Port Chalmers as my son's best friend from Aramoana, but when I quiz her about this coincidence, she titters and says I ask too many questions. My cream smells nice on her. I don't normally like lavender as a scent—it is too astringent—but the memory of my son is comforting.

I will come to regret giving her the ointment because it reminds me too much of the moment the child gets stamped by the villain Carmody Braque, in Margaret Mahy's *The Changeover*, another sacred childhood text. The little boy, Jacko, becomes sick when the stamp starts draining his mauri into Carmody. Laura, his older sister, doesn't realise Carmody is a demonic vampire before it's too late. And my apparition does in fact dress like a wild Pākehā activist. I wonder if she is going to Ihumātao, where my cousin is laughing at the white people building a barricade out of supermarket trolleys.

When I check the kēhua's Twitter account on the bus, I figure out her account is very fresh, less than 24 hours old. Which is unusual for an activist unless they get banned.

The kēhua wants to get off at Manukau too and asks me if she can come with us, but my cousin will not want this fresh information in her hatchback. I lie and say the car is full and she accepts this. So, I leave her behind—or did I leave her?

Maybe the kēhua did cling to me, because my cousin turns on me after three days as my usual lethargy becomes a strange exhaustion. She accuses me of showering in the middle of the night. I feel chilled by her paranoid accusation because I have not showered for a couple of days as I rework the story I am writing about Paul and cannibalism. I am dirty but I am telling the truth.

Before I leave her whare, my cousin makes a fragrant coconut curry, which she wraps in a tea towel for me to take to the bus station. I put the curry in the bin at Britomart because it is starting to soak through the tea towel. I feel seen when I do this, like she would *know*.

She lives out west, behind the phoenix palms across the road from a beach. Months earlier, in the last hot dregs of summer, we waded out to the pontoon and lay and talked for hours. I tried to tell her about Ben because I was battling the news he had just got married and she dismissed it by suggesting it was never the life for me. I was so sunburnt afterwards my face peeled, and the Aesthete, who I was still seeing, grimaced at me, feigning tenderness, when I knew my presence was starting to inspire distaste. It was hard work for both of us, pretending to be as attracted to each other as we had been in our epistolary emails. My cousin didn't want to let the Aesthete into her whare. But she lets almost no one in.

He picked me up from my cousin's, and we stopped for free drinks at a gallery opening. When I talked about Roman to the Aesthete he said, *Look at you, look at your face when you talk about him*. But I never talk about Roman to a mirror so I can't see the softness there.

*

I am back in Gisborne after a less-cosmic bus trip. Roman is sick of my misery, which is even more malignant now that I'm not speaking to my cousin. So, I start walking the dog through Gisborne's flat, depressing streets, which, despite all the palm trees, remind me of Tīmaru in 1952. Still, there are pretty houses, and one that reminds me of a Molly Ringwald movie. The ornate wood carvings on some of the Victorian villas feel like kōwhaiwhai. They feel Māori.

I stop eating, smoking dope and drinking booze, and then I decide to write about Janet Frame.

And the kēhua comes back. The kēhua is not the orphan on the bus, and not the blue shifting demon I brought back from the other side at the Sounds. The kēhua is all these things. The kēhua drains me like a battery, but that is only because my clamps are loose. She is not my nannies and not a woman with kawakawa leaves for a crown and not the red bridge with white swans crossing and crossing but never quite getting to the other side. She is not Nanny Shy, Nanny Lady, Nanny Picky, Nanny Glory, Nanny Why and Nanny Choosy turning into Nanny Bang. And she is definitely not Tūhoto Ariki—Isaac is long gone.

From the back step at Roman's, I ring Kerry, breathless and talking too rapidly, and she tells me to go to Pōrangahau, because I have told her there is a karanga course on there that weekend, but also I believe the dead are chasing me out of Gisborne and I need to get closer to home.

Kerry says it again. She says, *Go to Pōrangahau.*

I spend the night in Gisborne with Delphi, trying to convince her of the bad juju I'm bringing into her whare. I am so naturally high leaving her house the next day that the year I turned nine seems to be happening as I walk back to Roman's. A line from *The Changeover* starts to have a magical double-freighted ring to it: *It was the same, yet different*, as Laura Chant becomes a witch.

Outside the chemist I bump into the mental health worker I called to Roman's house when he was at work the day before. At the house she had a companion who had pale Nāti eyes and said, as he was leaving—standing in the hallway, which seems to shuttle and push me every time I am in it—that he was there during the troubles in Ruatōria. He asked me for a copy of the story I wrote about my father; I had it as proof on my father's table, which sits in Roman's kitchen, that I wasn't lying about being a writer, so that no one committed me—I just wanted some meds.

The mental health worker, this Pākehā-looking lady who sounds Māori when she talks, told him that he couldn't have my magazine, and she had looked askance at him when the first thing he said to me at my dead father's table was, *I know you Talia*.

The first time I fled the Aesthete for Roman, we then drove from Gisborne to Taupō to pick up Paul's heavy wooden table off a rich retired Pākehā couple. The woman had wondered out loud how close I was with my dead father.

We collected the table before I was fully decided about leaving the Aesthete, who was telling me to come back to Auckland, that he could get me a job as a housekeeper for his rich, troubled boss. Before I went back to the Aesthete, after collecting the table, I slept with Roman for the first time in a decade and it was so good I screamed. He laughed at me as I ran back to the couch from his room to read another email from the Aesthete.

I did drive back to Auckland but only lasted a few days with the Aesthete and then I was in Hamilton screaming at Mum about my life being her fault.

I went back to Roman. I was still pretending the dog was my only real reason for returning. Roman had new Sailor Jerry tattoos. He had two swallows diving into his chest. He had a cobweb on his elbow and a mermaid with a carp tail where the name of his sweetheart is still blank and waiting to be filled in.

And now, of course, I'm mad again.

Outside the chemist, in the mental health worker's car, there is a wahine instead of the man who thought he knew me. The mental health worker, who I trust, is wearing an anorak like Jim's and she gives me a script for the meds that will help me come down.

She says, *I was looking for you!*

Inside the chemist, all the little vials of organic oils and moisturisers I have ordered in specially seem to want me to drink them and eat them—and then Delphi is in the chemist too, buying something for her kid's friend's birthday. We start chuckling and laughing from distant sides of the chemist, because it reminds us of when we took acid at nineteen and she crossed the road to stop our thoughts merging, but we still knew what the other was thinking. And couldn't stop laughing about it. We later collapsed in my grandparents' conservatory in a pile of glitter.

As I get my prescription, 'If It Makes You Happy' by Sheryl Crow comes on the chemist's radio and I'm elated instead of deranged. The song makes *sense* to me. If it makes me happy, it can't be that bad. I don't question why my spiritual experience is being defined by someone as mediocre as Sheryl Crow.

Outside the chemist, I sit on a park bench and crack the tab of my giant can of Monster Energy to swallow my meds. And I realise how much the nice woman—who was happy to catch me wandering, insane, around Gisborne—at the random right moment reminds me of my grandfather Jim.

*

In *The Changeover,* Laura Chant has to go right under the water. She has to give in to being baptised by the absence of air, before the darkness will let her rise up, changed over into a proper witch. Laura is transformed by her love, Sorry, and his mother and grandmother, and she is ready to save her brother from the shrinking bald man and his stamp.

Even Mum has a third nipple; she used to put a face cloth over it when women came in to tell her their problems at Dorking Road while she lay in the bath.

In Roman's bath, I rise for air. Roman tells me I leave a mess like a little girl when I have a bath and does an impression of all my splashing around that makes me laugh and laugh.

But even with Roman's jokes, I just want to get out of Gisborne and away from the haunting, which he, of course, is partly conducting. Roman will come to the back door and tease me, using Nanny Shy's voice, to ask me what's for tea. Copper, his bitch, starts making strange gurgling noises like she is being buried alive when I try to smoke on the stoop that reminds me so much of Westra's Māori girl with her guitar.

I can feel the beautiful feathery arms of the dead at the invisible portal in front of me and I long to join them. I take my pills instead. And I imagine Jim, my Pākehā grandfather, being thrown around in the afterlife by these warring friendly kuia, like the Snoopy I carried everywhere at four until its neck was so long it dangled when it should have snapped.

Ladies of Pōrangahau

I dreamed the landlord would find me at Roman's with the kurī, and the next day his property manager is there; Tonka barks his stupid tiny head off when he knocks and we are caught breaching the lease. He tells Roman that Stanley and Copper will have to go, or me and the dog. Roman tells me he can't give up his dogs. He chokes on the word dogs: a rare emotion. I had already intuited that they would come first in any earthquake/tsunami situation. Plus I was a bit nuts—Stanley always retained his composure.

As we leave Gisborne for Pōrangahau in my son's van, Roman stops for gas and I buy a pair of wayfarer sunglasses crassly emblazoned with kiwi and the New Zealand flag. The sunglasses, when I put them on in the van, are also to let Roman know that I have gone insane and not to speak to me. For once, he does not tease me or push me past my limit. Plus, I use my lighter to cut the sunglasses' stretchy tag before I put them on and this impresses him.

We pass Waikawa, where Polly lived and Riria mourned. I look down at my leopard-print tights and I can feel my haunting changing spots. I am getting closer to where I belong, after some trade-off between kinder women. I can still feel Paul, and behind him, Jim.

But the van starts making a strange noise near Dannevirke, and when we get out I cower at two pīwakawaka hovering in the park. Roman is disgusted by this as he fixes the cambelt, and then stiff when we say goodbye in Pōrangahau at his sister Gina's place.

I walk around Pōrangahau possessed by my idea of Riria and Polly and encountering people who wear some better version of my face. Almost everyone in Pōrangahau is related but I am just an interloper.

Mugwi told me I reminded him of his grandmother Polly once, and I treasured this. I named my son after hers. It is sort of a mistake to mention Manny's name in Pōrangahau, but the name Manaia keeps coming back at me when they ask me who I mean by Manny, or I hear it when a little boy, about ten, runs across the road to the shop. I thought it was the girl, also ten, swinging from the phoenix palm beside the coffee cart.

Sitting in a homestead kitchen with Gina, I ask a relation, Rose—another of Riria and Nicola's thousands of descendants—what the name of the place means. I thought it might be something nice and metaphorical to do with weaving: raranga is to weave. But Rose tells me Pōrangahau means 'crazy wind'. I ask Rose if I should bury my father's pounamu cross and dark anchor, which I have put in the pocket of his puffer jacket and which I wear like his body and to protect me from the kēhua. Rose replies that we bury too many of our taonga—I could just get it blessed. She tells Gina's girls, who are fiddling with her muka and ribbons in the next room, that they better not be having a tutū with her stuff. She taps her cigarette.

Kerry's Nanny Wiki was a Rōpiha from Pōrangahau. Before I knew about the connection, when Facebook was still a novelty, I tagged her in a portrait of Polly and her siblings with their Rōpiha whanaunga in Pōrangahau. I write underneath it: *the lady with the bung eye looks like you, because she is so good at pulling faces.* Vika responds with the cry-laugh emoji, recognising Kerry and her gift for funny faces. Ole Bung Eye.

Vika was about to have another baby when I fled to Pōrangahau, and Kerry and I were worried about her. She

had a rare thing with the placenta and had joined a Facebook group where other expectant mothers swapped their fears about bleeding to death. She was on bed rest in Brisbane and resigned to the fact that she was going to die.

In Pōrangahau I walk towards Raina, Piri Sciascia's sister, the woman who can karanga to the whale, and she calls out the name of a recently dead girl, her niece, mistaking me for her, because the sun is behind me and she can't see how haggard I am.

I escape Raina's karanga workshop and end up at the pub with Gina, who works for Raina's daughter in the only shop. I fled Raina's karanga workshop because the prayer bowl they were using during the mihi whakatau sang too loudly above my head, and I thought the other women would know I had brought bad juju from Gisborne. During the pepeha a woman with a moko rae and a moko kauae said she was Uepohatu, the same hapū as Nanny Shy. As koha, I left them my copy of American *POETRY* magazine, which had the story I wrote about Beau and Nanny Shy.

At the pub Gina says one of Vika's Tongan relatives lives nearby. Then I am happy sharing a joint with a cousin who tells me I look like the dead cousin he used to kick with, even though it is another, recent, tragedy. An older woman, his cuz—the right fit for me—but this problem still, of arriving somewhere haunted and being told I have the same face as the dead. I was ready to walk into traffic in Gisborne, but only because I was trembling with a weird joy as I experienced my past as hundreds of simultaneous events.

It is Gina who makes everything okay. I take a photo on my phone of her tamafreaky smothering her as she holds up the wooden spoon as a family joke. Later she lets her man back in the house even though he turned over tables at the pub, and they waltz and jitterbug around the living room and I take photos of them, pretending to be Ans Westra again. He is suspicious of me, his new cousin, because she has used me to kick him out.

There is an ex-mobster bulldog called Fatboy who comes over and tries to maul Tonka and stares deep through his squished face into my eyes and I decide he is Paul, such was my thinking at the time.

Our cousin Orlando's horse-float coffee cart is so pretty with good retro it reminds me of my old aqua lounge in the deadly village where Kerry, Vika and I used to laugh ourselves stupid at my oval table. Orlando's cart reminds me so much of me that I have to take photos, even of the Three Wise Monkeys beside the coffee machine, refusing to speak, see or hear evil from behind the fake peonies and the small gilded portrait of Frida Kahlo. Gina says, *Look, it's so you, Tali. It's aqua.*

I take a photo of the golden elephant clock keeping time on the wall. 'Dreams', a song that always reminds me of Roman, comes on while we wait for our flat whites and I'm dumbstruck.

When I arrived in Pōrangahau, Gina showed me a film she got developed from Roman's; the old roll had been on the mantelpiece with my father's pounamu when she'd stayed with us a few weeks before the kēhua. The film was from the year Roman was born.

In one of the photos, Nanny Shy grips the wagon wheel of the stagecoach in the Otago Early Settlers Museum. There is another photo with a blue bead of light on a spider web, and the bead is my son. And I try to know, because there is so much luminosity in all her dark invasions of my head, that Shy is done with me. Even better than this—she is trying to send me home to my son.

But I still know four other things in Pōrangahau. Two of the intuitions are frightening and two are reassuring. Before she goes into forced labour, Vika posts a pic of herself at three in a blue McLaren stroller, like the one I had when Jim cooed over me. The photo feels like a tohu: there is a little girl coming. I try and pray, for me and our friend.

But I didn't know then that Kerry's Nanny Wiki was only three when she was promised as a bride into another whenua. I did not yet know that her purpose was peace.

Vika lives after the blood of two other people, pints and pints of it, is pumped through her almost-lifeless body.

She will call her baby girl Manaia. It is another surprise.

The matriarch

After the haunting is over, the craziness lingers, and I turn up in Blenheim at my grandmother's on Father's Day. My grandmother likes the dog, which is a miracle because she is fastidious, and I start to really like her. She is a warm, no-nonsense person and, unlike me, she has some self-respect. Luckily, I'm curious to know everything about Mugwi, whose large portrait sits above the flat-screen TV. Her eyes flick back and forth from it as we chatter over the bottle of chardonnay she opens at 4pm on the dot for just a glass or two. Paul is not a touchy subject, either: we agree that his death feels all wrong.

She offers to buy me a plane ticket to Dunedin, the place I'm desperate to get back to, but I'm embarrassed by the expense of transporting the dog so I get my grandmother, a woman in her late eighties, to drive me to Nelson instead. I'm lucky she is so capable; she can tuck her legs up underneath her on the big leather chair facing Mugwi's huge portrait because she's still supple as a girl. He's probably frustrated she finally has the remote and his portrait can't watch any sport, especially from behind the television.

She takes me out for lunch in Nelson, and even though I loathe this tiny city of retired National voters and hippies, the lunch is very nice. I try to ruin it by oversharing about my failed love life—especially the latest, the Aesthete—but she doesn't choke on her BLT. She admits that we've never given each other a proper go, which seems a fair summation of the situation, if I were to see it only from her perspective.

She drops me at Jaq's, my old tolerant flatmate with the fork issue. Jaq is a schoolteacher at a high-decile primary school, so she gets a lot of emails at unreasonable hours from parents who think their child is special. It confirms for me that, even though I whakapapa to Nelson, Pākehā have made it a deeply hateable place.

Jaq lets me stay for days. I make her a roasted carrot, almond, cumin and cauliflower salad to take to her reo class for shared kai. After I drop her at the class with her bowl, I take her Subaru station wagon straight to the drive-thru at Burger King. She tells me off when she sees the wrappers in the car, but is only half serious. It's not the mess that upsets her—it's the fast food from the global corporation. Yet somehow, we are friends.

Jaq was the sensible one who was wrong when she said I would regret burning Ben's box of memories. Ben and Jaq had tramping in common. After he filmed me trying to cut my throat and left the house he rang Jaq so she could come and look after me. She reminds me of this, the 'caring' phone call, and I tell her about the filming to remind her that Ben is Satan. I still can't bear it when anyone tries to humanise him.

In Nelson, while Jaq is at work, I am ruminating over being a failure in love and a failure at life. I have been reduced to floating around the country on foot believing I'm haunted, with my unmanageable dog in tow. Suicide starts to seem like a good option, virtuous even, but there's a difference between leaving BK wrappers in a Subaru and leaving your body in an old friend's house. So I ring the psychiatric service telling them I want to die, and they tell me I'd better come and see them. I talk for two hours about my curse and they don't commit me, but they do prescribe me meds to help me sleep. And they send a Māori around to Jaq's to make sure I'm alright. I put the jug on. I can still remember to do that much.

She arrives and kisses my cheek and we sit on the veranda as the creek tinkles behind the trees and establish that she is an Elkington. One of a large Ngāti Koata family in Nelson. She already knows that Paul has died. She seems to know who I am, too, but it doesn't bother me—not just because I have no filter but also because I know that my curse won't seem alien to her. After I finish raving at her, she tells me to be careful what I write about.

*

Elkingtons are often Mormon because they descend from an exquisite-looking matriarch, Wetekia Ruruku, who married John Arthur Ratapu Elkington. Wetekia Ruruku grew up on Rangitoto Island, or D'Urville as it's known later. The island was part of Tūtepourangi's tuku whenua after he lost the battle of Waiorua. After the war, Ngāti Koata and Ngāti Kuia lived in peace together. There were marriages between us on the island and at Wakapuaka near Nelson, so basically the woman sitting on Jaq's veranda was a relative—although not quite by blood. I am related to some Elkingtons and some Hippolites but it's confusing even for me, when I have spent years trying to figure out where everyone fits in for my grandfather Jim. A forest of family trees.

The Elkingtons and the Hippolites are already familiar to me because Mum went to Church College in Hamilton with both these whānau. They filled her American-style yearbooks, which I used to pore over. They had thick straight hair and long attractive faces. And their names sounded biblical, another offshoot of the Israelites.

The story of Wetekia's conversion to Mormonism is not quite typical. The Mormons differed from the other missionaries who arrived in Aotearoa because they were willing to accept the full extent of our manaakitanga. They didn't turn up their noses when we insisted they stay the night in the wharepuni with us. It was conversion by stealth and a full stomach.

Before the missionaries arrived in large numbers, visitors to Te Tau Ihu had already noted this hospitality. Louis de Sainson, an officer and painter on Dumont d'Urville's ship the *Astrolabe*, wrote about this in 1827, after spending a night with a group of Māori at Tasman Bay.

> *When it was time for sleep, the savages invited us into their huts but we were careful not to accept their invitation . . . you have to crawl in and there is nearly always an extremely foul smell to them* [shark oil and ochre]. *We preferred to lie down at the foot of a small tree by the beach, but we could get very little rest. To our great regret, a certain number of natives came to keep us company, and we had the pleasure of serving as pillows to these gentlemen, who found it very convenient to rest their heads on our outstretched limbs. How could we sleep amid the snores and restless movements of such neighbours?*

The smell, of shark oil and ochre, was a cultural thing. Plus, it probably kept the sandflies away, which are everywhere in that part of the country. More bloodthirsty than Te Rauparaha, whose heke-turned-taua had already done some damage by the time Captain D'Urville arrived.

Wetekia had a gift for prophecy. When she was fourteen and living on this southern Rangitoto, she had a dream:

> *I was standing on a very wide and beautiful plain. Around me were many people standing in many small groups. They appeared to me to be very sad. I wanted to know the cause of their sadness but could find no answer to my question because none would speak to me. While doing this I heard a voice far away but I couldn't understand the words until the voice was almost over me.*

She reported hearing a voice speaking in Māori say,

> *'O house of Israel, how oft have I gathered you as a hen gathereth her chickens under her wings and ye would not—I will gather you as a hen gathereth her chickens under her wings, if ye will repent and return unto me.' When I heard these words I looked up and saw a white dove flying over me saying these words. I clapped my hands and looked up and said, 'Yes Lord, I will repent and turn unto thee.' The white dove then turned into a book, a book with the pages opened out towards me. I woke up then shouting those words, I was so happy. My father rushed over to me and asked what was the matter. I told him of the dream and he said to me, 'It is a good dream, you are blessed of God.'*

Much later, when a group of missionaries descended on them, she recognised two of the men as being the figures in her dream. Which is serendipitous, since she seemed to have been quoting the Book of Mormon at them before she knew what it was. The germane question then becomes: did Māori absorb Mormonism into their way of life or did the church teleport our wairua and the tithe up into theirs? The answer seems to be both. Initially, Mormonism was much more popular among Māori than Pākehā.

Around the time Wetekia's looks, self-belief and charisma allowed her to convert hundreds of my people to this new faith, Kaikaiawaro morphed into Pelorus Jack and started assisting Pākehā instead of us. Then, one night, Wetekia's teenage daughter became very sick. Wetekia rowed her boat in a storm to the mainland to get help. The sea was rough, and her daughter was lying in the boat; it was a dangerous gamble to take her as far as Nelson. Suddenly, dolphins started appearing to hold the boat afloat as it threatened to tip. Wetekia made it to land and medicine and her daughter lived. Later, her daughter wanted to marry a man Wetekia didn't approve of, but eventually she gave in. He was a Whiro, a Hemi, and a relative of Kipa.

*

Ruby, the friend who helped me escape Isaac, is a Whaanga. Her relative Māui was Jim's best man. He hides behind the freesias on the cake in my grandparents' wedding photos. Ruby and Māui's ancestor, Hirini Te Rito Whaanga, grew up on Mahia Peninsula and Waikawa, where wānanga were held. Another seer who was baptised a Mormon at Nūhaka and was used to the strange traditions of an island.

Ruby feels like Kerry to me; when we met it felt like I'd known her before. By the time the Sciascia family arrived on Waikawa it was known as Portland Island and there was little left of the former wānanga where warriors had learned to fight and think. Wānanga were tertiary and abstract; they were a place to pass around the old cosmologies and raise your rākau at fighting angles to the sky.

Even though I'm still drifting loose around the country, more aimless than Isaac, I seem to have all this help. But it doesn't mean I take their advice—especially when they tell me to be careful what I write.

Ruby was baptised in the chapel the same year Mum left me there as a baby. It is another dazzling Dunedin coincidence.

Sisters of mercy

As I drive up the country to escape Isaac, I am writing to the Aesthete who reads Kierkegaard and whose letter was on my table that Saturday when Isaac showed up swinging the cricket bat:

> *I stopped at Koputāroa yesterday because there was this tiny graveyard on a rise over the train tracks. There was a child's playhouse out the front and two large stone angels in the centre of the cluster of graves, some headstones further down too at broken angles, like bad teeth. I have*

had relentless voices (some badgering version of my own insisting death is the only escape) all the way up the country and my hands shake and my heart bothers me. But it was briefly still there in the eye and some drawing up through my feet to my hands which instead of shaking started to wiri. Snort, I'll take anything I can get. They were my relatives but another whakapapa line, one of Teone McGregor's daughters from the second marriage further down amongst the bad dentistry, and a tacky kind of kererū on one of the graves with one of those old red fabric roses in bits on the grass. It all felt significant. I missed Kererū Marae, which I wrote about in the Isaac thing, but found it the second time round. I got lost after the turnoff to Taihape from Bulls and ended up in Whanganui instead. It is so leafy and pretty and old fashioned with that big slug of a river running through it but because Isaac returns there a lot and was born there I can never live there. It feels like there are so many places I'll never be able to live now and that makes me very angry and equally hopeless. Then I got lost in Vigil *country and instead of going mad my first poem in weeks started coming on. Before this my sense of direction has been uncanny so maybe there is hope.*

The dog is getting old and after about six hours he gave up panting and dribbling beside my ear and even rested his head on my shoulder. I started chatting to him from about Taumarunui because he means a lot to me and I'd like him to live forever.

But once I arrive at my mum's in Hamilton I am insane with anger. I am insane in the MSD offices of Hamilton when the manager is fetched to tell me there is little they can do. I am insane in Hamilton's suburban libraries while I charge my phone so I can fight with my mother some more by threatening her with walking into traffic.

I write to the Aesthete again, high on the idea my tīpuna are looking after me. I write this from a psychiatric respite facility:

> *The woman from the refuge who met me today, the bird was her name, felt familiar from the beginning and I wondered briefly if she was a McGregor. It was safe to talk about the magical thinking in that context and she had just said your tīpuna will be looking after you, that things were hectic and she motioned to the air with her eyes while I stared at her moko kauae. I mentioned Isaac then and stopping at the cemetery in Koputāroa. I also mentioned Hokowhitu (Teone's son and Kererū Marae's carver) and that I'd already written about Koputāroa in relation to Isaac so the tīpuna thing made sense. She said, Cousin I come from Teone's second marriage through the daughter. The one whose grave I was standing at the day before yesterday. She hugged me and said, I am going to tell that nice cop who rang me about you that I am looking after my cousin.*

*

The only other time I feel like I am with living kindred spirits is when I am in the waiting area of Hamilton's acute psychiatric service. It was a lively wonderful place that waiting area, and even with my back against the wall I didn't mind the large unwell Māori man with sweaty eyes inviting me for a coffee. Such interesting cross-conversations happened as people swept in and out of the door. People facing the bright of the day and looking out for one another despite the hardship of being mad or homeless or both. The sunny use of the word 'bro' when describing living in their car.

It's only later that I realise, when I got lost in Whanganui on the way to Hamilton and I am parked outside a house by the river—a house so ugly it is almost beautiful, a flat-roofed monstrosity incorporating many bad design elements—that this was the section where Captain Jock McGregor had one of his houses.

I should probably travel overseas. These coincidences would seem more avoidable then. But then again, I'm the one who can't stop seeking them out.

The good brother

In January 2020, just before the plague, I am in Hamilton again, staying at Mum's. I am scrolling through my phone on her deck, baking as much as all her thriving succulents and the shaded heavy purple taro. A cousin posts on Facebook that Piri Sciascia, Jacinda Ardern's advisor on all things Māori, has died after surgery. He looked a little indigo in the lips in photos online the day before, but fine, surrounded by his whānau after a lunch. I cry at the news, and then feel embarrassed by my reaction because we never met, despite being Facebook friends. I wrote him an email once asking for permission to use the studio portrait of his great-aunt, Polly, with Hoani and their children—Elsie, Enoka, Manny and Jack—before Jack went off to the Olympics. It was for the article I wrote, with Isaac in tow, for *Mana* magazine about the beach sale at Awaroa. Piri's reply was immediate, generous and friendly. He made me feel like I belonged in a way that was less fraught than my immediate whānau. I wanted to print out the email and get it framed.

I decide to go to his tangi—to go back to Pōrangahau. I know that I will want to write it all down and I'm pretending that I won't. I can't help myself or seem to be stopped.

I have visions of helping in the kitchen, which is equally absurd, but fits with my tendency to try to sneak in through the back door instead of being welcomed through the waharoa, to dodge the hongi line because I've had a ciggie. And I'm cack-handed in a kitchen these days, a side-effect of being a bit homeless. The ghost of Polly would slap me around the back of the head because I forget the little things, like putting up my hair so I sweat less and don't get incriminating black strands in the food.

On the way to the tangi I am enjoying being one of the people on the bus. The feeling kicks in for me just before Tokoroa, even though I'm seated beside a young man in white trainers, white socks, white shorts and a white hoodie who is watching white fascist protestors in America on a live stream. I decide I am seated next to a potential terrorist not a cricket player and change seats after Tokoroa, where I go to McDonald's because there is no Burger King that I can see.

We stop again in Taupō and I watch a Māori mum with three kids wrangle them so she can use the loo. She tells Dillinger to watch his younger brother. This detail, his gangster name, is as delicious to me as the bizarre architectural pavlova of the old Putāruru post office we passed on the bus. I take a photo of a gangsta in a hoodie and feel like a camera instead of a person, a human recording-machine, but with every detail begging to be taken in. I am a terrible photographer. I can't make the magic puncture the screen like Ans Westra.

The bus sighs when it lets us down in Napier and I walk into the centre of town, where the surreal little square plays a chiming version of 'Putting on the Ritz'. I wonder if the music is in my head at first, but Napier is famous for Art Deco and I try not to hold this against it. I go to the gorgeous scalloped pink soundshell and walk across the perfect lawn to take a selfie with the statue of my tuakana, Pania of the Reef. I look very pale in the photo so I hide this by overstating it with a *noir* filter when I post it online. The question of whether I am white-passing or not has started to plague me, because before I met my father there was no question whether I looked different from Mum, Jim and Gwen.

I find a Burger King and eat my Whopper Jr and cheeseburger stunner meal in peace. I order the same thing at Burger Kings all over New Zealand. It's the only habit I have that passes for a routine as I drift semi-homeless. I am drifting to Piri's tangi.

I find a cheap and nasty backpackers' in a decaying Deco beauty because my travel budget is almost non-existent. On the balcony, looking over the pretty, manicured streets of Napier, a little Indian boy who lives at the backpackers' tells me he is going to be a doctor one day. I tell him my son is at medical school and his surprise is so cute I ring Boy to tell him. I don't realise I'm being listened to but afterwards, an older woman and her young companion call me over to sit with them. I am drinking good Cuban rum and they say they didn't realise I was a native until they heard me *using*

Māori words on the phone. She says that I look too Italian. They assumed I was just a backpacker.

I'm not enjoying their company but the young one, who has snaky eyes and hips and is called Wyatt, after the cowboy, can get me some weed. While he goes and does this the older woman says there are two things she doesn't talk about: politics and Maoris. As if they aren't the same thing. I realise too late that I'm socialising with a racist.

Since breaking up with Ben, I have become unpredictable around racists. I used to tolerate drunk white people saying racist dirt to me but now that I imagine I'm damaged by Ben, instead of my own inaction, there comes a point in the evening with these random stand-ins, after I've drunk enough to untie my tongue, when I'll tell them they need their white head cut off because they are a cunt.

And some Pākehā laugh then, and some—like this woman, this beaten down, hurt, mean Pākehā woman—narrow their already-vicious eyes and tell me I don't look Māori enough to be defending my own corner, that I look too much like Amy Winehouse to be the real Mowree she has the bald nerve to complain to me about. She says we are taking the houses, fucking up the backpackers' with our shifty ways, that we are not *grateful* enough. Blah blah blah. She says the local iwi has all the rentals, the housing crisis is their fault—stupid bloody Maoris—and so on. She tells me she lives at the backpackers' with reduced rent because it is her job to keep the Maoris out. Calling me over to join her on the balcony makes a different kind of sense then.

All of what she says is deeply fucking wrong and full of malice. And all of it is impossible to argue with. I often think of colonisation as this abstract discourse, because I define myself through Paul's early absence, but it is in our pores.

I tell her it is our fucking land and stalk off to bed, but when I get to the feared shared bunk room there are two hulking, snoring Germans in it and no mattress on my bunk. I take photos of the sleeping Germans like it's a crime scene and lurch back out into the main lounge of the faded Deco lobby. I've just managed to find the candy land of Napier charming but now I think, Fuck Art Deco. The woman and her unlikely companion Wyatt woo me back over to the balcony, which is sort of nice of them since I have called them white cunts—but really, they are hustlers.

I find myself giving her the rest of the good Cuban rum I bought to survive the communal sleeping arrangements. I don't know where either of these impulses comes from—to give shit away to people when I am pissed off with them and to shout about my land—but it's a stolen place; it lurches from hurt to hurt.

I suspect the woman also suffers from a hurt more specific than all her racist venom and I ask if any of her kids are Māori. *Two of them*, she replies. She tells me she can't figure out if she likes me or hates me. Join the club, I think. But we have this foul staring contest too, and over the next few days I can't get rid of what was in her eyes.

Really this poisonous feeling has more to do with waking up after an hour and a half of sleep with a stinking hangover and missing my very early bus, carrying my big black sports bag as I run with the booze smell coming from me everywhere at once. Bus missed, I lie in the quaint square with its fountain and pretend to be homeless using my bag as a pillow and 'Putting on the Ritz' comes chiming on again because Art Deco is evil.

I have breakfast in McDonald's and throw it up later as

I try to hitch out of Napier, then give up to lie behind a bush near the motorway. I realise my hangover is making me overly dramatic and catch a taxi back to the bus stop. I suck at hitching because I'm better at giving stuff away than asking for something for free. I can't manage to stick out my thumb and eyeball the traffic. Fuck tourism, fuck Art Deco, fuck everything—especially asking a stranger for help.

When I study the photo of the sleeping Germans on my phone, I realise what happened to my mattress—that greedy, oblivious tourist used it to double up his own bed.

At the bus shelter I make a note of the other potential passengers. News of the plague has started to spread out of China and I wonder who is a tourist and who is slumming it in fugly middle-class sneakers and who is used to catching the bus. The answer to the latter is the Māori around me, who all either seem to know one another or are about to know who their relations are.

I make it to Waipukurau, forty kilometres inland from Pōrangahau, in a tenuous state. I'm still carrying the woman's hate with me as well as my unsightly hangover and I am close to giving up on getting to Pōrangahau, which, despite being geographically isolated, is not the end of a flat earth. I'm so anxious about hitching that I'm wilfully useless: I refuse to charge my phone to make things easier for myself and for Gina, who is expecting me in the middle of a massive tangi while she does shifts in the shop over the deep fryer.

The tangi is attended by the governor-general, other dignitaries and Jacinda Ardern, but not me. Instead, I eye the crossbars that bisect the park benches on the main drag of Waipukurau. The bars are acts of civic hostility that kick the homeless when they are already down. The bars mean no one can sleep on the benches and be seen. The Māori who are homeless on their own whenua. I think of that woman again and what she said about the Maoris; our vulnerability is contagious and something we are blamed for, when colonisation, that terrible heavy abstraction, is best revealed by things like that park bench. These small-minded acts of council cruelty that make it impossible for Māori to find a place not even to thrive, but just to survive another day after a decent sleep.

I walk in the hot air and heavy sun out to the end of Waipukurau and stick out my thumb. No one stops; I don't blame them. Even with my theatre degree I fail to impress them with my need. I turn around and start back to the town centre with the sports bag, which has started to feel like a boulder. A bright yellow hatchback pulls over, and a well-dressed woman in black asks if she can help. She's just come back from the tangi and confirms that I've missed it in my wretched state. I lie on a park bench without a bar through the middle, because it's not on the main street, and pretend to be homeless again but eventually Gina picks me up, and I'm the kids' weird auntie chatting nonsense in the passenger seat of the seven-seater. This is why the woman hates us so much: we still know how to look after one another.

Gina takes me to her place to have a shower and change and then to the marquee where all Piri's whānau are winding down after burying their father, brother and uncle. I sit with the niece who led the haka in the matrilineal tradition Piri massaged back into the area and she is the one who tells me Riria and Nicola, our tīpuna, were a love story.

People start to laugh and sing and dance. After all the sadness there is so much good feeling the tent bulges with it.

I take photo after photo I will never share. Gina introduces me as her sister-in-law, and I explain that Polly, Nicola and Riria's daughter, is my connection to the place, although Gina is the reason I have a backstage pass.

In the morning, Gina's partner, my less-reluctant cousin, makes a loud speech that seems partly for my benefit about how the real work at a tangi is done by the people cleaning up, and I don't take the hint and go back to the queen bed Gina has given me and eat one exquisite local golden peach after another and wonder what I can write about being here. The peaches are so good I decide to write about them. There is also the harder issue of deciding what I will have to leave out and what I can put in. I decide to leave out the koro who told me he was kicked out of the kaumātua flats for his crack parties because this detail is riper than the peaches. I add it to the list of things Pākehā must not know about us.

I wonder if I can include sitting beside Piri's brother, who was telling me that Piri was the person people went to if they didn't know what to do. He asks me if I believe in kēhua and mākutu and wonders if it was really his brother's time; the last thing Piri was working on before he died was a speech for Jacinda to make at Waitangi.

The bourbon and the deepness of the brother's conversation make me reel; I am too hungover and messy to be partying again. I walk over the bridge into the village in the dark by myself. I always feel safe walking alone at night—it's no different here.

The urupā where Piri lies freshly covered with his relatives is twinkling with fairy lights. It reminds me of the rainbow phosphorescence I saw once in the Sounds, the place all these Sciascia of Pōrangahau whakapapa to through Riria, like me. One grave is sparklier than a drag costume and I am lucky my phone is dead because what idiot takes photos of an urupā in the dark? I would just be asking for trouble again from the dead, who deserve their privacy, which is partly why we bury them.

Although, our Ngāti Kuia kōiwi used to be trussed up in trees in the Sounds before Christianity changed how we do tangi, turning them from an eternal haul to a three-day event like the Resurrection. I read in a Treaty claim that our bones were later taken to the mountains near Nelson, where there were two lakes bluer than the sky reflecting in them. The bones were taken to the wai to be chanted over and scraped. One lake was for the wāhine and the other was for the men. The dead need privacy but they also need to be clean.

The sky above the fairy lights twinkling in the urupā is unbearably clear and crisp with stars. The constellations Nicola Sciascia taught to his children from the lighthouse and that Jim gave to me.

I manage to leave Pōrangahau with ease. Gina is going to Tokoroa to visit her father and there is a mix-up between them on the phone about what day to come. He says, *Aww, not on a Friday.*

But as a staunch Rātana he means that his eldest granddaughter shouldn't be getting her hair cut on a Friday when we drop her off in Waipukurau on the way. Driving there we pass the sign for the longest place name in the world, and Gina's children know it so well one of them is known to sing it in her sleep. They chant it to me in the seven-seater: *Taumatawhakatangihangakoauauotamateaturi-pukakapikimaungahoronukupokaiwhenuakitanatahu*, which describes the hill above Pōrangahau where Tamatea, their Ngāti Kere tipuna with the big knees who slid around and climbed summits, plays the nose flute, the kōauau, for his dead brother. These girls speak their own tongue with such rhythmic confidence because of Piri and the mahi he did to give ourselves back to us. It seems a more important and profound act by their uncle than when he made Barack Obama and Prince Charles feel so welcome. But I will never be a visiting dignitary: I will feel like I have truly arrived only when I can stick out my thumb to beg for a lift.

And I want to tell the bitter, mean woman at the backpackers' that there is nothing here without us—there *is* no *here* without *us*—but instead I leave a one-star review and complain that there was not even a mattress to sleep on. I don't mention the woman for the sake of the little boy who wants to be a doctor. His parents managed the place and maybe she was lying about doing their dirty work. Tauiwi are not responsible for the finality of her statement about politics and Māori. It was a poisonous, Pākehā sentiment and I will not carry it inside me when I can instead billow like a tent with all my good feeling for us.

I tell Gina's girls in the backseat that Kim Kardashian is our cousin because her mother is a McGregor, like Riria Sciascia, our tipuna. Finally, a receptive audience.

Hello America!

I do not like Sam at first. In fact, I think I might hate him. I let Isaac know where my new house was because I needed him to help me shift and within a day this became a problem. He introduced himself to Sam, over the road. Sam, the highly organised pirate with a dungy silver Nissan, and within minutes they were off to score some weed.

Isaac says he has never felt so instantly comfortable with someone, and I wonder who this guy over the road is who claims to be a counsellor when his house and its raggedy ruin suggest that he is an old addict.

It turns out Sam is both things: an ageing but eternally youthful addict who knows he can't work as a counsellor. Methadone allows him to maintain a routine. He lets his huntaway bitch fly in front of the car on her morning run and, before we are friends, when I hear her excited bark, I think, At least he walks the dog.

Isaac threatens to tell my new landlords, who seem very nice and very straight and live right next door, that I am also a drug addict. It's bad enough that I am on the benefit and this is why I ask him to leave. Isaac, the eternally abandoned, abused child, threatens me some more and takes the rest of the weed off me. He is staying at Sam's over the road. There is no getting rid of him.

This new house by the sea was meant to be another fresh start. It has many redeeming features, including a deck with a view miles up the coast past Karitāne to the old deadly village by the sea. I can't believe the walk-in wardrobe with the light that turns on when you open the door.

By day two in my new whare I am in the wardrobe, hiding from Isaac. I have already locked the dog in the car by accident because Isaac was chasing me, and I had to call the fire service to get him out. Isaac had a go at hitting and kicking me as the alarm was triggered by Tonka in the hot car but it was a pathetic effort. It's the threats that have worked their dark magic.

My new landlords, who are just back from a Springsteen concert, must have already been asking questions about the woman who said she was a writer. Just because I have been on Kim Hill doesn't mean I remember rubbish day. When my landlord takes my rubbish out for me I leave him some scorched almonds and a note to say thank you. The note really means do not touch my rubbish again.

Isaac had been chasing me because I had stomped over to Sam's in no bra with my wild hair and whatever version of pyjamas and kimono I was wearing that day and raged at him about sheltering my abuser. Sam's eyes lit up at my tirade because I'm some fresh information and he tried to help me by pointing out to Isaac that *the relationship was over*.

Sam does in fact talk like a counsellor—a good one, albeit surrounded by happy squalor. Later I will come to adore his whare: it is the safest place in the world to me. I become more placid there than lying on the lake.

But I'm determined to make an enemy of Sam, at first, because I am trying to get Isaac banished, so I point out that Sam's seventeen-year-old daughter isn't safe around Isaac. That he will try and fuck her. This is when Isaac chases me back to the house.

Sam calls out, *Naww, don't do that,* but like the king of a pride he rarely moves unless he has to, and he isn't aware, or is choosing to ignore, that Isaac is tormenting me. But Isaac then makes the mistake of getting too comfortable too quickly and tells Sam's daughter that she can sleep on the couch with him if she wants to. It's a mistake because he does this in front of Sam.

Sam realises it is time to drop this hōhā waif off; he has run out of money for beer anyway. I am hiding over the hill at Mum's amazing old vicarage in Port Chalmers and Sam later tells me that Isaac sat outside my new house all night crying *I love you Talia* so the landlords could hear. Sam dropped him off on the motorway and wished him luck, which also means don't come back, you useless pile of trauma. But of course, Isaac does come back.

I manage to have an amicable relationship with my landlords despite this initial fracas, although, after I get back from Paul's tangi there is chopped lettuce in the toilet. Like someone has emptied out their Big Mac box in there. I don't ask why but my landlord comes over to explain that he had to feed my septic tank while I was away, and I wonder if I will ever recover from this conversation. Plus, I have to hide my dope smoking and my habit of playing slit-your-wrists music too loud after 11pm. My son thumps from the top floor when he hears me crying to Andrew Bird and one particular song by Aldous Harding, and I insist loudly that they are happy tears.

We become friends, Sam and I, because I don't know where to get weed and Sam, like Isaac, knows where to get anything.

Like me, Sam becomes naturally high if he has a few days off substances and I know he is in a good mood for no reason when he shouts *I love you Talia* from his deck that resembles a ship, because he thinks it is funny to take the piss out of Isaac. I love him too. I love it when he is having a better day than usual and shouts *Hello America!* before he shifts the kurī—who loves to slouch right into him on the couch—and asks me if I have seen the remote.

A deeply platonic love that is better than having a father. I can sit on his couch with the dog between us while he watches his box sets on Sky TV in complete comfort and silence and he doesn't care where I ash, even though he managed to give up smoking years ago.

Sam is also a Leo like me. We understand each other to be big-hearted and misunderstood. We might be wrong about this but our pride of two is self-sufficient.

When I arrive back at Sam's ten months after leaving the house over from his, when I am returning from Pōrangahau to be with my son, he says, *You never should have left*, meaning over the road. Even though the Aesthete flew down from Auckland and helped clean my oven so I could move; he thought any minute Sam would be bringing over some drugs. Sam immediately distrusted him.

But it is possible for a man and a woman to just be friends.

When I hear the news that I have won a writing prize, I start gushing at Sam about how we are just like Marvin Gaye and Tammi Terrell. Sam is only really interested in Elvis, INXS and the Stones but he listens.

I have a thing for Marvin Gaye: one of my first records apart from Madonna's *Get In the Groove* was the single of 'What's Going On'. As a teenager I listened to the whole album over and over with Dieter, the Dutch boyfriend who liked jazz. But it was Mum who had the album of Marvin's duets with Diana Ross and his very good friend Tammi Terrell.

Marvin's duets with Tammi were special. Then Tammi developed a brain tumour and died and he became permanently more famous without her. Tammi's death marked the beginning of Marvin's long coked-out decline: in the first year after her death, he didn't leave the house. Then Marvin left the Midwest, and erratically raised his son in London. At least he remembered to get him an ice cream to have in the back of a cab amid the chaos.

Marvin could still sing like an angel; there are no words for the way he could sing other than this old cliché, whether the lyrics were about getting it on or saving the babies. Marvin was a fallen Black angel. He said he used to hear music everywhere but then it went someplace, right after he sang in a church like its acoustics had the ribcage of a whale. Marvin was almost too much to come together in the fragile shell of a human being. The looks, the moves, the voice! No wonder he was doomed.

He ends up watching porn on loop upstairs in his parents' house and coming down for dinner only to be shot by his father for asking him not to speak to his mother like that.

Before his father murders him and Tammi dies of the brain tumour, Marvin was singing at the Apollo Theatre in Harlem with Carla Thomas. Tammi was in the audience. Her head was freshly bandaged and swollen from another surgery that wouldn't save her life. She endured listening to their songs but eventually stood up and started singing in a shaky voice to her best friend. Marvin left Carla on stage and joined Tammi. The song was 'You're All I Need to Get By'. Duets are always sentimental.

Sam says, *That's beautiful*, and tells me that I've done very well for myself. Meaning the prize. He's proud of me and pats the dog's head. He asks if he can unpause *Special Victims Unit*, which is his favourite spin-off from the famous thudding opening of *Law & Order*. He can never quite decide if Jayne Mansfield's daughter Mariska Hargitay is beautiful or not.

*

In another of the coincidences endemic to Dunedin, Sam bought the house I feel safest in from Jim's friend John. There is a photo of Jim and John wearing kilts at the hui-ā-tau where Jim would escape Gwen for the music.

When John was dying of AIDS in the eighties my nana nursed him. She has never let her beliefs get in the way of looking after someone, or any opportunity to out-care Mother Teresa. Maybe we have this in common—except I require too much care myself for this to be even close to the truth.

When I had my abortion and woke up in recovery, I realised it was Gwen who would have held the women's heads in day surgery as they re-entered the world after doing what was best for them. Recovery nursing was one of her many specialities. In the sixties, she passed brain surgeons the scalpel. We would wait outside Day Surgery to pick her up, but I never noticed any pro-life picketers—just Jim listening to the Concert Programme.

I thought Gwen and Sam, a man as kind as Jim and as gregarious and generous as Paul, would get along. I waited for him in the supermarket carpark once as he nattered on to a woman who was living in her car. Within five minutes, and a quick trip to someone he knew who lived round the corner, Sam found the woman somewhere to live.

When my sister wailed at me down the phone that Paul was dead, I ran over the road to Sam's but I wasn't in danger and the kurī was already halfway up the steps.

Sam is white-passing. But he carries my worry as easily on his back as Mere Harper, his tipuna, used to carry people from the boats to the beach at Karitāne. She helped Truby King, the reasonably benevolent overlord of the Seacliff Asylum, set up corridors where new mothers could feel looked after as he forced them into routines.

Sam lives up the road from the beach Ben wanted his ashes thrown into. Up from an old pā that has such bad juju from the kai whanauka, or cousins eating cousins, feud that I never go there.

Except Ben took me up there once with the children and it made me want to push his daughter into the water because, unlike his son, who had hated me at first, she set me on edge. I found her saccharine and irritating and couldn't admit this to myself. She found my son *distasteful* but he was the only one of the three who knew who Jackson Pollock was, because Roman likes art. Boy was in disguise there in the back of the car between his new siblings in his daily stubbies and sticking to his zero-shoe policy. I also battled the urge to throw myself off the pā because I get vertigo. But it's only my fear of the void. And this fear of shoving and being shoved.

Baggage claim

Just before Matariki in 2021, I'm en route to Wellington for a second attempt at learning how to karanga in Pōrangahau. I have a feeling that the plane's onscreen quiz, which is meant to distract passengers from their impending fiery death or a view of the clouds, is going to ask me a question about Ben.

And there it is, on the screen: *Who directed Excalibur?*

The answer is John Boorman, and it was Ben's favourite movie. He used to rhapsodise about Helen Mirren's breasts, which was hardly original of him, but neither am I for being fixated on his death. This was one of the endearing things about him, though—I can remember this now with no pain: his enthusiasms. Except for when he used to talk about how 'dishy' his mother was. Ben said Kiwis were repressed. But wanting to fuck your parents is not normal. Despite what Freud said.

The descent into Wellington is smooth, for once, and at baggage claim I recognise Ben's mother from behind, by her dark, coarse, short, dyed hair. She is waiting, like me, for her baggage. And I'm not surprised to see her, even though she lives overseas and the plague has made travel difficult.

I come up behind her with a sinister giggle and she must have already seen me because there is something guarded about her back. When she does turn to face me, she pretends not to know me when I say, *That's what you get for calling my son a n****r*, hinting with my venom at a curse I am not capable of.

And she starts to laugh my same insane giggle as she walks away. I wish she had tried to scratch my eyes out; she is known for her own frightening yet impotent rages. I judge her grief to be insufficient. I feel whakamā starting to rise pale under the red fury, but I also feel like I have done her a favour—what I've just done is so wrong it might make her feel better later. But that wasn't my intention.

After the Uber into the city, I wait for Kerry on Cuba Street, outside the hotel, which she ends up covering the cost of because my writing invoice hasn't been paid yet. Almost thirty years after meeting Paul here, Wellington still feels like my city, and I am still poor.

The next day, after a launch for Tayi Tibble's second poetry collection, *Rangikura*, we are late to the karanga course at Raina's, because I can't book a rental car until the invoice clears. Maíra, a Brazilian friend I stole off Mum, agrees to drive us. When we arrive at Gina's in Pōrangahau I find out we're still invited to the course, despite being late, because of our Sciascia and Rōpiha whakapapa. But also, the course is free because it's funded by the government so

Māori women can learn about crystals and calling to the dead.

Instead, I spend three days getting wasted at Gina's with Kerry and Maíra. Gina is turning forty, so we choose to celebrate life instead, plus I'm not sure what to do with Maíra—it seems wrong to leave her there after she's driven all this way.

Maíra has just lost her own mother—witnessed her painful death in fact—and she and Kerry are horrified when I confess what I said to Ben's mother. Kerry has always encouraged and snorted at my verbal carnage after the fact, delighting in my self-soothing stories of losing my shit in public, but she is subdued. *What did you do, Talia?* This is her usual micro-encourager.

But this time she isn't laughing when she says, *Oh Talia, you didn't?*

I did.

I confess my only real regret is hinting at the curse and when Kerry asks why, I reply that I'm now worried it will come for me. They both look at me like I'm a bit sick and viciously self-centred, but we still we have a great time getting on it here in Pōrangahau.

As the night wears on, Kerry turns to me, her grin flashing in the dark, and says, *I am bulletproof*, meaning that she is, and I am so happy she is having a break from thinking about the man who is disappointing her—I can feel her invincibility blooming inside us.

When Ben was still alive I told Mum I wanted to shoot him in the face, and I must have seemed like I meant it because she was genuinely concerned. I even made a plan to drive to Queenstown and do it, but I am scared of guns and you can't smoke in prison or a forensics unit. But I imagined it a lot. I dwelled on it—his bald cowardly head exploding like a watermelon in pink mushy pieces when it would not have been a pink situation. Mum wouldn't let me do anything as self-defeating as shooting Ben in the face and I resented her more for it and raked my arms with my nails to let her know how unfair it was that I had to live. My left arm still has the scars, which have turned brown as dirt.

How can I explain or even justify this extremely bad behaviour? This inability to let anything or anyone go? Who can I blame?

I blame it on my blood, this minestrone boil-up of being Italian and Māori. A friend said my scorched earth policy when it came to his family was called an omertà but I realised later she probably meant vendetta. And then there is the reciprocal nature of utu. I think of the way intellectually wise Māori underplay the meaning of that word now. It is not safe yet for me to call to the dead; I might use them to do my bidding.

There is so much good Māori food in Pōrangahau I hide my plate full of hāngī in the cold oven for later. I eat the indigo-green pāua fritters and wait in the morning at the horse float for Orlando's good coffee. Later Orlando mistakes Kerry for me. I drink whiskey and smoke the cousin's good weed and take a video on my phone of Kerry as she endures Roman's cousin Hilary's lecture on Stan Walker and Michael Bolton. Gina stays out of it and sways in my leopard-print jacket to 'Sitting on the Dock of the Bay'. Kerry disagrees about Michael Bolton, despite the fact crossing cousin Hilary is a foolhardy move. She is still too pretty at forty-two for her stubborn streak to register with Hilary. Kerry is older than me by six weeks, a fact that smarted when I was asked if I was her mother while on my annual visit to the tavern in the deadly village by the sea in our twenties. I blame it on the chignon I favoured, on looking like a matron before my time. But Kerry's whakapapa is older here in Pōrangahau. She is the Rōpiha.

When I post the video online Vika writes underneath it, *I miss that cackle*. Meaning me laughing at Kerry and Hilary, relentless in the background.

Hilary is from the same marae as Roman, related to him through both her Pākehā mother and her Māori father. A South Island thing, when the men came south to shear for Pākehā who would let them come to the front door for their wages instead of to the back door of those large Pākehā homesteads sitting on whenua that used to belong to the door-knockers.

I have *Rangikura* with me, which Tayi leaned over the counter and signed for me at her launch the night before. A homeless man outside Unity Books insulted my looks compared to Kerry's but I still bought a bud off him for ten dollars. I don't like getting stoned in Wellington because I get paranoid about when the Earthquake will happen, and what will come first after the big one—the gas mains blowing, or the tsunami from Raukawakawa. But I still have a toke and rave on to an unsuspecting poet about the musket wars.

In Pōrangahau I peel through *Rangikura* like a shearer as we lie about in the garage and former kōhanga out the back of Gina's, which is filled with double beds. I tell the other girls how good it is. I remind them Tayi is from the same marae as Roman and my son.

Every time I come to Pōrangahau I seem to encounter more of Roman's people or bring them with me by accident and I don't know what it means. Like when I left the story about Beau and Nanny Shy in American *POETRY* magazine as a koha the first time I tried to learn to karanga. It was worse than a humble brag because their story, or rather the road trip from hell, gave me the cover.

This time, Gina picks up a book from Piri's other sister about the old connection between me and Kerry. Lying in bed beside Kerry I read that a cousin knew death when black kutu fell from his comb. My period arrives two weeks early to line up with Maíra's, and then Kerry's too.

Ben was bald and enthusiastic about disco. He was enthusiastic about *Dune*, *Zardoz*, the Black singer Sylvester, black pudding, Kate Bush, engineering, yachting, Sister Sledge, rugby, electronic music, the British Empire, tanks and machine guns, James Bond, tramping and *Chitty Chitty Bang Bang*. He thought the Falklands was a *noble* war. But I'm choosing to retrieve this information, and with ginger fingers, as though it's rotten instead of a dissonant list of contradictions that I tolerated, was baffled by and that were a complicit part of my engulfing love for him.

Sam asked me once if I thought Ben might be a bit . . . gay? We both knew his dealer and I said it seemed strange that when Ben talked about buying us a mansion, once the start-up really took off, he said the dealer would move into the bottom house as the gardener. Maybe they were in love—the dealer had red hair. Ben used to spend a long time in his little hut when he was just there to pick up the weekly $100 bag. I decided that Ben was English and fucking racist, but not gay. That would have been preferable.

Bea did not want Ben joining her at the Asylum after Jasper flaked on her with his new wife. Her husband said he talked too much and would try to run the place.

My real curse is I always love the sisters more than the men. Or rather, my love for them is adoring and uncomplicated. But I don't have the tenacity to be a proper lesbian. Mine is a sanitised kindred-spirit version of lesbianism. The kind you get from reading *Anne of Green Gables*, *Anne of Avonlea* and *Anne of the Island* far too many times.

Here, getting on the piss in Pōrangahau with women I love, the loneliness leaves me briefly alone. And I still think about my abandoned plate of hāngī in the oven when I'm hungry and it's two days before my benefit hits my account with its brief bounty and there isn't enough to eat and I have to do something creative with lentils. Lentils are a lesbian staple from my childhood, when something as simple as barbecues, and the atomic clouds of men, were ruining the world.

Cousin Hilary describes Roman and Gina's mum as a radical. She plays us 'Melody Fair' by Lulu and tells me it's her song. It makes a change from Duffy; cousin Hilary has played 'Warwick Avenue' many, many times. But it's another song I like.

Another woman staying at Gina's sings along to 'Melody Fair' in a voice better than Joss Stone's, who she also cracks. Her son has a Mormon prophet's name and waves his arms in the garden at the invisible chickens because he is Nephi. When we tell her she can really sing, she is sly when she reminds us, *Someone needs to be able to* ***sing*** *around here*.

It is not time for me to learn to call to the dead and ask their permission to enter myself through the tongue rolling the ochre carpet out through the waharoa—I am still too busy crying *burn, motherfucker*.

Ben would reheat my jokes in the microwave of his mind and use my quips as a centrepiece. We entertained well as a couple; maybe that's why all of this is so confusing? Maybe lack of originality is the original sin?

I still have too many questions that can't be answered by attending a course. Even though I suspect he is in Māori kuia hell I still want Ben to explode like a can of hairspray in that odder thing known as real life. No closure: just this wet mist.

On our last day, I watch Gina dance with cousin Jolene to 'Flowers' by the Emotions, their movements mirroring each other even as Jolene catches Gina when she stumbles because we've been drinking since 10am. I video them secretly, sitting under the grapevine, because it is one of my favourite songs, the prettiest disco anthem in the world. I am worse than Ans Westra at asking for consent, because what if someone says no?

Raina's daughter has given Gina a pounamu for her birthday. The pendant looks like it has a narwhal trapped in it, and an angel hovering in a cloud. I touch it and take a photo and tell Gina it's beautiful, and she says she wasn't sure about it at first. I reassure her how rare and ethereal the hard jade is as I hold it in my hand away from her chest; but she is too pissed on her birthday to care about aesthetics.

When Gina is given a photo of Fatboy, who must have gone into the river, and who she would tell with love that he stank, she cries.

Baby, this isn't Wonderland

I moved in with Alice because the rent was cheap and the eco house with its curved roof and painted red beams was metres from the beach. The whare was in the wonky style transplanted Germans seem to favour. As if having a composting toilet in beautiful parts of Aotearoa could undo the Holocaust.

Alice was not German, but the owner was; much of the house had been built by her eccentric ex-lover, who was battling the council about his right to have an ark out at another remote section by the sea at Aramoana.

I moved in with Alice because I was desperate, and Alice said the dog was welcome. It was becoming a real problem, the dog and his suitability as a tenant. I scanned Trade Me after my Covid-fucked writer's residency, searching daily for anywhere to live, and almost everywhere said *NO PETS*. But I wanted to settle and not just *stay* somewhere, as Isaac put it. I'd been rootless for two years; the dog was the only constant. I suppose my reckless idiotic devotion to the kurī is why I kept verging on homeless as I drifted around the country, and it was perverse that I imagined he was the only thing keeping me alive apart from my son. Plus, my animal husbandry is erratic: the dog was *lucky* to be alive.

Alice was thin and pretty and brownish all over, with a sideways profile like a doe. She had a dog too—Matilda—a large old spaniel that was also brown and faun all over. They matched.

And I was stunned by the house, its curved earthy red pod and wraparound deck and the large Buddha squatting under a dwarf bay tree in the garden. Inside, the vast open-plan lounge had a wooden dinghy tied to the recycled timber beams as a boat bed. Facing the sea, under the deck, was the obligatory hippy outdoor bath to burn your bum and where strangers might find you naked.

The bathroom was also beautiful. There was a large leggy begonia planted in the generous indoor rockery and a curved timber-slatted path, which led to an outside door that split in two and was fit for a horse to poke its head through. There was a large zen-like circular window behind the begonia that faced into the master bedroom, which was lined with varnished plywood and had wonky Caligari angles. That was Alice's room. Mine was constructed out of an old shipping container before doing this was hip for a year or two. Like Paul, the German and her lover were ahead of their time.

The kitchen was built out of a house truck that they had first parked on the gorse- and flax-filled section in the nineties, sticking its rear end into the southerly. It was hobbity with uncleanable crannies and it was already stuffed with Alice's clutter, but it was still bewitching and had wide dark teak floorboards. It had a breakfast nook where, below the string-of-pearls plant, the sea could smack you in the face with its nearness. And Alice could display her basket of kale, leeks and cauliflower.

The rocky surfing beach below the house was sheltered with sloping golden sand like something out of a British adventure story but, really, Kuri Bush is a very old Māori place—spooky in fact.

I kept seeing flashes in the garden but did not mention them to Alice, until Sadie, the other new flatmate, did. In an email, after I'd answered the ad for the house, Alice wrote that the fact I was a writer 'made sense', and I was hesitant then because the Trade Me listing had also stated she was into yoga and permaculture. There is nothing wrong with either of these things, in theory, but the practice of them by Pākehā can be troublesome.

Alice mentioned seeing a pod of dolphins, about a hundred of them, off the beach the morning before I moved in. And then three that morning. I made eye contact with my son but didn't say anything about dolphins to Alice, which he knows is not my style: I spill.

I was anxious, after I'd agreed to move in, that Alice might also be vegan but I bumped into her outside the health food shop where she worked and she said life was too hard for that sort of thing. So I warmed to her. I didn't realise she was a zealot about organic food and the cheap rent would be made up for by having to buy really fucking expensive milk, which admittedly seemed creamier.

Alice surprised me by listening to Jewel on a tape deck as she sang along in a wispy voice. I felt transported back to the late nineties, which was also the last time I'd had anything to do with festival culture, traipsing around paddocks with pious hippies. But my flatmate with Jaq had decks to mix her trance on. She was fun.

Alice was lo-tech on purpose. She avoided Facebook and Twitter but floated free as a cosmic fruit loop in the goop and glitter of new-age Instagram. She seemed harmless for an Aries, so I wondered when the raging baby within would show itself.

In the composting toilet Alice had pasted up the CD liner notes to the *Into the Wild* soundtrack, that wretched film about a white man who dies when he becomes stuck on his spiritual, monkish journey.

Back in the lounge, I sat stoned at the table and asked Alice if she had enjoyed *Into the Wild*. She had and, sitting in the lotus position on her long sofa, she confessed to loving Pearl Jam too. I gulped down my intense hatred of Pearl Jam. I told myself it is better to just let people *like* things.

I wondered whether I would be able to live long term with Alice's music, her batty talk of nodes and retrogrades, her art and—most fundamentally—the troubling places she had stuck the art on the walls. There was a plate with a Franklin Mint version of a Native American princess in the kitchen and I tried not to sneer at its romantic, washed-out image. Like what Christians did to a Jewish Jesus. My inner alarm was so loud I remained deaf to it. I excel at ignoring my intuition.

I told myself Alice was as harmless as the ineffective coffee she brewed with the antique German grinder and round screaming kettle on the gas stove. I squashed down the contempt I felt at the militant sylvan effort she put into making such weak, insipid coffee. I like my coffee strong, milky and far too sweet.

There was a solar heater for the water that wasn't effective in winter, at all, and I would wait and watch the thermostat climb high enough to wash a dish or have a shower. I also fed the fire with its wetback to heat the same water supply. The wood was free, from a besotted neighbour, and the outdoor bath had been built by an ex for the crime of leaving her. Alice was so pretty she got a lot of free stuff. Men used to give me cars and chickens, but I don't remember it being a happy time.

When Alice got home from work she praised me for feeding the fire in the same way she talked about her kundalini being set free. She said when she worked in hospo she was drawn to the fire of the pizza oven because there was so much fire in her astrological chart. I suspected that Alice just liked people looking at her bum, which was impressive for a thin Pākehā.

Alice was proud that the house took so much work to heat and to have hot running water. She told me I wasn't allowed to use my good liquid detergent that smelled delicious and actually washed the clothes. The powder I had to get was like dirty chalk, and my sheets would have been cleaner if I had washed them in a puddle. Alice liked to turn the internet off when she went to bed, which was early, and I like to fall asleep listening to YouTube videos about the history of slavery, late.

I ordered expensive clay-coloured sheets online and waited for the tsunami to come. When I questioned Alice about how she coped with living in fear of the sea and its constant nearness, she said, *But what if the tsunami doesn't come?* Once you get caught in the tumble dryer of circular logic at least it's warm and fluffy.

There was no dryer at Alice's; there was a wooden rack on a pulley above the fire. Everything was wooden in her whare, even the dish brush.

Alice had invited Sadie to move in around the same time as me. The German had been giving Alice a rent holiday because her man had left her after Lockdown 1.0.

Alice and Sadie had worked together at the bougie eatery with the pizza oven. When I told Sadie, who was only twenty, and exuberant but likeable, that I had itchy feet she said that would be my earth chakra, so I asked her if she knew where I could get a fifty bag. I may as well give in to these kooks, I thought, if they can get me weed. Alice was very excited she had brought these two witchy wāhine into her whare—it was like she had orchestrated the whole thing!

One night we were all chatting and drinking weird nettle tea and Sadie was telling us about her chickens and the spiritual moment she experienced when one of them died in her arms. Sadie knew then that inside the chicken was the spirit of her grandmother. She explained that this was why she had become a vegetarian. The bit about her grandmother being inside the chicken made sense to me but I still eat bacon. Even though Alice was there I told Sadie about Jim, and how I think he transitions through the afterlife as a dolphin. I told them about Fatboy and my father locked inside his chuggy bulldog walk back in Pōrangahau.

Sadie's grandmother had died in a hospital room in Christchurch during the earthquake. Her uncle fled from the others in the waiting room during the actual quake, only to come back for his new sunglasses. Sadie's reaction to her uncle was *True, cuz.* It was Māori cousin housie to find out we were related through Ngāti Kuia—the dolphin people, no less—and that she had been at kindy with my son.

Alice had chickens: three Sussex whites with splashes of black that pecked around the red beams and the wheelbarrow with their red combs and reminded me of William Carlos Williams. One of the chickens was broody and didn't come out in the morning for its special organic feed, which included an expensive linseed, almond and sunflower-seed powder that had been ruined at the health food shop.

Sadie would romp around the garden before work wearing headphones and her dressing gown, and singing loudly and tunelessly, smoking the dart she had cadged off me. She'd arrive at the house in her shiny Subaru with the heavy dance music pumping. After too much whiskey I told her she was beautiful by complimenting her large, froggy Ngāpuhi eyes. I got lost in the dunes that night in the dark. I truly stumbled but said nothing after I managed to drag myself back to the house.

Sadie knew she was gorgeous and was dismissive of the frog remark when I apologised in the morning, although she did tell me I reminded her of her mum. Her pole-dancing big sister, who made a mint on OnlyFans during lockdown, was also beautiful but far more fearsome. When she wasn't performing kinetic feats on the pole she was happiest with horses. I told Sadie I wanted to take photos of them and their Ngāti Kuia hair, using her good camera, as I raved at her about Ans Westra and showed her the images in *Maori.* Sadie was open, intense and hilarious. But she also kept immaculate boundaries.

I helped her with the zip of her jumpsuit before a party and took photos using her camera for the gram and she slayed it wearing my Fenty red lipstick under the begonia. I was happy to be around someone stunning and young, and to have the house to myself later as she went off for lines of MDMA at an engagement party in suburban, straight-af Fairfield.

Another night, by the fire, Alice thought she saw colours around my son, but he was only challenging her for believing in astrology, testing what her limits were, and when she announced that she could see the *colours* he'd just said something a bit frightening to see how she would take it. Alice brought out Roman in him. Alice called him 'young man' in a way that made my teeth curl. But when I gave in and asked her what *colours* she saw around my son, a voice not quite his own, maybe Nanny Shy's, said, *Don't ask that question.*

The firm opposite of her voice coming through Roman, needling sweetly for her tea.

Megan Dunn, a Pākehā I like—who commissioned my Ans Westra essay and who was working for City Gallery—sent an email and offered me a free plane ride to Wellington. I was to give a talk at the gallery for Te Wiki o te Reo Māori. My reo was so bad I accepted the offer because deep down I like a challenge. Here was a chance for me to humiliate myself in front of expert speakers! I hate flying, but the thought of the hotel room for the night made me excited. As long as there is no balcony, too high up. Otherwise, I would have intrusive thoughts of throwing myself off, precisely because that's the last thing I want to do. It's just the fear of the void again.

I was nervous about giving the talk about my taniwha Kaikaiawaro, and Jim, and babbled about it on the way home with Alice in the car after a rare trip to town. We chatted quite well together; Alice was a good listener.

At Waldronville, a few kilometres before Kuri Bush, Alice said that soon she might have to go to a rongoā thing for the health food shop. She glanced at Saddle Hill and asked if she could use it in her mihi as her mountain, since she grew up in Waldronville, in an eighties subdivision by the sea, in one of the barely there suburban houses down a cul-de-sac as generic as *Neighbours*.

I told her I was Māori and I would never claim Saddle Hill as my maunga in my pepeha because I am not Kāi Tahu, and that Saddle Hill was part of a sleeping taniwha, Meremere. It knotted Kāi Tahu firmly in place here. It would just confuse people if she claimed it as hers; plus she might get in trouble with a Māori running the rongoā workshop, a fate worse than death.

I mentioned the Treaty; I mentioned Oranga Tamariki; I gently questioned her about why she would claim something that belonged to other people, when Oranga Tamariki kids are often separated from their whenua and might only grow up to learn their pepeha in prison. I became smug and said that Māori belonged to the land, not the other way round. I sensed no white fragility because I was feeling too fragile myself—or maybe I am just a tremendous fuckwit. I also told Alice I'd heard rumours that Waldronville had a Satanist cult, but her eyes were back on the road by then. It had gone well, I thought; I had done her a favour by letting her know Meremere was not hers.

The next day I was still battling feelings of fraudulence and decided to take magic mushrooms with Alice to *help* me write my speech. It was just a micro dose, but I made the fatal mistake of playing Raina doing the karanga to a whale to Alice who lay in front of the ancient speakers like she was praying to Mecca. When I went outside there were two kererū in the hedge.

Just then Sadie arrived home in the booming black Subaru station wagon with a big golden retriever in the boot. I felt overwhelmed by the totemic significance of all these tohu and waved my arms up and down at Sadie while I raved about the two kererū: they were our wood pigeons; we could have one each and there was no need to worry about any tsunami now!

I went inside to tell Alice, thinking, Alice loves a sign! But when I told her our Ngāti Kuia totems had arrived as kaitiaki she had a face like the underworld on her. She must be upset Sadie brought out her dog, I thought, because Sadie had got bad vibes and taken the kurī back into town.

Then my son arrived and I gave him my new bed so he could take me to the airport early in the morning. I spent the night on the boat bed, nervous as anything, and when I woke at 6am, Alice was standing over me, rocking the dinghy with her knees and accusing me of being the reason she had not slept at all.

Alice wanted me to know that, even though Sadie and I were welcome and had been invited by her, she was the one who really belonged there; she had grown up in this area and she was called here to this amazing house. Alice didn't really relate to colonisation. She said everything between the beach and Saddle Hill was hers. I was about to catch a plane funded by the taxpayer so I could give a talk about my mountain, awa and whenua and here was this new-age vampire standing over me, suggesting I was the threat—that all that meaning, and this tax-funded talk I was fretting about giving, really belonged to her and her anxieties.

It was so out of line, it actually helped. It incited rage—which is when I feel the least fraudulent—because these talks are only tax-funded because of the grabbiness of her ancestors. No wonder she would try to identify out of that, leech onto our stories and tie a saddle to our taniwha.

But I was too consumed by my impending talk to confront the fact that Alice was as hateable as her Native American princess plate, and another much more frustrating realisation: I was probably going to have to move out when I got back from Wellington.

When I tried to figure out why the raging baby had revealed itself, I realised it was my excitement over the two kererū, flapping my arms up and down like I was one of them, that had probably pushed Alice over the edge, not Sadie's golden retriever. Nothing good happens for me if I express any kind of joy.

In Wellington the next morning, after checking out of the hotel, I was photographing my second eggs Benny of the day in Olive, after the talk went quite well! But then I had a pesky intuition: I realised Alice would have let the dog out the horse door by accident on her way to work. The eco-shack was unfenced and by a fast country road. For the rest of the day I catastrophised that the dog was dead. At least then I can move out, I thought.

I distracted myself on the flight back by imagining him dead on the road; I was resigned to the plane crashing as a solution to all my anticipatory grief. I'd felt the same on the flight up: I had consoled myself with the thought that if the plane crashed, I would not have to embarrass myself in front of other Māori, giving a talk for reo week about how I have almost none. Whether my fellow passengers deserved to live or not was not included in my anxiety-versus-death spiral.

But Tonka was asleep in the wheelbarrow by the front door when my son dropped me back at Kuri Bush. Tonka raised his tail and thumped it, weakly, like he hadn't been expecting this sweet reunion either. He had got out the horse door but he wasn't dead.

The day before I told Alice I was leaving *her* whare, the dogs didn't come back when I called them from the deck. It was mid-spring and warming up by then—the solar heater was almost effective—but I was wearing my fluffy dressing gown when I stalked up the narrow road after calling their names for an age on the idyllic, rocky beach, and only Matilda returned. Then I heard Tonka barking: he is loud for a small dog. I followed the sound down the side of an established house and garden on the other side of our beach.

Peter, the neighbour besotted with Alice, let me into their bed and breakfast through a door near the accommodation wing of the house. Their kitchen and its glass jars were so wholesome! Peter told me he ground flour for his own bread, and his wife was as welcoming as him, although she had a reserve that made me curious. I also just wanted to get out of there, so I didn't have to pretend to like Alice. Who seemed to be blaming me for the mould on the carpet under the giant monstera near the boat bed.

I was perched on one of their bar stools, braless, sweating as I clutched the dog into my dressing gown so he didn't piss in their house. Knowing full well it was too late for that and they would find his puddles later. Peter was talking about the potter's shed out the back and some local history because

I told him I was a writer. And I felt the tender prickle I get at the back of my neck when I know someone is about to tell me something tapu and transgressive. Peter said when he dug up the foundations for the shed he had found an old human leg bone. And instead of getting it blessed and buried he had put it on the shelf in his little potter's shed. I was horrified by this fresh information because the bone would likely have been Māori, and ancient, and therefore this nice motherfucker had cursed himself. He may as well have been grinding bones into flour for the bread.

Peter had started seeing a figure in the mirror in front of the potter's wheel—or a guest did. And other people hadn't felt right in the room, either. I thought of the flashes Sadie and I had seen from the corners of our eyes. The buried woman Isaac had wanted to help across the Taieri River up the road. The bones there were as old as moa.

Eventually Peter got a kaumātua in to bless the house and bury the leg bone. So at least he got something right.

When I told Alice I was moving out, she was once again standing over me as I lay in the boat bed at dawn. It was hard to be lethal from a lying-down position but I gave it a crack.

I asked her why she was so frightened of Māori, after I told her I was leaving, and she replied that she was frightened we would *take her house*.

I said something pious and unforgiveable then: I told Alice I was not willing to *give* anything to racism.

Peter's wife caught me down at the beach the next day, before I left, indulging in the ritual of singing goodbye to the sea with one of the few waiata I remember from school.

*

I wanted to fictionalise this story, to prove to myself that I could. I wanted to be generous to that doe, because I liked Alice in the beginning. I wanted to be generous to Alice and especially to Matilda, the spaniel Roman's son called stupid in front of Alice. Because I couldn't believe I had met another oblivious racist. Even when her initial email should have raised all the whero flags. There could only *be* one witch.

Matilda had taken to sleeping on my bed because I'm always keeping it warm; she started doing this even when Alice wasn't at work. I woke up once at 3am to Alice reaching into my sheets and carrying the large old spaniel in her thin arms back to her bed—and this was when it was still fun to be there. But if I think of this story from Alice's sideways profile and the danger she was sensing around her—a doe sniffing the air for the Māori taking over the place—I can only, truly, feel my own gaze. My eyes are firmly in front, like a ruru, but not like a super predator; Alice was wrong about that. Mine are the front-facing eyes of the haunted.

And I'm only attempting to set some inner record straight. Even my son remembers the talk of colours differently than me. He says Alice saw yellow all around him when I was thinking the colours must be blue and better kept to Nanny Shy. The yellow would have been Paul and sunny optimism.

I was so angry at Alice the day I left, a raging red, that I finally told her something I really, really shouldn't have. I told her the colours around my son didn't like it when his world was disrupted and Alice finally found some mettle and said, *Don't tell me what I saw.*

And I replied, *You don't know what you've seen.*

Alice went to work and I went out to check the mailbox. Inside, there was a typed, friendly invitation from someone who had been driving through Kuri Bush and was desperate to buy the house from the German—who Alice thought she would convince into a rent-to-own situation. But property prices were soaring on the coast. Alice only worked at the health food shop part-time.

Kuri Bush, that exquisite spooky place where JC Sturm's husband was born. I drew a big smiley face on the bottom of the leaflet, and wrote one word: *See*. I left it on the table for Alice to find.

Eight months later I'm sitting on the bus just before Ōamaru after coming back from Pōrangahau with Kerry and Maíra. I am trying to remember what I did with the three sixties African wall plaques I left in one of the houses I was shunting through during the two years I was semi-homeless after leaving the house over the road from Sam's.

Sadie sends me through a DM as I'm sitting with my ham, cheese and pineapple toasted sandwich in the tearooms in Ōamaru. It is a photo of the plaques. She writes that she is leaving Kuri Bush and do I want these back and can she keep my cream jacket? She signs off with 🩶✌️.

When Sadie drops my wall plaques off at the house Mum and Lisette have bought for me and my son, we share a dart, and, after skirting around the subject of Alice, Sadie says she wanted to smack her one by the end. Alice refused to let Sadie's tuakana stay the night in case her new man found the sisters, alike as twins, too hot. Sadie said she never wanted to talk about astrology again, and that she had started reading the Bible in front of Alice or avoiding her by wearing headphones through the lounge on the way to the nooky kitchen. A good Māori girl, the cousin who lasted longer than me. I let her keep the cream jacket because I adore Sadie, but also I have no idea which jacket she means.

Sadie and I cohabited well. We kept a respectful distance—for cousins. I ask her if she remembers seeing the two little plastic Māori figurines, which used to come in cereal packets, that I left on the window sill of my shipping container. More treasure I took by accident from the man's house in Riwaka. I gave the blue one to the Aesthete to pass my demon on; the other two were red and brown. But Alice must have done something with them. She was not into plastic and would never have put them in the log burner: too efficient.

Later, I remember it's a subtle cream Tocca duster coat Mum picked up for me in London that now belongs to Sadie. I am always giving away Mum's beautiful, thoughtful things.

The coat I gave Alice, in the heady few weeks when we were *all* allowed to be witches, was another type of jacket, also bought in London for me by Mum. It was more Alice's kind of thing than mine. I'm not a hippy; I'm a witch with no waist and a dicky neck from lying in too many beds on the run.

House music

Ben threatened Roman once. He was frustrated that Roman didn't give me enough money. But it was the first time in fourteen years that we were sharing equal care of our son, which included all the sports stuff Roman paid for, and all the time he gave him, and the cold steamed kūmara he put in his lunch box. Roman, the health food junkie, passing on a love of tuna and kiwifruit.

But still, Ben made me ring Roman. I was reduced to shouting at him down the phone about giving us more money while Ben earned a $150k salary with Koru Lounge benefits. Roman was his usual tricky self, but he was in the right for once. Secretly, I agreed with him. This is why I was yelling. But also, Roman is very good at making me scream.

Ben grabbed the phone from me and told Roman he was going to do him in. Gee, that temple of his liked to throb. He was on medication for his blood pressure by then. Then Ben the Brave hung up on Roman and turned on me saying I had brought this type of *low* person into his life.

The snobbery enraged me so much I warned him, *You're a fucking idiot to threaten Roman.*

Only our son knows how to handle Roman when his eyes go black, a fact Ben hated being reminded of. He stashed his air rifle in our sons' bunks and hid for the night at the only friend of his who regularly came to the house. He had the key because he was meant to be feeding their cat.

When he arrived home the next afternoon, after leaving me to potentially deal with Roman, he was not sorry; instead he was quizzical about what I had done to his life. Ben forgot he hid the gun in the boys' beds—I had no idea—and his son found the gun.

Dad, why is there a gun in my bed? he said.

It didn't quite become a family joke.

When I remind Roman of this, lying on the comfortable corner of his couch in Gisborne, Roman admits he did briefly think about coming down the side of the house and, in his words, *fucking that cunt right up*. Then he whinnies and says it wasn't worth it and goes back to YouTube. He is watching the moment Marina Abramović runs into her ex at one of her 'performances'. Roman is far more of a snob than Ben and has the whakapapa to match. His tastes are even more eclectic. He is silently waiting for me to ask him what he thinks of Marina. Fuckable, would have been the answer but I study him instead. The old silky game between us.

He brews good strong hot-milk coffee in the Italian Moka every morning at 6am before work, and puts it beside me on the couch. I tell Roman the hi-vis vest he is wearing brings out his complexion, that it looks like a cocktail dress because his shorts are so short. The orange with the reflective stripe glows like a buttercup under his brown chin. Delphi refuses to visit the house unless I promise that Roman is wearing trousers.

The other thing Roman says to me in Gisborne, with a touch of bitterness, is, *Look at you—you're thinking about him*. He does not mean the Aesthete. But around the time of Nanny Shy's and Beau's unveilings he sees the box of Steinlager in the boot of the Audi and asks me a question, rhetorical in flavour: *Who are you fucking?*

He knows I'm not much of a beer drinker, that the box of beer would belong to someone like Isaac. But this isn't who he means now. When Ben and I were still together, Roman's voice would be venomous and mocking on the phone before he gave in to our old banter. He would say, *You sound like him when you answer the phone, la-di-fucking-da. What has happened to you?*

Roman is proud of the old Cornish tattoo on his shoulder, the one he got at twenty-one like the rest of his Nāti cousins. It is of a head split by a sword and the Gothic text circling it is the family motto from the crusades. Translated from the Latin it means 'the cross is my spur to faith'.

Justine introduced me to another friend at university, Luna. Luna was the one who ended up offending Paul with her hat. We bonded over Armistead Maupin even though she had heard I was crazy and scary and told me so.

Solomon, my old school friend, called us 'the unholy triumvirate' because we talked about postmodernism in the smokers' lounge. We thought science and the truth were great jokes. We read the dictionary of philosophy together and made subtle Lacan jokes about children seeing their reflection in an oasis in their 'mirror moment'. Postmodernism is not very funny. We slummed it in McDonald's and I told them that fast food had always made me happy. They had onion rings instead of a flame-grilled patty when we went to Burger King because they were vegetarians.

At ARC, the new hippy dive, Luna screamed in a young man's face that there was no such thing as biology. It was all bullshit, she told him—ALL OF IT. The idea that nothing meant anything made Luna euphoric. Luna had taken too many drugs at the Gathering and mistaken it for an epiphany. Reading Donna Haraway and Judith Butler didn't help her feel any more at ease in the world. Nor did anything else for that matter. Luna was from Nelson. Her parents were therapists. There was no way this terrifying, smart, honest young woman could help herself.

Before she had a nervous breakdown from knowing too much, Luna took up boxing and saw Roman sparring at the gym. She went on and on about this amazing-looking Māori man and what a ruthless boxer he was and I said that it sounded like . . . the guy I used to follow around Wizards, the video game parlour, while he played Street Fighter II and pretended he wasn't in love with me.

She was very taken with how aloof he seemed. Brown boys were her one soft spot. If we were still talking, I would tell her this is gross and racist. One of the reasons she was so loveable was she genuinely enjoyed hearing terrible things about herself. I do not.

Roman did in fact remind me of Rocky when we got together, which is funny I suppose because my namesake played his wife. Mum lifted my name from the credits in the movie theatre after almost picking Hannah. Paul said to call me Kahu but that's about all he said before he took off.

At Bath Street, the best dance-bar in town, Roman would clap along in a beat-driven, super-gay way to house music and dance like a Nāti. He used to tell the girls leaning over the bar waiting for their jungle juice or chocolate shakers to kiss his tattoo because he loved showing off his arms.

You can't be serious? I laughed. *I remember you.*

And then he made a move, right into my neck, nuzzling in behind my ear and said I smelled too good to be bothering with that much makeup.

The She Tree

I can't believe my luck. After my essay about Roman, Ans Westra and the kōtiro playing the guitar is published online, a book offer falls into my inbox. I'm living in Hamilton again, which moderates the lucky feeling a little, but this is also the day we are driving south as a family to pick up another Audi I have bought after everyone told me not to.

Paul's cousin, my new favourite cousin, offered me some money to buy a car. I'm not good at accepting money from anyone except Nana, or Mum and Lisette; in fact I am often asking them for money and use being a writer as an excuse. But eventually I gave in to my new favourite cousin's random generosity because I found a *bargain* on Trade Me. She is silver with plush blue velour seats and she purrs and hugs the road in the heavy reassuring way specific to German engineering so I christen her 'Dallas'. A good Māori name. I thank my new favourite cousin profusely and write something mad about my father looking after me. I don't add that he seems to be looking after me better in death than he ever did when he was alive because she will have already deduced that I'm a toddler hiding in a middle-aged woman's body.

Mamie is also enjoying some success. She is modelling after being spotted shopping in Karen Walker and even made it onto the social media pages of Italian *Vogue*, the only true *Vogue*. I refuse to be cynical about diversity in fashion. Mamie is all Beyoncé and *Yasss Queen*, and she dances as well as Mugwi when he used to glide his new honey around the dancefloors of Halifax and Bradford after he had switched from playing for the New Zealand Maori to professional rugby league in England.

Sometimes it does feel like Paul is somewhere nearby pulling helpful levers. I still wear his puffer jacket when I feel like I need the spiritual insulation. A beautiful, monstrous closeness.

I put the dog in his new cage so he doesn't fuck up Dallas's upholstery and he stares at me through the bars with his beady flea-coloured eyes, panting with a Jack Russell's human fury. He is used to being a free-range maniac in whichever car I'm ruining mechanically and aesthetically. I'm trying to set some boundaries for us this time, but I know they won't last.

I didn't learn to drive until I was twenty-six and it altered my interior too; I became a better mother, because Boy and I could go places then. Driving is when I get to 'woo the distant parts of myself', as Alice Munro wrote about in her short story 'Miles City Montana', where the narrator's children almost die in a pool. One of those incidents you dissect later, sick with relief.

I drive Dallas to stay at a bach in Aotea that I have booked with the rest of the money I was paid for writing a profile of an impressive wahine Māori. It seemed ridiculous that I was asked to write a profile about someone else when my only subject is myself but I went along with it and let her read the piece before it was published because Māori women remain terrifying to me. I was let into her inner sanctum, briefly, because I went to school with her man.

As a lost princess it is important that my lying down occasionally achieves a brief alignment with the fantasy, so money goes through me faster than piss. The holiday house was expensive. But I am drowning in work offers, not realising they won't last.

I have Te Rauparaha's son Tamihana's book, *A Record of the Life of the Great Te Rauparaha,* about the musket wars with me, because I've been commissioned to review it. It keeps my stolen copy of Ans's *Maori* company on the passenger seat. It is an impressive-looking black book, lined with red like Paul's Comme des Garçons jacket. And I'm curious as to how his father's rampages have been told, when I know the musket wars story is basically one glorified massacre after another. I find it *interesting* that it can be translated by one of Te Rauparaha's descendants, Ross Calman, and beautifully produced by a university press.

I know before I even start reading it—and I was both hungry and wary to read it—that the story inside the high-end embossed hardcover will make me feel sick about what happened to my people and the uncomfortable fact that my other taha helped do it to them. It's not the sort of book Pākehā should read and yet I know they will be the main consumers of it, when really the only audience it is intended for is Ngāti Toa.

I don't know anyone else who has read it. For such a beautiful product there was very little fanfare around it. It appeared in the odd curated bookstack and did not enter the chat. It is the kind of book racists decontextualise to use against us. It seems exhausting to try to explain all this in another online essay, so it's another review copy I get to keep and absorb without writing about Māori histories.

Pākehā have recreated Māori history from their own projections and anxieties and decided we were fairy folk holding hands and tending our gardens and following the moody phases of the moon. Māori have to go along with it if we want any funding. We also have to go along with it to stop them from taking our children off us.

*

There are only two monuments to the musket wars. One is a tall concrete cylinder at Kaiapoi, where our Rangitāne tipuna Hohua was released from the shame of slavery to fan the flames by using his Ngāti Kuia power to karakia to the wind and make it hurihuri in the direction of the pā. On my way back to Dunedin in Dallas I splash water around myself at the gate to the old pā and take a photo of the tall concrete pou and I don't go in. The dog is still in his cage.

The other monument is in Mataura, near Gore. It states the Māori war ended there with Ngāti Tama's failed campaign through the Haast Pass, thoroughly defeated and disgraced by Kāi Tahu. Te Puoho is finished but Te Wahapiro, who shot Tūtepourangi, makes it out alive.

My friend Jesse says his aunties spit on the floor of the wharekai if you mention my family at Tuahiwi marae near Kaiapoi. But we were taken there by the taua as fallen birdfolk.

Now we have a new holiday for Matariki. I'm not complaining; I just never heard much about it singing 'Tutira Mai Ngā Iwi' at primary school—a poor central Wellington school that was so brown and multicultural my Samoan nemesis, Taleai, treated me like a ghost. Although, maramataka has been a Māori revival and, like the Tower, it is helpful to know when the moon is in Whiro. If in doubt blame a higher power.

And yet. The musket wars probably shouldn't be taught in schools on stolen whenua, and this makes me feel frustrated and confused because the number of dead is anywhere from 20,000 to 50,000. Nobody really knows, which is why I feel I have to write about it. The wars involved seismic shifts in our geopolitical landscape. Iwi boundaries that were centuries old were erased and redrawn in thirty years.

The musket wars were full of slaughter, cannibalism and our own mutable brand of slavery. Tamihana, who was only a child during the wars, describes victors taking forty slaves each. The irony of the introduction of muskets to Māori warfare is that the cannibalism stopped making sense. The killing became too easy; there was no real mana to be had by extracting it from the heart of your enemy or keeping their mokomokai as a trophy. Tikanga must always play catch-up when the bodies start piling up with their stink.

We should have some more hui and talk about it amongst ourselves, I suppose—an internal reckoning. Maybe Paul would feel restless in his grave and scoff at this; he would say, *All hui, no doey*. But Mugwi used to sit quietly at hui and make stuff happen, only speaking when it was necessary.

I feel uncomfortable trading on this story too, knowing that, like Ross Calman's exquisite translation, it is trauma that will be read and processed like cheese in plastic, when the pages are dripping with red. Trading on our trauma is a tricky business for Māori.

Te Rauparaha made a killing trading in our heads, keeping new slaves in pits and tattooing them while they were still alive to make them look like nobles for overseas collectors of these formerly meaningful curios. But the photo that sporadically circulates online of Horatio Robley sitting in front of the heads from the North arranged like a collection of macabre kabuki masks doesn't quite tell the full story.

Because one of my taha turned my other taha into non-talking heads, I am the skull that can speak. And I would like to carefully posit that the horror in this instance truly belongs to Māori. The repatriation ceremonies, where kōiwi and mokomokai are returned from overseas museums, elide this truth with a tikanga that's too solemn. But also, the image of Horatio in front of our heads, its discombobulated toothy display, is a white obscenity. None of these museums should possess our bodies or their divorced heads. And I state this as someone whose favourite exhibit as a child was the Egyptian mummy at the old Dominion Museum in Wellington. I was captivated by the toes peeking through the bandages. I loved the canopic urns with animal heads. But now I know that these anthropological displays are as problematic as Ans Westra's images.

There is something sentimental inherent in Westra's photos in *Maori*; despite her ethnographic project, her images cross the line into art with a touch of kitsch. And it is prudent to be suspicious of any white person's image of us, even as I make the distinction of her being tauiwi rather than Pākehā. Tauiwi means her bones are not *from* here. I believe this is why she couldn't stop taking photos of us. We were exotic to her on our own whenua. But it is the gaze of Māori in her images that does all the heavy lifting to get her over the line, beyond sentimentality, beyond kitsch, to where we are too beautiful to behold.

And my suspicion of her gaze is double, because for thousands of struggling Māori whānau who come under the watchful cyclopic eye of the state this suspicion of Pākehā—or any white person taking from us as they imagine they are doing us a favour—is drilled into us at birth.

The state is yet to acknowledge it is holding the drill. Or that its all-seeing eye is still a distant monarch.

*

In Aotea, the bougie bach I've arrived at is even better than it looked in the photos. It is called Ruru Cottage. There is enough pink light left in the day that I can see the great expanse of grey over the turquoise water of Aotea Harbour. The flatness of it intrigues me; the whenua is dead-looking and ethereal.

There is a massive broken pōhutukawa between the immaculate cottage and the main house. Parts of it collapse down the bank below and I mistake the branches for new shrubby growth.

The dog makes straight for the pōhutukawa and pisses on the trunk and I think, At least he won't do that inside the cottage, but he pisses on the corner of the bedspread too, imagining he is doing me a favour. People who let dogs

into their bougie cottages are good people but you also have to hide a lot from them. One of the fights Ben used to rightly pick with me was over the fact that I was reluctant to get the dog's balls taken off. I still had Roman in my head telling me he would make a great sire. Ben beasted the dog so much he would piss himself under the bed instead of cocking a leg. 'Beasting' was Ben's word for the animal abuse he indulged in when I was at work, and sometimes in front of me. He overfed him to see if his guts would explode. I think that might have been his attempt at a joke and my feeding of him was already erratic so the dog would wolf it down. Tonka got utu on Ben when he took in the brand-new Nilfisk to get fixed and they found dog piss all through its parts. He followed me around the house shouting the full price when I knew he'd got it on sale. Jack Russell utu was not covered by the warranty, but the dog is still scared of the vacuum cleaner.

In the morning the caretaker asks me why I've come to stay in Aotea. I show him the book and tell him I am writing about Te Rauparaha. He shrinks back a little and says Te Rauparaha is known as a terrorist in these parts. He points to the green terraced ridges, which are still visible on the hill to our left, and says it's an old pā, the site of one of Te Rauparaha's first battles, which saw him driven out of Kawhia over the hill. I feel the familiar shiver even though I have come here for such an experience. I am at ground zero of Te Rauparaha's heke; I'm a red pin on the war map.

The caretaker asks me where I'm from, and I tell him *I'm a Macdonald.* But he mishears me and says, *I wondered if you were a McGregor—you look like my first wife. She was a McGregor*. I explain that I'm a McGregor *and* a Macdonald and he looks pleased about his hunch being correct. Then he says, *You were brought here by him*.

The caretaker says it with the same woo-woo as the whirring sound effects in *Once Were Warriors.* It is a bit much for me to hear because I agree with him, so I change the subject to the tree, which proves to be even spookier.

He tells me the tree the dog has been pissing on is tapu, which makes sense: Tonka will be the death of me. Then he tells me the pōhutukawa is a woman and she was the anchorage spot for the Aotea waka when it arrived from Hawaiki, before the iwi were pushed south into Taranaki by the Tainui people, who I descend from but don't feel close to. This is my third or fourth time in Kawhia and Aotea, and I still feel like an outsider, despite my Ngāti Rārua whakapapa and a whanaunga connection to the Ngāti Koata. Riria was half Ngāti Raukawa; they came south later and were close cousins of the terrorist. Polly sat on the pae with Princess Te Puea and had stayed with Rewi Maniapoto when the Sciascia family was at Kawhia. She met Te Kooti, who ended up in possession of the hei tiki Te Maungārongo, the peacemaker, after a tohunga advised our tipuna Pukekohatu to gift it to Te Rauparaha on a slave girl's neck.

The caretaker says the tree is so ancient she is being carbon tested to see if she is older than the one in Te Araroa. I tell him Te Araroa is where my son whakapapas to, or maybe I was wise for once and withheld this? The name of his tree is Te Waha o Rerekohu. It is upright, whereas this tree has collapsed four ways. The caretaker tells me why—another myth—and I don't tell him the dog pissed on her.

As the caretaker is talking, I'm desperate to get rid of him so I can write it all down. He directs me to a book in the cottage that is full of all the old pā sites in Aotearoa. It was written for keen hikers—or as I call it, walking for no reason. The book is a boon of names and places and I want to give him something in return. I offer him Tamihana's account of Te Rauparaha, the terrorist, to read.

He is almost impolite with the son's account and returns it after a couple of hours, like I've given him a sticky old *Penthouse* to read. This magnificently produced book, with its faithful and arduous translation, is war porn that no one wants to whack off to. Although Tamihana became a Christian the only real distaste I detect in it is for the old cosmic ways, the deeply held suspicions shrinking like a vampire before a cross.

Each leaf of the pukapuka is split into the Māori and English versions of the text and when the English I understand too well becomes tu meke I flit over to the other side to make sense of the reo, because then all the killing sounds vague and beautiful.

Tamihana indirectly ridicules my people, the Kurahaupō iwi, for submitting to his father's invasion. He mocks our habit of using kawakawa leaves to cover our eyes when crossing between the waka and the ika of Aotearoa. His people adhered to our tikanga before they slaughtered us. The kawakawa leaves were to stop us looking into the eyes of Te Wheke, which were plucked out by Kupe and then shapeshifted into two stubby rocks, called the Brothers, at the entrance to Tory Channel. If we looked at the rocks too directly the waka would tip our people into the moana.

Tāmairangi, an ariki and descendant of the patupaiarehe captured in the Sounds, was allowed to look, as the maiden at the rear near the taurapa, and the kererū feathers trailed behind her from the carved stern post to bless the water.

When the caretaker returns the book I remember to ask about the expanse of grey sand over the aqua harbour hovering like a UFO. It looks even deader in the daylight. He replies that it's a mass grave for the Māori who died during the 1918 flu pandemic. He says nothing will grow there.

The caretaker's talk has added to my high and I wander the grounds of the cottage. There is a phoenix palm, which I stop to admire because I love these semi-tropical pineapples. But then a starling drops out of it with a twisted neck and starts twitching on the ground in front of me before dying. I take a photo because otherwise I might not believe it happened later. I find a long black feather on the grass, which is as tidy as the dyed coconut lawn in front of the gingerbread house the man in Riwaka made for me. The feather with its white tail and stem like a straw has appeared out of nowhere and I tuck it into my copy of *Maori*—not into the book about our massacres.

I decide to go for a walk. Everything is starting to vibrate and shimmer and the green is too *green.*

I stop at the DOC sign for the pā, the terrorist's old battle site, without climbing up into it, because I'm frightened of the bad juju I keep seeking out, but also, I'm quite unfit. On the walk back I take some more photos of the hill behind the cottage, which has a few tall unbroken pōhutukawa clinging to its side. When I scroll through the photos later it looks like there are bodies hanging like giant bats from the branches.

The caretaker told me they used to hang bodies from the She Tree. But he was insistent that she is a good woman. However broken she is, the tree does seem to resonate with a magnetic peace.

I drive over the hill to Kawhia to get away from the feeling threatening to overwhelm me and to get some supplies, because everything was shut the night before. But I'm wearing my red Adidas slides and my black kimono sack, so everyone in Kawhia stops and stares at me outside the general store because who is this Mongrel Mob bitch who has turned up out of nowhere in an Audi? The dog barks and barks from inside his cage, which is normal behaviour for him. Alert, alert! Whero flag!

I am a tremendous fuckwit to draw this kind of attention to myself in Kawhia, a Māori, dainty, seaside place. It is so remote that when I took the Aesthete to the pub my second time here, eighteen months earlier, the air was thick with menace. I blamed him for our hostile reception and decided I would have had a great time if I'd gone by myself. On the drive back to Hamilton the Aesthete talked about how special his ex was, because they still maintained their habit. I had talked about Ben so much I deserved this intolerable conversation, which was saved from being a monologue by my unhelpful interjections and my having to negotiate the manual transmission of his ute.

The more the Aesthete told me about himself, the less I liked him, which is not my usual pattern. I hated that he was potentially protecting a rapist, his boss. It makes me feel guilty about escaping Isaac, because the boss has a taste for pretty, damaged men. The Aesthete's only good work story is about the cock ring that flew out of a painting the boss had brought in to be cleaned at the gallery. I hated that he didn't understand 'Halo' by Beyoncé is a great song. I hated it the first night we were in bed and he told me he loved me, because he was lying. I lied and told him I loved him the morning after he left me to visit his ex and I sat there crying about Paul. Love is very close to hate so the lie was as small as his. He sat on the end of the bed and flinched when I told him, like he'd been pierced by an arrow, but he fucked like a plank.

Back in Hamilton, after failing at the pub in Kawhia, Mum and I exchanged a fatal look after the Aesthete announced to the dinner table that he and Jacinda, then prime minister, had almost been an item. In a tender, breathy voice he explained that he felt drawn to her because she turned up for a meeting at the gallery with wet hair. Mum could tell I was not really that into him. I'm a snob about grasping social climbers. As a lost princess who imagines myself to be one of the people it is not my task to be rational in my dislikes. I squirmed when he lamented that his life could have been different if he'd gone to the *right* school in Christchurch. Oh, you are serious, I thought.

During the night, I woke up and wondered who the stranger was in my bed and how I could get rid of him. In the morning he asked me if I wanted to go to the zoo but seemed kind of antsy. I told him I just wanted to stay where I was, lying down. I needed to save up the idea of going to the zoo and the Italian Renaissance section of the Gardens people told me about when they consoled me about living in Hamilton. He wanted to go to Miranda, a place he'd never been but liked the sound of, because there were pools.

I am a tremendous and incredible fuckwit who knows when someone is lying to me and themselves but can't manage to use this knowledge to protect myself. It's an annoying trait that gets me into scrapes. 'Scrapes' is a euphemism for living with my mother in Hamilton as a failure in love. I could feel Mum nodding and giving me another one of her wry looks.

*

Eighteen months later, none of this is Kawhia's fault, or Mum's. The general store in Kawhia does its own baking and the cream buns have an impressive shiny glaze and the blessed blob of raspberry. The apple turnovers and lamingtons rival the portion sizes of Ōpōtiki's and I buy a pork-and-watercress pie and eat it in Dallas. The pie is very good; the clear gravy is peppery and the dark pink wild pork falls apart in my mouth. The empty promise I made to myself to look after the interior of Dallas is already over as I drop pastry flakes like buttery confetti.

I drive down to the waterfront where Māori boys are doing manus into the water from the jetty. It's another Ans Westra photo happening without her. The dog is panting and still in his cage—but, by his calculations, not for long.

When I get back to the cottage, I take the sleeping meds I use when I'm feeling too good about myself and can't stop thinking. I am glad for once that I don't have any weed. Because of the daylight woo-woo and the broken She Tree of Aotea, I know that I will freak myself the fuck out if I get stoned here at night. I'm still reckoning with the starling and its twisted neck. Mickey always said they were filthy birds and would chase them out of the guttering and the roof of the house he was building for us.

*

I often feel around in the junkyard of my head for the red, blooming She Tree. I ruminate about her and the way the day twisted more than her knotty branches when they got caught in my hair. I wonder if the cleaner found the piss stain on the bedspread and if I'll have to use another name to book the bougie cottage if I ever go back. It seems unlikely that the dog, who is fourteen, will live forever, but that doesn't bear thinking about. I will have to wear him as a stole around my neck once he goes.

My son tells me Tonka sucks up all my sadness and anxiety and it's crazy that he's still alive considering all the cortisol he's had to absorb. I tell him the word he's looking for is stress. Boy says we have to get another dog before the kurī dies because otherwise my grief will become a burden for friends and family, who all despise his breath and his habit of marking their spot. Except Sam.

My son is one hundred percent correct. When I get too sad or anxious this wretched animal, the other love of my life, lies with his back against mine and it's the only thing that helps. To lie like a parenthesis facing away from him and from the central problem of myself. It's a shame the world isn't ready for people to marry their pets.

I don't know why I'm being trite like this, why my tone undulates from sad and scary to poor attempts at jokes when I write about hard, indigestible things like slavery and cannibalism—the very things in our histories other Māori seem to know not to touch. It's harder still to write about not being loved. I suppose it's an affectation that hides the fear and the horror I have of being me and this bizarre thing known as life. I know I appear more solid to people than I actually feel. Most of the time I am not even here. I bump into things and bruise easily, swaying around the house like it's a ship because the rooms disappear with my dreams.

I still ruminate over the caretaker, wondering if he was like the kēhua on the bus, from another dimension, or just another figment of my faulty imagination and dumb craving to be spooked. I can't really be trusted. My lust for vengeance is probably disproportionate to the crime and my belief in the supernatural as a means of exacting utu is grandiose.

I will admit the more I try to understand the terrorist Te Rauparaha, the more I find we are just the same or, rather, have a lot in common. We could have told war stories together. I could have been liberated from the pit on Kāpiti before being decapitated to be sent overseas when I became lippier and more elliptical than Scheherazade. When my pain started to repeat itself like a meal.

I feel more akin to the terrorist than my Ngāti Rārua ancestor Pukekohatu, who Mugwi's mother, Horina, came from. Pukekohatu was known as a measured and peaceful warrior even as Ngāti Rārua rampaged through Whanganui Inlet, killing Tūtepourangi's brother. But I'd make a hopeless war general. I am too hot-blooded and impulsive to make those kinds of clinical calculations.

Even though I refuse to be erased without a fight.

After he bailed on me, I told Ben he shouldn't have sex in the missionary position because of the sweating and his drippy man titties. But he insisted he was in better shape than me. The last thing he said to me—before he paid me to leave his home, and I'd made sure the money I didn't want was coming to me—was that I was no better than shit on his shoe.

When I ran into Ben's father during the worst break-up of all time my blood was already boiling, and I pressed the button for the window of Ariel to ask him if he is proud of his son. He replied, *Yes I am, actually*, and I screamed the n-word at this Pākehā expat invader in his seventies. He turned back towards the safety of the bar filled with normal people forgetting their problems, and he dismissed me with a chuckle. *Talia is making up stories again.*

But I'm hoarding one of my only remaining opals. When Mamie arrived home in Auckland after coming to my graduation ceremony, she told Paul that she did not like the way Ben treated me or her nephew. It doesn't sound like much, but I have so little proof. Which has been taxing for my son, who was also *there*.

And it's the rātā tree at Ben's that used to drop random white kererū tail feathers through its branches as I sat there staring at my roses, the flowers Ben claimed to hate one day and tolerate the next. This is the southern she tree, which blazes redder in my mind than the true colour of the sun.

It doesn't hurt anyone for me to believe the white feathers falling from the rātā tree were a message from Jim, reminding me it was already the future—to say a little prayer, buckle in, hold on.

MAORI

Postcard from Ans and the cocktail hour on the *Underworld*

Ans isn't quite sure where she is. It could be her bed, it could be her Volkswagen—her back still feels hunched into it, even here in her coffin—and then Ans and her dream are on a waka and all of the people bear the heads of dogs. But she is an easy traveller; she has her raisins, Brazil nuts and little cubes of Gouda.

It could be a cruise: there is a kēhua here in the cocktail lounge who has had too many mojitos, too many piña coladas, too many tropical fucking drinks, and the kēhua wants to get to Hawaiki so they can send their brother blue feathers, but when Ans leans to her waist to help them there is a waka huia instead of her camera and the kēhua is swimming in the pool of it; the kēhua is riding an inflatable swan and Ans will never catch their mystery; where are her slippers, where is her breakfast, who will find her magnifying glass—ah there it is, at her neck on a string.

Other parts of Ans have flown off, they have scattered like slaters; the scrolls in the waka huia help her to remember the now, a photo negative is a shadow of the now, the image punctuated by a click. But where did she put her slippers, why are her keys in the freezer; she has started demanding answers from me. This is her dream so I am wearing my old caregiver's smock, and she tells me things; she says, *People forget I have never seen a windmill in my life,* winks, *I hated clogs,* clicks, *I left the place! I did not ask to be born so tall!*

Hone Tuwhare, her old e hoa, says she needs to come and sit closer to the fire: it is bitter here in Kaitangata. He makes her eat the best part of the crayfish, and teases her about the tiny blue pot of mustard she wears around her neck; he grabs the little spoon and snorts from it like it could be cocaine. Hone sucks at the mussel but the best part of the fire is hers, for now—for the night, but maybe not for te pō. Hone reads to her and licks the stars into place and seals the waka huia shut like an envelope. *Have a moe*, he says, *have a moe*.

Ans sends me a postcard from the underworld. She says that she is happy enough on the cruise that never ends. She writes:

> *I get requests, I wear sequins and give in to being glamorous, I perform a nightly cabaret where I am draped, not hunched, over my Volkswagen and I glitter red under the stage lights, I chant every name of every Māori who has ever lived and hide these scrolls in the archive, safe from the fire. I am that sly and beautiful, and dead, I think I can pull off all these ridiculous favours, so they let me float with them a little, but the little feels like forever and someone is singing* give it back—*what do they want from me? Maybe it is something deeper than photos or money.*
>
> *Talia, I told you the name of the man in the singlet in Te Kaha, his face is carved into the prow of this waka, but it is the woman who takes off her dog mask and turns to tell me to adjust my sequins so no one can see your bruise.*

I am missing my camera. The waka huia is ready for the tomb. I cross my arms over the blue feathers they gave to me, and the rare honesty I will have to give back. I owe the ferryman some coins too, and all your gold poured back into the mouth of the taniwha whose gaze came from inside the children, I could have stopped taking the pāua from their eyes and admit I did not know what I was seeing, I did not know what was really happening, which is that for every click, every time I pointed my camera at Māori staring back at me, it was me who was being clocked, it was me who was seen.

Open it, open up the waka huia, please take it from my hands so they can bury me. I am tired of cocktail hour. I am tired of this cabaret. I am tired of chanting silent names.

One path to the sea

I did and didn't live with Ben. I rented a crib in Aramoana for two years when we were together, but there was no wifi and the water tank ran dry and we used it like a holiday house. He would butcher the name of the place, calling it 'Aramoingy', which contained his affection for me and our score. As a middle-class person, having a holiday house was important to Ben. An easy way to infuriate him was to accuse him of being lower middle class. Preferably during *Downton Abbey.*

Our first night in Aramoana my son makes a friend. They are like me and Kerry, with a friendship more instant than coffee, but they are not girls; they are eleven and bond over an impromptu skate ramp near the bus stop under the cliff. I moved there in late spring and it's only in winter that I learn the cliff cuts off the sun before 3pm.

I try not to fixate on the massacre that happened here in 1991, when David Gray murdered thirteen people on the thirteenth day of November. It is easy to avoid the historical fact of it when we discover the pretty community garden: its planting is done in spirals and there are cosmos, rainbow chard and nasturtiums.

Later, I find a crib in the village I prefer to the one I'm renting: it has a large rambling section filled with outbuildings and is painted a faded pink. I covet that crib. I decide it has a nice feeling. I'm willing to take a stroll around Aramoana with Ben because it's flat, but I refuse point-blank to go tramping with him. Or to climb the cliff where David would sit pretending to be a sniper. Something Roman told me about after sex in the dunes a few years before.

I avoid walking the length of Muri Street, where David Gray did most of the shooting, because I am trying not to be a ghoul, my natural inclination. Solomon, my old school friend who lives halfway between Port Chalmers and Aramoana, told me his school bus was half empty the week after the massacre and that David used to hit the side of it when he cycled past on his savage lonely rides into Port Chalmers. I imagine him wearing fingerless gloves. I have not watched the movie—I agreed with the locals who endured it that making a spectacle of what happened was wrong, and that viewers should choke on their popcorn. But here I am writing about it anyway, with the thinnest excuse that I chose to live there.

Solomon also tells me that the night all the sirens were heard screaming down the Port road to Aramoana, Mungo Lewis, one of the large Lewis family, who lived in a tiny shack below the harbour wall, said, *That will be David. Blowing his top.*

But, after I run out of rest homes that I can storm out of, I look after a woman in Port Chalmers. Dot worked with David's mother at the shirt factory on its main street. She claims David's mother was a quiet, mousy woman. She says when David was a boy he would come up to the top floor of the factory to see his mother, and the girls could send him down to the shop for anything.

The first time I meet Dot, this tiny woman in her nineties, she hugs and kisses me goodbye. The hug becomes an unavoidable part of our routine. It is sort of inappropriate, right from the beginning, so eventually, after dropping in on her daily for months, I have a dream she is kissing me passionately on the mouth. I feel even more awkward about her affection after that. She married late, and tells me I'm pretty when I least expect it. Ben has started saying I'm not as good-looking as when I met him; he pokes at a fat roll bunching up the caregiver's smock that I wear visiting people so they can stay in their real homes. I remind Ben that I can always lose weight but he will become balder and balder.

Dot opens her wardrobe and shows me her bridesmaid's dress from the forties, which is a rich crimson velvet, and the fall of it is like a curtain dropping in a theatre, or hair. We agree that the newer velvet doesn't fall like this.

After I stop working for the care service I pick Dot up and we drive out to the mole at Aramoana to eat battered oysters and we stare at the water glistening with light while we chat. After she is put in a home I visit her again. She repeats herself, the thing you are allowed to do once you are in care. I wasn't being paid to look after her anymore and we went halves in a dozen. Like Mamie, she is tiny but a good eater.

*

When I first moved to Aramoana I sought out the monument to the victims. It is not signposted, and I had to walk through tussock and thick, creeping ice plant to find it, surrounded by yellow lupins. The monument is a steel construction in the shape of a pyramid and has all this air around it and inside it. There is a quote from Kahlil Gibran tooled into the central post listing the thirteen victims: *If it is for your comfort to pour your darkness into space it is also for your delight to pour forth the dawning of your heart.*

It's not for me to say if it is a fitting tribute, and I understand why David is not listed as one of the dead. But the part of me that absorbed Dot's story of the willing shy boy, keen for extra silver coins at the shop, wonders. How did he morph into a lonely figure scoping his marks from a cliff? The wrong kind of gaze.

I also found out the crib I was so fond of was the place David hid in all night, paranoid and listening to the radio, before he emerged to get shot in a blaze of non-glory. It was the only solution to the fact that he had shot and senselessly killed so many people.

Nana's favourite, her pōtiki, was out there that night, a good cop lying armed in the dark.

Maybe it's important to note that Aramoana, which means 'pathway to the sea', was never a kāinga or pā. Probably because of the lack of sun in winter when the other side of the harbour is sunny as anything. The ghosts at Aramoana are fresher than folded laundry sitting on the arm of the couch.

Ben used to put laundry on the table and I would say it was wrong to put clothes somewhere that was intended for food. But we ate in front of the flat screen, not at the table.

Any time we did eat at the table I would take photos. To pretend this was our life.

Historically, Kāi Tahu would paddle over to Aramoana from their kāinga at Ōtākou to collect shellfish and other kaimoana on the salt marsh. Not all beaches are amazing—some are extremely depressing in fact—but Aramoana is so glorious it aches. It has four different beaches. Standing on the mole, which cuts the sea in two, and looking across to Taiaroa Head and its lighthouse, watching the freight and cruise ships come into the harbour opening, you can forget that anything bad ever happened there.

I would walk the mole scanning the sea for dolphins and watch the terns lift off before the kurī could get them and think, Yes, birds. Dainty as fairies, terns fly every year from pole to pole. I spent a lot of time trying to decide whether birds with a large wingspan were the giant albatross from the lighthouse at Taiaroa Head or just really big seagulls. But one weekend I used the phone Ben paid for to snap one albatross after another. The wind was *high.* As usual my photos didn't capture the better scene happening in real time.

One day, midsummer, after my first year in Aramoana, I'm sitting in the sunroom making a quilt, because having patchy internet has made me take up crafts, and a big-boned looker arrives at the door, delivering my crying son. He was having a water fight with his friend and some other kids, fell off a washing machine and chipped off half a front tooth on his way down. Because he is vain like me and Roman, the first thing I tell our son is that the tooth can be fixed—he'll still be beautiful.

The looker introduces herself as Chiquita, and tells me she is living out here again. Chiquita, the girl who survived the massacre. My son's tears and shock over the tooth seem slightly embarrassing after what she went through. I tell myself that if she can live in Aramoana without feeling haunted then I am just being self-indulgent.

Boy's tooth gets fixed and then the cap comes off when he concusses himself going in for one of his kamikaze rugby tackles, which are both impressive and frightening to watch as a mother. He's old enough by then that I don't need to tell him it can be fixed. Life is becoming something he can understand on his own terms.

*

After I got back from Gisborne and Pōrangahau, Sam found me somewhere to live round the corner from his and I met another survivor of the massacre.

The visitor told me that the day before it happened, another hazy Sunday by the beach, he had been towing some of the other local kids in a trailer behind a farm bike. He took a corner with too much gusto and Jasmine, Chiquita's sister, chipped her front tooth on the pounamu she was wearing when they all fell out. In shock after losing this essential part of herself, she had told him something bad was going to happen now. Before he told me this story I had told him I was a writer and that I couldn't be trusted, but there was tequila instead of tikanga.

After listening to his story I told him about my son, who was a similar age to Jasmine when he lost his tooth. The visitor looked at me like he wanted to rape me or kill me because I had the audacity to think sharing this story would fix it for him. That it would recalibrate his old grief that was still livid and his intractable sense of responsibility. It was not just the unlikely synchronicity that bothered him, it was that no one was allowed to talk about that terrible day, or the day before it, except him. Which seemed fair enough but, because he claimed to be an atheist, I told him they were just kids. None of them were responsible for David. Jasmine was just testing out her powers in her broken mouth. Children tend to believe in omens and spells.

But when I looked up the tragedy online, I found that the pendant Jasmine was wearing was reported as a crystal. It helped identify her body after David set her father Gary's house on fire after killing him first—Gary, his formerly friendly neighbour. After David killed Jasmine and Rewa too, Chiquita turned up at Julie's door, barely alive. Julie, who was Gary's partner and Rewa's mother, drove Chiquita out of Aramoana.

Even atheists want to cling to tohu, even if the tohu makes them suffer. I wonder who has it wrong—or whether she changed her pendant.

It turned out I had it wrong. I took my son out to Aramoana just before Easter 2022 to visit his friend Aaron, who he was reconnecting with. He told me he loved Aaron, but he was fucked off with me and my constant panic, the fear that had come back because I hadn't dealt with my grief over Ben. Boy told me he was going to hitch home.

I walked the dog on the beach and he pissed on a log that turned out to be a leopard seal who was too sun-baked to bother chasing him. I drove home and smoked and worried about nothing.

Then I drove back out to Aramoana and caught Boy trying to hitch. He grinned at me when he got in the car and said, *Good timing*, even though my anxiety was a waste of petrol and I had been cruising around the village waiting for him after he'd told me NOT to do that.

Out of nowhere he said a first name and a surname and I said, *Wait, what?* Because it meant nothing to me at first. So he told me it was the name of my birthday *kēhua*. She hadn't just been talking in insane riddles—she did go to the same school as Aaron—and my fear over her shrank to a harmless human size in my mind. I had spent all that time not managing my own derangement and had puffed her up into a poltergeist.

My son said he recognised her in the story being told at Aaron's because of the pointy teeth. The bleeding gums in the Joker mouth that had disturbed me so much. I regretted not asking her name when I gave her the ointment on the bus; as a Māori I had been too busy trying to figure out where she was from, and she said such strange, discursive things that I got distracted.

When I punched her name into the search engine it gave me nothing, so I held on to the nightmare. At least a bad dream makes a strange kind of sense. The name my son gave me was from a series where the hero could get himself out of scrapes by making something out of nothing—and he hated guns.

But that was too close to what I do, and *MacGyver* was a great show.

In one episode, Murdoc, whose real name is Dennis, fries in a vat of oil or flaming water and, watching it at age eleven on TV, living in Foxton Beach, I thought, Surely that is the end of Murdoc. But MacGyver's nemesis keeps reappearing from one season to the next. Before he sinks into the flaming water, Murdoc directs a play and falls in love with Teri Hatcher's character, Penni Parker.

And in another episode, MacGyver and Murdoc finally join forces to beat a common foe.

Murdoc's sister needed their help.

Roman candles

I am pregnant and neither of us owns a car. I am twenty-one and I don't know how to drive, but Roman does. We are on the bus heading out to South Dunedin and I'm unsure if I should be having a baby with him. Our son was Roman's idea.

He taunts and seduces me with stories about the arranged marriages they still practise on the Coast, and how he is being lined up for one. Later I learn that Beau and Shy were one of the last official Nāti arranged marriages, a ritual that involved walking a path from their respective hapū to meet in the middle of a place I don't know the location of. These marriages would still happen if the kuia remained in charge of everything. We signed a Treaty with a queen, not a king. And we were already pretending our power didn't exist as a matrilineal force when mostly men signed it.

And maybe these marriages do still happen. Whatever, I was the only one stupid enough to fall for Roman's line that I was the perfect person to have a child with. I was finishing my theatre degree but Roman had already decided which role I would be playing in the play of his life. I was told I was a terrible actress finishing my first degree and it must have sunk in. I was told I should be a director instead, not a performer, but maybe neither of those things is true. I took being able to write for granted and wanted something else—something bigger I couldn't name. Maybe the theme song from *Fame* was still playing in my head, because I loved Leroy and legwarmers. After our son was born Roman used to play 'Emma' by Hot Chocolate to me, the boyfriend's lament for a failed, doomed starlet.

On the bus, Roman has something to show me. It is a black-and-white photo of his father holding him. His father looks a bit uncomfortable holding a baby, but is too good-looking in the photo. Roman does and doesn't look like him at the same age, and baby Roman has big eyes and lips that are puffier than fruit jubes. Roman looks like his mother too, but he hates being told this.

I had never really considered that Roman could have been a baby. Something real has just happened between us. He is not trying to insist his whakapapa is superior to mine, for once. He is exposing his one vulnerability.

Usually, he is calling me a Ngāi Tahu princess because he knows that, as Rangitāne, this infuriates me. Our ancient uncles used to play rugby for the New Zealand Maori together. Roman has decided I am the right mare to breed a thoroughbred super-athlete from. This is really how he thinks: humans are inferior to the organised mysteries of animals, and like any good Nāti from the Coast, he thinks in terms of breeding. Roman is a bit disturbed when he realises I'm unco and as dangerously clumsy as a lawnmower flipped on its back with the rotor still running, because I'm already pregnant by then.

'Dreams' by Fleetwood Mac is playing on the bus radio but the spell is broken when the bus stops near the house Mum and Lisette bought when we moved back to Dunedin from Foxton Beach in 1991. We get off the bus at the same stop without having our usual fight about whether it is time to get off. He hates South Dunedin and likes to make sure I'm getting enough exercise. Roman believes South Dunedin is too low to the ground. He gets superior about the weirdest things.

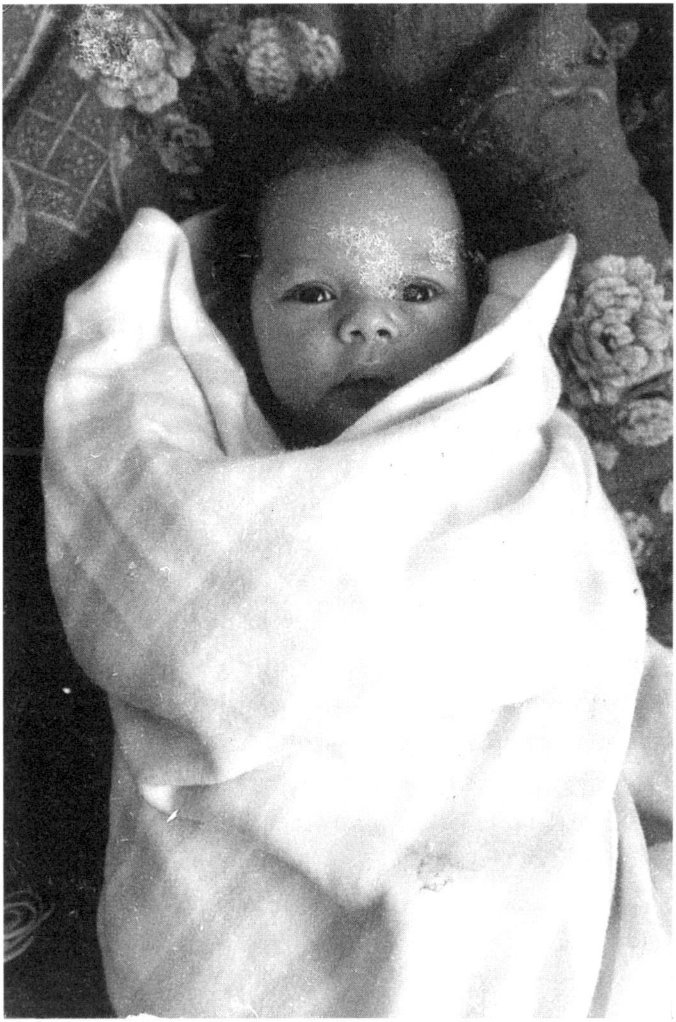

*

'Dreams' becomes *our* song, I guess. And I get annoyed during the plague when it becomes popular again and I start hearing it everywhere because of a man skateboarding down a freeway drinking Ocean Spray cranberry juice. I like the video of the man: it's the freedom of it while the rest of us were trapped in rooms where the state held the key, locking them from the inside because Jacinda was becoming relentless about being kind to one another. The problem is everyone else likes the TikTok too. Maybe the only thing Roman and I have in common apart from our son is that we consider ourselves unique.

'Dreams' was written when Stevie Nicks fell out of Sly Stone's bed; it was already right there waiting for her. The trick was to get it down in time. Like she was a divining rod for the song, a conductor of crystal visions. No wonder I dress like a hippy. It's not just the fact that I no longer have a waist and didn't have much of one to begin with. The poems that come on like a trip are always my best ones. But also, I am just incredibly lazy. My dreams come first.

In 1991, my friend Timo from the Mormon church I've been dabbling in to meet boys tells me his friend Roman has a crush on me, so I start stalking him around Wizards, the video parlour. Roman will tell me in bed seven years later that my eyes were scary in Wizards, that I looked desperate.

In 1992, I go with Mum to a noho marae and Kerry comes too. We make friends with the other kids and teenagers who have been dragged along to this barest university imitation of Māori life. Behind the makeshift Ngā Hau e Whā Marae we watch a sheep in the paddock haemorrhaging from its vagina. A big pink bubble comes out of the glassy-eyed ewe and a trail of bright crimson red, but no lamb.

Later, in the whare, Kerry and I leaf through a book about Māori heroes. There is a picture of a man so good-looking that we agree about it—we are only thirteen but we already have different taste in men. The man's name is Moana-Nui-a-Kiwa Ngārimu. He was the first Māori winner of the Victoria Cross, and Nanny Shy's brother.

Roman says when he met his Nanny Shy as a teenager, he reminded her so much of her brother that she called him 'my Moana'—although he was known in the whānau as Mo. In a documentary, Shy describes laughing at Mo because the horse he was standing on to pick plums left him dangling in the tree.

But now it's the new millennium and we are on the bus doing our worst impression of humble because Roman has come back from going missing in Australia. He said he left because he was going to make some money for our baby. He was drilling seats into the stadium for the Sydney Olympics and ringing me from Coogee and then I heard nothing. When I finally tracked him down and told him the baby that was coming was a boy he said he'd have to come home. As a Māori and a Sagittarius, Roman is good with children—he is a favourite uncle. But I still don't know if he would have come back if the gender reveal at my scan was pink rather than blue. Another man that didn't want a girl.

My mother was also convinced she was having a boy, but these guesses are always fifty–fifty or at the border between the two, a silver dollar being tossed in the air and landing on the tail. A pendulum going back and forth like a metronome, or moving in a circle if you tie a ring to a string and hold it above your wrist. An unborn child is just a series of guesses. A coincidence is when the guesses land, and we rub out all our other hunches and intuitions and write the version that matches over the top.

*

My friends Luna and Justine read Judith Butler at university. I tried, but only really absorbed one crucial element of her thesis: I understood Butler's girling of the girl and that we are more than noughts and ones. That gender is named rather than born into our bodies.

It's true Mum had to perform our sex while growing up in a cult posing as a church. It damaged her more than she wants me to say. Partly because she had such a good time at the chapel or at the lake with her family and friends before Paul came along at eighteen, staying with the whānau whose daughter ends up replacing my Audi forty years later.

Like Rhett Butler, Paul doted on my sister and her girlness. He tried to let me know once that everything he did for her was about what he didn't do for me. But she is the one who makes it impossible for me to feel anything more complicated than love for her.

He told me about the things-he-did-for-me-through-my-sister on the holiday in the Sounds when I was twenty-eight, where I managed to be a quick study for another ghost. Under my breath, for the sake of the children, I said to Paul, *Well that's a win–win for me*. We have just been in the Picton supermarket and my son is amazed by how full the trolley is and how Paul let him put whatever he wanted in it.

When Paul rang me to tell me he was having a baby, I hadn't yet told him I was pregnant so after telling him to fuck right off I hung up. Mum was the one who told me to get over it. She said she and Paul were both only eighteen. She went to one doctor after another, but they kept telling her what she didn't want to know.

My sister was born five days before my son even though she was due after him. Finally, the correct birth chronology.

The kind of lateral synchronicities in family trees that are not unique to Māori. Look at Irish Catholic families, examine any culture, and you'll find multiple ways to either absorb or discard the spares.

The unnamed babies in communal graves remind us that humans are not good people. Being a good person is extremely hard labour. It certainly doesn't come naturally to me.

At six, my baby sister already knew she could taunt my son about being his auntie, even though they were the same age. The other way she taunted him, when we were staying in the Sounds with Paul, our father, was by saying *I love you*.

When Paul found out I had named my son after the great-grandfather he didn't like he booked a flight to Dunedin. He fussed at me because he didn't think I was gentle enough putting a grey, fleecy trench coat on his grandson, the jacket he brought back for his moko from LA or France. We took him to meet Manny's brother, Enoka—Polly's pōtiki and her other son.

Enoka used his hands, which were elegant and long-fingered, like a cradle when he held him.

Before Roman went AWOL in Coogee he took me to a park beside a church and tried to tell me that I was the best thing that had ever happened to him, that the baby didn't really matter—I could keep it or not. And I snorted like a tricky mare because I didn't believe him or that I might not find someone else with bigger aspirations than having a son.

I was trying to decide about keeping the baby, whether the inevitable 'he' would ruin my own dreams. Mum was furious I was pregnant because I was still living at home and she had just turned forty; her liberty was finally in sight.

When I confessed one Sunday in spring, she said, *I'll support you in whatever you decide to do*, and then, before fleeing to Lisette's for three days, she said: *Don't forget to feed the cat the mince.*

Neither of us are cat people.

I'd never nursed any fantasies about having a child, maybe because I had no illusions about being a solo mother—a fate I didn't want to share with Mum, or the world that shunned and ostracised her for it. But this faulty, punitive heteronormative set-up, where a woman was only worthy if a man wanted to keep the baby, the very thing that was expected of her, was also what allowed her to flee and join the free lesbian army.

She moved to Wellington, taking me with her, and became who she'd always been. The love letters to a girl named Echo, which got her sent home in disgrace from Church College in Hamilton—finally getting to dance all that shame out to 'Smalltown Boy' at the gay clubs of Wellington.

When I am in labour with my son, induced for being two weeks late, Mum comes to the delivery room where I am walking in circles to fight the pain and she asks me how I am feeling. *It hurts*, I say. *It gets worse*, she says, and walks out and goes home until he is born. She can not be that person twice.

Mum was in labour for thirty-three hours after I was three weeks late. I was due near my absent father's birthday. I got stuck in her birth canal for four hours as she lay on her back, the worst way to deliver a baby. Nana was still thinking I might bring shame to the family so I'm not sure her presence at my birth helped any more than Roman's at our son's.

My midwife booked me in for an induction while she was delivering other babies because I seem so sturdy and predictable, despite the protein in my urine, but she has gone home exhausted from the other births. It is just me and Roman until the pushing stage, when another midwife and the obstetrician appear like useful wise men and make Roman seem helpful rather than punishing. I am only in active labour for four hours and the first thing I think when my baby locks eyes with mine is, You are kind. Changing his nappy after the black meconium comes out of him I realise he is the same shape as Roman.

After he is born, Nana floods into the room and scoops up my baby like he is the ultimate treasure. When she finds out I have named him after Manny, the godfather of Blenheim, she hands him to Jim and goes to wait in the car, because in her generation women didn't learn to drive.

Manny's mother Polly and her taxi purchase were an anomaly. Maybe this is why I named my son after hers: driving her old taxi routes into my difficult future has been one of my chief rescues and pleasures. Paul was right—the Kaikōura coast is one of the best drives in the world to risk cutting corners. The place I see our taniwha with my son.

It takes Nana three days get over my rebellious Māori naming because she wants her expert mitts on my son. Roman wanted to call Boy 'William', after his favourite uncle, but I win. Really, he wanted to call him Prince William because that's how fucking funny he is.

When Roman dematerialised to Australia, I was shocked I might be doing his idea alone and I was often blank with fear of the future. But one night, before I'd located him, sheepish in Coogee, and I was in that liminal space before you fall asleep, I felt all these kuia clucking in reo around the bed. Cooing and clucking in the language I only half understood. I got the gist of it, though, even as they were bickering about who he belonged to: everything was going to be alright.

I woke up in the morning determined to name him after my side of the family.

*

In 2016, I give in and admit I might be a writer because Ben doesn't want me anymore. This is an embarrassing sentence, because I'm finally telling the truth. He probably knew I would finally leave him if he was vicious enough to me about my son. It's my thirty-eighth birthday and I am staying alone in the Sounds at a shabby crib, waiting for Isaac, who I do not want. I am writing a book review on Atholl Anderson's thesis about our first migrations and the Rangitāne bones at Wairau Bar. The oldest bones that we know of here.

A gruff German man called Walter runs the 'resort' and gives me a small blue cod he caught with his grandson. I put up some pretty rainbow honeycomb lanterns and take a photo of the sandwich I have made from the cod floured and fried in butter, some lemon and an avocado smashed into good brown bread. I post the photo on Facebook and pretend to be happy and grateful surrounded in a shack by my tat. Writing about my whakapapa on my birthday.

But I am so depressed that when I get up in the night and see rainbow phosphorescence on the water and then three orca, and then, further out, a solitary dolphin, I just meh at the navy iridescence. I go back inside and lie down on the bunk bed that looked cute in the photos but is as comfortable as a WWII army barracks'.

I fight the urge to die as I stalk Ben online and discover he has flown to Malaysia for an elaborate Indian wedding. It makes me remember the first credit card statement of his I'd ever opened, after the break-up, where I found he'd subscribed to the premium version of an Asian dating site. Love costs, but so does self-deception. After six years together I still didn't know the pin for his bank card. Ben said I couldn't be trusted with that kind of information. What an asshole—I can't be trusted with any information.

From the hut, using the dodgy internet, and instead of slitting my wrists, I get in touch with Ian the archaeologist, to ask him some questions.

Ian was Mum's last boyfriend. He came right before she entered her radical period, taking me in a taxi with Sue at night to spray *The Treaty is a Fraud* outside my future school on Tory Street. The OG Queer Warrior, with her brown four-year-old in tow.

It was Ian who took us on the camping trip to Tutukākā when I was three, where we found the kuia's fresh shrine in Whale Bay. Her belongings had been left untouched. There were still jars of preserved peaches and baked beans in the cupboards; her crochet blankets were folded neatly in triangles or over chairs ready for her midnight rocking.

That was the time my voice echoed across the valley. Maybe it was then that I started to believe in magic, the dream we're forced to relinquish as adults when we commit to the ordinary.

Over email, while I sit in the hut in the Sounds, Ian and I acknowledge that we should never have walked through the whare before the valley and disturbed the kuia's things. He starts the sentence and I finish it as I'm reading the email.

Finally, a man I can agree with. Mum says Ian was very

fond of me; it was her who didn't love him. In 1981 they took me to *Quest for Fire* at the movies on Queen Street in Auckland. It was an anthropological film featuring prehistoric rape. Maybe this is why I get haunted by blue demons when I am unwell, because, when I look up the plot, trying to understand why I feel so disturbed by the memory, the frozen still of Ika, the girl painted blue with a black stripe across her eyes, that comes up in the image search reminds me of the kēhua that first followed me back from the Sounds. Those periods when I can't look at a piece of fruit without believing it has more layers than an onion. When I split on myself instead of acknowledging that I share the responsibility for some of my life.

I remember pulling the hairs on Ian's legs, and Mum's too, during a conversation where they told me people die. I was very upset by the idea. I was only three. I still haven't recovered from what happens to Bambi's mother.

*

Any time I have tried to insist to Roman that I love him too he gives me a look that is colder than a freezer. He is a suspicious person anyway. I'm probably piling on the meaning and twisting narratives with magical thinking instead of allowing for his basic character.

Two weeks before I learned the name of the kēhua, my son drove me to the twenty-first of one of Roman's favourite nephs. As usual I was desperate for any kind of sign. Stevie Nicks came on the radio as we drove around Dunedin's centrepiece, the Octagon, which has four ways in and out: east, west, north or south. Roman believes in the restorative, hopeful light of the east, in turning towards it and making offerings to the birds in the morning like Jim with his bag of crumbs. But on our way to see his family we went up Stuart Street instead of Mount Hikurangi. The song by Stevie was 'Rooms on Fire'.

And I DO believe there is magic all around us; I just need to curb my bad habit of thinking I know where to look. Roman doesn't have to walk into the room anymore for me to tuck in my sticky beak.

He doesn't need to whittle a stick down to a tiki head with its tongue sticking out and tell me that if I move the stick I will die.

I remember him years ago, before I had any real trouble in my life, telling me that his grandmother didn't like the way I talked about *them.*

I keep the photo of Nanny Shy holding Roman in a box with the others so nothing bad can happen. I have already been in rooms where everything was on fire, but it was the silence that truly frightened me. This is the only hole I belong to, and its sliding obsidian walls are just my fear. Nanny Shy holds the flower to get between one place and the other. Her gloves let her scale any tower and are made of the same silk as spiders and her strange version of help.

Whāngai is not just a way of dealing with babies whose parents can't look after them. Traditionally it was also the opposite—it was about giving back what is owed. This is possibly part of the reason that Oranga Tamariki, that re-naming of CYFS, which is like lipstick applied to a gash, has been such an epic failure.

Paul did not want me so I had to find another way in: these cousins I come across insisting I am one of them. *True, cuz.*

Whānau refers to the four branches of a family tree. It is the north, south, east and west of your grandparents that form the Octagon, or wagon wheel, of the child. The circle of te ao mārama, the snake eating its tail. But we don't have snakes here so a lizard will do. Lizards are only cold-blooded until they find a sunny stone to lie on.

At the twenty-first, cousin Hilary's sister Lala comes over. Lala is from Uepohatu too, via Hiruhārama, and she slaps my son on the legs while she cajoles and berates him about the fact that he *has* to be a doctor. No pressure, but someone in the whānau has to succeed. Her mother's lasagne made from pasta bows is very good as I tell Aroha, Roman's other sister, that I haven't eaten or slept in days, and she gives me a Vodka Cruiser. Lately our son has been wanting to be an artist.

I can't think of anyone else who would get away with that—the slapping—except for my nana, who slapped him on the back of the head (tapu!) as an adult recently for eating all her almonds. This is not like her—she is getting a bit demented. Nana may be Pākehā but all the children and grandchildren who walk into her whare open the fridge first to help themselves. Being Mormon meant they were used to sharing: there are so many Māori in that church it has rubbed off on them.

But when Moana-Nui-a-Kiwa Ngārimu's parents were asked how they felt about having a medal instead of their son they replied, with a great deal of dignity, that it was an honour, but really they'd rather just have him back in Ruatōria with them. Moana was special, but there is something even more universal than war in what they were expressing: the desire to keep your children safe forever.

Lala was the only one from Roman's family, apart from his sisters, who visited us in the hospital when our son was born, because she worked in the kitchen and saw my name on the meals list. Roman had told his own mother to stay away. That was the coldness after I snorted at him in the park. He'd intuited correctly that the person I was then might not think she and her Pākehā clan, who raised Māori men's babies in state houses, matched my middle-class aspirations. I am so impressed by them all now I struggle to find the right words for it. And I like George McCrae much more than jazz. In the Crown Hotel playing pool with Roman before I was pregnant, I surprised him with a favourite of his dad's, 'Rock Your Baby'.

Roman's mother, Boy's nan, has ended up an ally to me, and I trust her even when she is on the turn. Roman threw my car keys into the long grass once and she helped me find them. When my son was four months and grinning at me as my milk collapsed out of his mouth, she rang me slurring and said, *When am I going to see my grandson?* Roman didn't take him home to her for three years, even though she would leave his dinner in the oven. We could never cohabitate for longer than a few days in Mum's house without a fight.

But he would also devise games for us in the lounge, dividing it into a court. The eternal trickster playing foursquare, a ball game I loved at school, and breaking Mum's lamps while Boy slept. Sometimes Roman would say I showed real potential as an athlete—I had such good legs—but it was a shame I couldn't catch anything smaller than a netball.

Roman would let me chase him down the streets of Caversham in a yodelling rage, while our son, who had frequent ear infections and would need multiple sets of grommets, laughed in the pram as the wheels went *whee*. My big brother and chief tormentor, very rarely showing me another, singular vulnerability.

Which was when he crumpled in the hall, after I'd pummelled him lightly for saying I should be a perfect stay-at-home mother to our unborn son, and he cried and said, *You don't know what I've seen.*

Our son is twenty-one, too—his pāua key to the future belongs to all of us as much as him. What a terrible burden.

We live in a valley now on the sunny side, which means the sound of the horse in the paddock in the old quarry over the other, darker side carries across to me. Our son can hear it too, and I explain to him that's what valleys do. The sound carries. It means the neighbours can hear everything.

I tell him about the whare I shouldn't have walked through. I tell him Mum had another boyfriend apart from Paul, an archaeologist.

And I have another confession to make: I ate all the almonds. It was me.

Young man crying

I felt myself turn into a wharenui once. When I was writing about Isaac.

Mum's oval table was on the deck at Taieri Beach and I was alone because Isaac had taken my car to work at the abattoir. I was quite stoned, for once.

I felt my spine turn into the ridgeline of the whare and my ribs spread out flat as butter knives to make the rafters ready for the kōwhaiwhai. My arms were the same, spread out like a kererū on the downbeat as I hunched over, my head turning up to become the tekoteko and my fingers the manaia at the ends of the maihi, because I was writing about the whare at Pōrangahau. And the way Isaac and I pronounced Pōrangahau differently.

It was good weed but I'm not a tipuna yet.

When Māori come home for a wedding, a twenty-first or a tangi, everyone sleeps inside the body of their ancestor, as the other ancestors and pou holding up the shelter of this body watch over them too. The pou have the direct gaze of guardians.

Our pou would have seen us as kids, bouncing on the stack of mattresses the first time I can remember staying the night on a marae. This was in 1989 at Koputāroa down the road from Foxton Beach. I was there with Kara and there was a big twenty-first on. There was a tarpaulin between the wharekai and the wharenui and a Nomads gang member taught me how to pour beer from the keg. He told me not to get too much ice cream on it, meaning the foam. There was Foxton Fizz on all the tables in the wharekai, like plastic jewellery in glass bottles. And there were fake flowers in vases placed over the newsprint that covered the tables. I still found hāngī too smoky when I was eleven but went crazy for the pudding.

This was the marae that took Riria to Pōrangahau with her brother Hokowhitu. It is called Kererū Marae. Or rather, it's the whare that stands over his original whare. Hokowhitu's pou are on display in the Palmerston North museum. They are black-and-white, and graphic as salt and pepper.

The whare in Pōrangahau, Te Poho o Kahungunu, is the place I've only been out the back of, for Piri's tangi in the big white tent once the dignitaries had gone home. In the kitchen I took a photo of the menus on the whiteboard. It seemed a lot to organise and all of it fucking delicious.

Māori scholar Charles Royal described entering his ancestral whare as 'feeling himself enter his self'. And I think I need to do this too. I feel that the only way to cure myself of the volcanic anger, dragging grief and endless anxiety is to learn how to karanga, to call and be called onto this marae that is Ngāti Kere's but full of my whānau and that Riria helped build.

But I'm still not ready. I would still rather just get on it with the girls.

Gina comes down from Pōrangahau to Dunedin with the kids and then both Roman's sisters are sitting at Mum's oval table in the valley. Aroha is telling us she introduced Dunedin to Amy Winehouse and everyone laughed at her at a neph's first birthday over it. The neph is named after the man who plays the nose flute for his brother.

On cue with the snare, Aroha starts singing along to 'Love is a Losing Game' and Gina reminds her that Amy is dead and Aroha tells Gina to get fucked but doesn't miss a beat and out sings Amy. Aroha then pauses to say she has her portrait of Amy above the rubbish bin and that she's a pivotal part of her life. When Gina tries to interrupt my song again—I've asked Aroha to sing Amy to me—Aroha says, *We'll be off to rehab soon, so watch it.* Her voice though. I ask her to sing along to their mum's song, 'Melody Fair', but Aroha tells me she prefers Lulu's other song, 'Morning Dew'. *It's so simple,* she says.

I find the version with the lyrics and it is aching what Aroha does, outsinging Lulu, and I decide I would be happy to die right there just listening to her. Aroha hits the beginning of the line from the base of her spine and sends the note right up into the dome of her skull, but it's her plaintive slide at the end of each phrase that wrecks me. Her voice is a miracle, but Aroha can't be fucked being famous.

Gina tells her sister to *sssh* so she can put another song on. Gina says, *Coming in hot, coming in hot*, as she hijacks the Bluetooth speaker. Coming in hot, coming in hot—there is no stopping her—but she is a bit hard of hearing so leaves most of the singing to Aroha.

It is the first time I hear my son play guitar while his auntie sings, but my phone battery is dead and I don't get a video of what they do with Al Green's 'I'm So Tired of Being Alone'. We agree Al Green looks a bit like Roman—horsey on it.

Boy tells Gina she's a psychopath because she reminds him eleven times of something he said to her five years ago about her being smarter than him but that, sadly for her, she lacked his work ethic. I am allowed to throw stuff at him for once, for being disrespectful to his auntie. None of us can stop laughing.

Gina does an impression of Roman's other ex—who I call the Moa—that is so funny, tears are rolling down my cheeks. She does it on and off all night and I tell her she has to stop or I'm going to piss myself as I slap my leg and cackle and howl. This is what I needed. Just this. It's news to Aroha that Ben has died. I stopped talking about him online using his real name years ago, and the talking I do in real life isn't unbearable to listen to, I hope. I grin and say I'm finally over it. Not his death—that's none of my business—but the life we had.

Aroha still says, *Oh well, Tali, good job*. Gina and Aroha call me Tali like Nana does. But they are not Nātis—as Roman's half-sisters from Ngāti Kahungunu they are the singers and the lovers; they rarely hurl mākutu across the pae. It is news to Gina, too, even though I have already told her Ben is dead and what I did to his mother at the airport when we were staying with her in Pōrangahau. Or did I? I have started calling him Ben by accident instead of using his real name and they ask me who Ben is. Maybe I have written a novel.

Gina tells me she still has fifty photos to develop from the film on the mantelpiece at Roman's. She puts on Paul's puffer jacket and says, *Gee that's warm, Tali—why is it so big?*

After my son drops Gina and her brood at the airport he says, *I've been auntied*. He says he will sleep for days. There has been a hectic schedule of activities for the children and he went ice skating with his cousins so he could show off his balance, which has always been good and is not something he gets from me.

*

Before I learn to karanga I need to learn how to karakia. To have a little faith without hurting my knees on all the eggshells.

In fact, I have done a karanga once before. It was when I was studying theatre, just before I got pregnant. A Pākehā lecturer asked me if I had whakapapa, and since I was the only Māori woman on our course I was roped into doing the karanga for a class trip. I must have botched it because the woman who taught me didn't make eye contact for the rest of the noho marae. At the poroporoaki I told everyone I was not sure that I felt Māori. Because of my father.

The kuia were about to get me good.

There was no young man crying. I never heard him crying through the sound of my own wailing at all.

The ruru

Jacob makes a birthday video of Angus singing along to 'Landslide'; it is this grungy version of the Fleetwood Mac song that Angus loves. Then Jacob makes another video where Angus commits a crime. Angus tells a dream story. Angus is holding a cup of tea and explains to the viewer that in their dream they acquired a baby smaller than a fingernail, a minuscule onion-head kewpie, but the baby was so tiny it fell into their cup of tea.

Angus was pōuri about turning twenty-eight. Angus was pōuri about not being hapū. Angus made Jacob film their dream story and their song. Angus was twenty-eight. Stevie wrote 'Landslide' when she was twenty-seven.

I cannot watch the videos. I can only watch another, earlier video where Angus is covered in pigeons at the Botanic Garden. I can listen to 'Landslide', sometimes—and if there is a singalong, I might ask for it. And usually, a few people groan. It is hearty but a little melancholy.

At Angus's tangi I stood outside the waharoa with Becky waiting to be called on. It was embarrassing that there were only two of us, because too many Pākehā had turned up at the wrong time. The kaikaranga must have been exhausted. During the kōrero, one of Roman's relatives on the board of this Ngā Hau e Whā marae insists we will still be running a writer's workshop at the marae next week. The one Angus was organising for us. I can feel Becky shaking.

I should have learned how to karanga. They would have heard my sadness and mamae then, if I had wailed. This business playing out in front of the mourners would already have been settled in the land of the dead.

I should not have played Angus 'Rooms on Fire'. It reminded them of their parents' divorce. And there is a baby in the video. The week before Angus died I was editing a draft of this manuscript, and listening to it on repeat. When I heard a ruru hooting five times in the dark, I turned Stevie up to drown out its warning. We don't get many ruru in this valley.

Becky tells me I should listen to 'Beautiful Child', but I can't remember where Becky's Dad's ruru is, the one that died and he had a tangi over and she then buried in the Botanic Garden, here in Dunedin, on the way to Rakiura. I wanted to leave the ruru at the man's door. But it's lucky I never got my hands on the ruru because if I had actually seen him, the man who hurt Angus, I would not have been able to stop myself. I would have ripped him apart. I would have used my claws and my teeth.

Months earlier, Angus had visited me, heartbroken, and at my table I told them that Saturn's return would not make life easier, like they had heard; I warned them that it would turn them inside out.

It took me three months after Angus died to ask Jacob if they had left a whakamomori note. He revealed what Angus had scribbled on the scrap of paper about the hazy ringed planet. But part of me already knew. We had a pact that it would not have to come to that. Ever. Now I avoid pacts.

Instead, I take Becky's advice and play 'Beautiful Child' and sing to Angus. This was the love story of Stevie's that Angus deserved. Instead of being head-fucked to death by a fuckhead. 'Beautiful Child' is the story of a sweet, brief affair Stevie had with an older sound-engineer guy.

Instead Angus fell from the Tower.

*

Angus's e hoa drives to Pōrangahau after the tangi. She wants to learn to karanga with my relatives, but she flees after one night because gender politics have been slow to reach Pōrangahau.

> I message her and she types: *omg I am sleeping in my car*
> I laugh and type back, *those are my cousins hahaha*
> then: *poor u*

Angus messaged me while I was in Pōrangahau the morning I was lying about, doing nothing, with Maíra and Kerry. I typed back that I was reading about black kutu falling from combs. A year later my period arrives a week early again, rare and weird, and I know something is off before Jacob rings me to say Angus is dead. Rain and sleet lash at the windows and I touch the cold glass to make sure the world is real. It is winter. Even my son cries.

*

I have won the Surrey Hotel residency—the one which caused me to rave about friendship to Sam—and I am meant to be staying at the mock-Tudor hotel in Grey Lynn. It is famous for its roast and I dream of it. But after Angus dies, I find that I can't get out of bed.

In Fleetwood Mac's 'Everywhere' music video there is a Tudor inn. There are horses. There is romance. My son used to wake up to 'Everywhere' when he was a baby, to its electronic tinkling. I am being haunted by Fleetwood Mac. A step up from Sheryl Crow, I guess, but they are good friends.

Eventually I stay at the hotel with Becky for another project, a writer's table. By Sunday I am too hungover for the roast, which, she later tells me with skinny glee, had *crackling, apple sauce and even cauliflower cheese*. I groan and tell her to *fuck up*.

In the morning, she buys me breakfast. I have eggs Benedict because I'm basic and she has the Works. Another tiny eater with an impressive appetite. The placemats are filled with New Zealand trivia. One of Roman's relatives stares up at me: the boxer Tom Heeney.

My uncle Martin dies suddenly in his immaculate nicotine-stained little flat. Nana, Mum and Lisette find him. At the cemetery the boot of the favourite's 4WD is open, and Martin's carvings and art are all on display. 'Tusk' is playing very loudly—for Martin, and Mum, and her living brothers.

The first time I am able to laugh at Angus for being a fucking idiot and leaving us, it is eight months later, and we are burying their ashes in Invercargill. Fucking Invercargill. It is later, alone, that I really laugh, then howl. There is another dismal version of 'Whakaaria Mai' at the graveside, when Angus did not believe in one God. But at least Angus is buried with their koro Gus, and I hear the name of a recently dead man from Ruatōria, who is mentioned in the whaikōrero before the burial. I whisper *Fucking Invercargill* in Angus's mother's ear as we embrace because her grief is unbearable to witness.

Afterwards, I hotbox a joint in the car with Angus's e hoa and there is an exquisite meal in an odd venue. It is the kind of creepy room Angus would have loved.

When I leave, the road is so slick with rainbows that I almost skid off State Highway 1 on my bald tyres. I stop at Tuturau near Mataura and take a photo of where Te Puoho died and Te Kiore lived. I take a photo of the end of the war. I make a promise to Angus to remember our enemies. And to never look a ruru in the eye.

I managed to mourn for Ben, once, very briefly, maybe five seconds, before I started cackling over my prosecco at the news he was dead.

Six months later I wake to a Facebook memory of the photo of my son on the web. But it's too late, I've already decided to use Stevie Nicks to fix my book and lift the tapu hanging over me since Angus died. I feel entitled to the cobweb's blue bead of light and the horses inside me storming the valley. My son says he is going to sell a painting down at the bar, and I know I will have to leave the house and buy the painting back.

Stevie wrote 'Rhiannon' after reading a book where the titular character is haunted. In the Mabinogion, the Welsh folktales that inspired the book, Rhiannon rides a white horse and three enchanted blackbirds in the tree of life keep her company.

Jacob makes me a heru, which breaks two of its five teeth when I try to shove it into my bun, getting ready to leave the house. My son had warned me months earlier not to bring it into the house. I have been hiding it in the pocket of my mustard trench coat.

Down at the bar, where I follow my son, haunted, stoned and benzoed up, the music is ALL Fleetwood Mac: someone at the open mic is having a crack at 'Dreams', and out back in the smokers' coven the speakers are blasting their *Greatest Hits* album. 'Everywhere' starts to tinkle. But Stevie the great white witch has nothing on the kuia. They take her anywhere and how. Five small spiders crawl from my son's head. And I cannot remember when Jacob gave me the heru—was it near my son's whakapapa being spoken over the dead, while two pīwakawaka flitted around the hedge as Angus and Gus were buried, or was it after the meal?

And does it matter that Angus and I had different versions of what happened, one day, when we were sitting on the deck of the house Sam had found for me to live in, round the corner from his?

In my version, Angus and I were having a spliff and splitting a bottle of pinot gris when a baby ruru was picked apart by sparrows in the air and flopped dead on the deck in front of us. It was an unusual event, but I wasn't in the mood to admit it. I was sick-to-fucken-Māori-death of manu as tohu but Angus was fully into it. Just before their birthday and death they brought up the ruru and I was still tohu avoidant, but as a budding paranormal investigator, Angus was always keen for any talk of omen and kēhua.

And I said, *It meant I shouldn't have been there, staying in that house.*

But it did not mean that. I should have listened closer to its crying in the dark. It was a message coming to me, not for me.

As for my darling friend's version—who I loved more than light and always will—the ruru locked eyes with them before it fell.

*

I scored the cover of *POETRY* magazine taking the piss out of Wallace Stevens and his 13 blackbirds because he is an idol for me, and I tease my idols. I could not keep my tongue in Roman's mouth. Even worse, I had used his marae.

My son starts to hate blackbirds and I can't think why. Even when one turns up dead with a twisted neck outside his room. Even when one manages to get trapped in the house.

Together, using his white sage incense we lead the blackbird out of the whare in peace. Unlike the number 13, the bird is lucky to be alive.

Rhiannon. Rhiannon.

E hoa, I'm singing to you:

Stay
My lotus
My child
My O

Our blue.

Today

I am lying on the bony ground in a tent beside Ben at Whanganui Inlet, just below Farewell Spit. It is down from where Mugwi will have to return from Hawaiki for his wife when she joins Paul and the golf balls in the grave, which are likely becoming worn as teeth.

It is New Year's Day and I can't believe we have found this extraordinary place—even Ben admits it's uncanny. The rātā are in full bloom and the air hums with the deeper stories I have been looking for outside myself, when they've been lurking inside me all along.

I am obsessed with my novel and how to write it. The world I'm trying to imagine seems very far away even as I lie on my own whenua. A swirling battle sphere that I feel for;

a bush court of ancient strategies and tricky, bloody tides.

Driving here with Ben through Tākaka and then Collingwood and Pākawau, I couldn't believe this place was even possible. How did I not know about it? I decided all the hippies were to blame. And I sneered at them as we drove past the Mussel Inn. In eighteen months' time, when I take Isaac there, I will discover they still use alfalfa sprouts—which taste like wet socks to me—and I will be relieved when he doesn't complain loudly about the food for once, content with his bowl of mussels. There is so much garlic on the garlic bread it feels like an alternative source of energy. But Isaac does not mutter *yuck* on the veranda of the Mussel Inn.

Earlier today, I was in a terrible state in the Terrano. Ben and I spent New Year's Eve in Motueka with Maíra and her kid's dad after visiting the man in Riwaka. We took Ben's Ecstasy. Maíra is so down-to-earth it seemed okay to take E with her, but now I am coming down for me and for Ben, who retains the Teflon quality that drew me to him. He said, *Darling, I'm having a terrible whitey*, but he was happy, really, driving the road beside the sea.

I finger the seams of the tent and picture the cliffs outside it and wonder how I can tell this story. I see Hinekawa as a kōtiro without a guitar, because even peaches hadn't yet arrived here at the very tip of the South. I see Hinekawa as being like Cassandra before the wooden horse rolls into the walled city of Troy, standing on the cliff looking up to Kāpiti with her cousin Meihana, knowing that trouble is coming. And I see Thom telling them to come back from the edge. He doesn't see the kererū with two heads that follows the children everywhere they go. The bird who can shapeshift into twins sharing a spine and whose heads face towards the past and the future.

But Thom can see Kaikaiawaro. That dolphin is kind of a fame slut, tbh. He spent years helping Pākehā get through our gaps. But he is my taniwha.

Ben and I are too wrecked to walk on the spit where either the whales choose to strand themselves or their sonar is fooled by the finger of sand stretching into the sea.

I am lying here in the tent, beside the ghost of the man I wanted to be buried with, asking myself if I should turn the story inside out to show the stitches or make the seams invisible. The places where I have stretched the truth to make it fit over the faded scars, and the places where it can still grate at me and itch at my neck.

But I'm not suffering anymore. I'm no longer labouring under a grinding daily affliction when I would rather be dead. After all these encounters with cousins and biting into golden peaches I've come to believe that being dead won't make the suffering stop.

I turn my back from the coldness beside me, ready to be touched by a hand that knows what it's doing.

But I care far less about being loved.

Really, I just want to live.

Karanga mai

The whales were the first tohu. Fifty of them stranded on the spit, and only five of them still alive. Our people were down there gorging and cutting, but Meihana and I stayed with Thom, Pāpā's mōkai. Watching from the cliff and up into the bright water of the other island, where Kaikaiawaro is probably hiding. Thom made me a playing kāri—a joker, a taniwha to take away my worry.

But now I am here in this big covered waka, and it tips and rolls like the sail I wash for the bed we lie in.

He keeps putting these words in my waha, Jocki does, by reading his two Bibles to me. I call the Bibles ngā kererū because they flap; the pages flap from their fat puku, and we rock back and forth in this waka, and he reads to me and he reads to me and I take to the feather quill and it surprises him, which surprises me because he knows by now that we are made of feathers.

I learn the letter *j* and to say 'Jock' instead of 'Kok', although really I am teasing him because Thom has already taught me the words and shown me the cards. And I keep my secrets from him, at first, and I tangi in the dark and my puku grows. I am carrying a kākano. *He kākano, he kākano*, I waiata, and Jocki says I sing in my sleep.

And I katakata, and I hold my waha. And I wear his white kākahu, which are softer than my mother's, but I miss the fingers of my whaea stripping the harakeke into muka and weaving, weaving, and there are both these things and they rock back and forth. I write in this pukapuka instead of weaving and then I get some harakeke and make an okooko for our baby to lie in against me before I carry him on the tartan on my back.

I cannot say that I love him like I loved Tawhi—all I can remember is the terror, breathing inside me like the sail inside the sail. But I was used to terror by then. Jocki tells me about Jesus, another J-word, and I katakata and say *Joki, ehara koe i a Jeeesus* you will do for ināianei and I tease him with the word 'aroha' and the way I never say it to him directly, and I roll my eyes.

I don't want to talk about what happened to my father, so we don't. Kāore kāore, but not how Te Kiore chanted it at us, because they mocked our death with all their life and tried to make me marry him. Kāore to him. Ka ora, ka ora to this new life. I will never understand how they beat us like they did. Or why, the more Jocki reads to me about Samson and Delilah, the more I lose sight of Rupe and the other half of my spine. The sight of Tāwhaki sliding into the bush with his tuatara on a leash. Meihana splashing me with moana and Kaikaiawaro letting both of us ride the kōkākō grey of his back.

I tell Jocki about Tāmairangi, whose feet were not allowed to grace the ground, and I tell him about Kunari. Exiled to Rēkohu. I spit on the floor when Jocki mentions Ngāti Tama and Wahapiro, who I call Te Kiore. We had no rats here, before he came.

I tell him about Hinepoupou and her lust for utu. After what happened I am scared of the water now. It turns to blood before my eyes when it should be blue.

Jocki calls me Scheherazade. *S* sounds are still new to me. I have my own ways of hissing.

After a storm—one I haven't called for—Jocki tells me about *The Tempest* and why his waka is called *Ariel*, to distract me from what happened to my people on the *Elizabeth*. How frightened they were when we found them tied up below deck.

I tell him about Meihana and Rupe, our kererū, the one who turned into the twins we became when we ran and ran, but the pages of his Bible are very still.

After Teone is born, we are not together for long before I split into thousands. I split into the hundreds of coloured dots on my moko's fairy bread. I blister and bloom into the hot pink and turquoise bleeding into the lard and then the butter.

I split into Tutu and her mother's sadness. I bust the tight seams of the tutu I wore every day before I started school and I prise open Polly's eyelids. It is lucky Wiki's girl is with her too, because those girls cannot be left alone—that is why they are always paddling together. It is why they were friends before we knew we were family.

Kerry is driving and singing along to Rihanna, who is begging the music not to stop. We are taking our kids to the beach, to the actual sea and not the deadly village where all the wives hate us.

They are squeezed into her Toyota Corona like chubby Kmart sardines. I am wondering how I can make this love I have for my friend, who is closer than a sister, last longer than forever but only music comes close to this. Even though the aroha we share for our children is bigger than the sum of our parts.

Inside the car, Mia, Kerry's youngest, likes the song by Lumidee as well as Rih's 'Umbrellla'. She is three and sings along to the *uh-oh uh-oh* part of 'Never Leave Me'. Mia is a perfect mimic like her mother. *Uh-oh uh-oh*, but it may as well be my heart. I would prefer that perfect facsimile of worry to the warnings—I am tired of them. Surely, if I stop talking about my trouble it will be over. The eels will stop sliding down the She Tree.

I could just be grateful for the days my son wakes up singing like Roman. The natural joy did not come from my taha, unless it skipped me like a stone on the lake that is deep but not without end.

When we worry about our children to each other, I remind Kerry that Mia was born as lucky as my son. And her eldest was born wiser than most adults. My son and her eldest pick on Mia, but also, Mia has a blister, which she takes out on her sister and Cam tolerates it because Mia is only little.

It is sunny, the day is fair and rinsed with the right kind of blue—why else would we be going to the beach again?

Polly and Wiki and all the other kuia ride on the roof of Kerry's Toyota Corona with its navy blistered bonnet, like duchesses at the opera being carried on a litter, but also like unruly hens squawking in crates. They do this for all the moko; they are everywhere and roam inside us as they keep weaving the net and it's no small thing that only a few slip through. The afterlife is hard mahi and the birds gapping it for Hawaiki have it better. The creaking sound of their wings is the release.

I cannot see these royal wāhine, even though Kerry possesses them in her desiccated skinny fingers and the fineness of her touch. But very rarely, I can hear them calling like Raina's invitation to the whale and the whale's long *aueee* back. The white kererū feathers trailing behind the waka and the balance of that blessing.

The same balance my son has from walking the fence in the deadly village by the sea. I would wait to piggyback him back to the start again. I didn't know how to play but I was a determined workhorse. Even after all that time spent lying on the lake.

I can hear them calling as much as Ruby could smell them when she refused to sleep in the wharenui on the noho marae after the man with the darkest āhua carried our mattresses in.

But I am not the kōtiro who can absorb them fully formed at Hiruhārama, just before Ruatōria. Nor can I be lured towards their darkness without turning myself into a stinking fool. They will scald and scold you if you try to send your hūpē through their pou and I do not want another growling. I am so easily spooked I'm asking for it in giving all my attention to the dead.

They do not belong to me; my son belongs to them and they need him *here*. I hurt myself with their spells and my false tohu and should stick to karakia. It might stop me from losing so much hair and I'd be able to tie it back into a taut bun instead of a life raft for my baby. The hair I kept losing in my nightmare to the drain in the shower.

Even when I was peeling a sink full of eggs for the salad in the kitchen after the unveiling for Beau and Nanny Shy, no one told me off for having loose hair. Roman was still contrite; a twisted sorry had come out of him near Dannevirke after he'd threatened me with the accelerator to shut me up. And he could be so gentle in the ways he chose to torture me, even with his tuatara side-eye. I was astonished to be there on the Coast playing his wife.

And then, two years later, to be sitting in the Ngārimu homestead while Roman's auntie queried the mood of Hikurangi after she gave us biscuits and tea from the urn.

The kurī nuzzling at our palms when we arrived and got out of the van.

I am rocking back and forth with the rightness of the wrongness of it all. But I have my hand back on the tiller. My uncle goes down into the cabin for a nap—it is just a lake after all. A lake inside an island within a lake within an archipelago within a sea.

And here is my karanga back to the kuia. It is reedy and it wavers but eventually I will be let onto the silk that runs through the cobweb glinting in the light between us and us. I permit—no, I *enjoy*—their shoves and the impossible task of admitting to myself that I am just a mongrel with desperate eyes and not a lost princess.

Hinekawa is me but I am not quite her: I share her with the other cousins. We are Polly and Riria too—or rather, I am on my way to fulfilling them. I am no longer Hinepoupou, swimming between islands driven by her desire for retribution. Driven so mad she tore off her kawakawa crown and turned her kurī to stone. I am demanding to see too much at once and blinded by the force of my feelings.

I am certain they are *there* as I wait sniffing around the waharoa instead of sneaking in again and again through the spotless kitchen of their heads and all that immense capability.

I know I am a hōhā and that I don't know how to stop having a tutū but it doesn't matter because in my marrow there are all these women, and I feel it is *them*, and the glimpses of their faces on and in the water . . . as I trail my hand from the waka . . . who will never leave me alone.

Author's note

Roman is a co-creator in this book. I could never stop being entranced by his stories, and his long eye on me, and there are parts that break into fiction through changed details and the deals I have had to make with all the beautiful tāne. I understand them, I hope—Boy's dad's pou and his stake in the sadness of the whenua, and the good fathers they try to be when there is no shining example, except the stars.

A number of the names in this have been changed—including all of those on Roman's taha. If I am talking about my taha, some names have been changed to protect private people.

*

There are multiple discursive accounts of what happened during the musket wars, which has allowed me to pick and choose the version that resonates the most with my imagination. The battle of Waiorua is a good example of this—dates and facts vary wildly. The description of Tūtepourangi and the emerald halo around the mere comes from W. J. Elvy's 1957 booklet *Kei Puta te Wairau: A History of Marlborough in Maori Times.* The book I was reading to Isaac in Riwaka that has the description of heads adorning the waka was Ron Crosby's 1999 survey, *The*

Musket Wars: A History of Inter-iwi Conflict, 1806–1845. I also took some information from Angela Ballara's 2003 book *Taua*, but took issue with the two versions of Tūhawaiki, because I had already read all the volumes of John and Hilary Mitchell's *Te Tau Ihu o te Waka: A History of Māori of Nelson and Marlborough*. I am conscious that the Mitchells helped advance the Wakatū claim in the courts and that Mugwi devoted the latter part of his life to this mahi and was on the board with Eva Rickard. I extracted the de Sainson account of a night on the beach from their work.

I also read *He Pukapuka Tākatu i ngā Mahi a Te Rauparaha Nui / A Record of the Life of the Great Te Rauparaha*, edited and translated by Te Rauparaha's descendant Ross Calman. I was unable to finish listening to the podcast on the wars because I found this version of events too disturbing, but I recognise it as a work of considerable merit when assessing the impact of the wars. And the key to understanding an old way of life that no longer exists here. The book also gave me the image of Te Rauparaha dreaming of the black hawk. But it does not mention Tūtepourangi, so this is my attempt to write my tipuna in.

I have read through many Treaty claims around Te Tau Ihu. The detail about the bones at the Hauhau ceremonies in the mountains is from the Ngāti Apa claim, which fed into the foreshore and seabed issue—as did Meihana Kereopa, who understood the relationship between the whenua, the mauka and the moana, and would never let anyone walk over his bones.

Some of the 'Pelorus Jim' chapter was informed by James Cowan's fanciful rendering of Kipa Hemi Whiro's tohunga role in the Sounds. It was published around 1912 in a booklet called *Pelorus Jack: The White Dolphin of French Pass, New Zealand with Maori Legends.* When it came to the story of Wetekia Ruruku Elkington, I borrowed the text from a speech made by Dr Debbie Hippolite Wright about her tipuna at Brigham Young University ('Living up to Our Legacy', September 2005). And the story of her daughter surviving comes from *Turning the Hearts of the Children: Early Māori Leaders in the Mormon Church* (2014), edited by Dr Selwyn Katene.

The Sciascia family website (sciascianz.com) has also been an invaluable source and I read Felicity Campbell's book about Nicola Sciascia in PDF form, downloaded from this site. It gave me the story of Punch and Judy, the account of the shipwreck and many of the details of Nicola's life, including the lost notebook. Again, this is an attempt to fill in the lost pages.

Thank you to Peter Meihana for his Ngāti Kuia scholarship and the proper name of the tohunga at Kaiapoi, and to Madi Williams for letting me read her history of our people. Rupe facing towards the past and the future comes from her.

I still have Ans Westra's 1967 book *Maori* and continue to look at it when I need reminding of who we are. I was also informed by 'Camera Antipode', Lawrence McDonald's 2012 thesis about her. He had many insights into her work and the context in which it was made.

Finally, the account of a night spent with wāhine on the beach and being carried back to their boats is from Augustus Earle's account *A Narrative of a Nine Months' Residence in New Zealand, in 1827*. He is an unreliable narrator, but then, so am I.

List of illustrations

Acknowledgements

Firstly, I would like to thank Megan Dunn for commissioning the Ans Westra essay and giving me 'art is a mother' as a theme, and a new lens to view Ans with. And thank you to Ans for receiving my criticisms with grace. She has left a rich body of work, one that we can argue over for many years. They are images that will age well. You are the beans, Megan, and this book would not exist without your magic tail.

Thank you to my first Dunedin poetry people, to Michael Harlow for teaching me and three other girls (including Kelly) how to be lyrical about wallpaper in 1992. To John Dolan, Katherine Liddy and Kay McKenzie Cooke. Thank you John, for telling me I should write like I talk, and for the permission to hate, and to scan for fakery with love. Thank you Kay for *lying in the lap of the mountains* and to Katherine for *Love, you are the lolloping black dog of my dreams*—both lines I remember from our Otago ENG 217 1997 poetry workshop. Katherine, thank you for turning up at my door that day! It's a climb and I value you more than I can say.

To Richard Reeve and Nick Ascroft, who were not allowed at the women-only readings in Dunedin—this is still LOL to me. Thank you for the arguments Richard, they have been excellent, and thank you Nick, you are a model of Dunedin discretion.

To Jeanne Bernhardt for setting a wild example and to Dean Havard, and the book of poems I still owe you.

To Emma Neale, you will always be my Glinda, thank you for being a Pākehā I can trust, and for your grit and graceful eye.

To all the English teachers who adored me and let me get away with murder, especially Ms Martin. Who loved Margaret Atwood, but I will always love Alice Munro.

Thank you Marty Smith and Kirsten McDougall, so cool to still know two wah from the O'Brien 2001 crew lol, and Kirsten I'm gutted I didn't get to taunt you with the words 'full powhiri' in messages about my launch—or Tayi Tibble, who also managed to escape being my publicist, but I would like to thank Tayi for being Tayi Tibble, and the kuia who assembled her on the Bratz doll line of the Coast to conquer the world with all-seeing eyes and matchless grooming.

To Marian Evans for the cheerleading and to Emer Lyons, Alice Tawhai, Carin Smeaton, Emma Hislop and Steven Rineer, thank you for being such good writing friends.

A special shout-out to Cousin Lynne, who bought me Dallas, and to Mary Ann and her manaaki and negronis, and thank you to Peter, for trawling through 90,000 images one morning in England so I could have Polly in high resolution.

To all the cousins who gave me permissions, especially Diane Taylor for the image of Kuia in Polly's fur coat. Thank you Diane for being with Paul in the hospital after he crashed his truck into the Manawatū Gorge and walked out of the upside-down cab with a broken back. And to my sister Mamie who had a warning of the crash in her sleep—I love you darling, Paul would be bursting with pride, and is, sis, I miss our dad every day. Thank you Tui Macdonald for the photos every time you visit down at the Island. It's where I want to go.

To Jenny, Barb and Trudy, thank you for being in Mum's life, and mine.

To Becky Manawatu, bitch, I let you in my life xxx And to Helena, you let me in yours xxx

To Kelly Ana Morey for all the support and for taking nice photos of the kurī.

To all my brown girls, you know who you are, and to any friend with a changed name in the text. Kelly, I had to make you Delphi, because Kerry and Kelly sounded and looked the same. Like we all used to. Love you my girls, and to Justine, thank you for not editing yourself out despite your wise counsel. You do matter that much to me. And to Masoumeh, thank you for thirty-two years of an amazing friendship. So amazing I did almost forget to thank you omg lol xxx Thank you for being my backbone in another country for over twenty years.

To Noelle McCarthy for writing *Grand.* It was so magnificent it gassed me up to write 50,000 words in a month. A true fairy.

To Steve Braunias, thank you for editing my first 4,000 words down to 1,000 back in 2016 with very little explanation other than I was a raving beatnik. I had never had my writing insulted with so many compliments. I called you a parsnip, later I called you a cunt, but you are my favourite whitey. Thank you for saving the reader from all my darlings and especially the ones I fight to put back in. Thank you for making Jasmine's job on this such a breeze. LOL. Thank you for my start and I am lucky to count you as a friend.

Thank you Jasmine, you are the most patient, sensitive person I have ever had the pleasure of testing. Thank you for being the waharoa to the Coast and being there when she held my hand and I finally had the permission I needed from Nanny Shy. You are a real dancer.

To all the people who contributed to my hustles to get this over the line, thank you, your generosity was astounding and embarrassing. Special thanks to Gerard Carter, who didn't even wait to be asked. And to BC, thank you for being so sensitive, I'm sorry I let you down.

To my son, you are the joy of my life, thank you for giving me back what my grandparents first gave to me. And to my Nana, who died days before this was due to go to print. You are made of magic and wire and I hope you understand why this has to be true forever and why I sent Boy to play the waiata instead of my sorry self. He looked like the most beautiful Italian waiter in the world with his guitar. To Jim and Gwen, my giants, my sparrows, nothing will ever hold a candle to your love. Thank you for never teaching me shame.

And to Mum, I love you, thank you for never letting me go. Except that time you left me at the church. LOL.